PRAISE FOR
THE DIABOLICAL TRINITY

Wrathful God

Tormenting
Hell

Sinful
Self

"Mark Karris' *The Diabolical Trinity* not only explores the deeply violent emotional and spiritual damage done by Hell indoctrination with true insight and compassion, but also offers a real path to recovery."

— **DAVID BENTLEY HART**, *THAT ALL SHALL BE SAVED: HEAVEN, HELL, AND UNIVERSAL SALVATION*

"People like us—who grew up in hellfire and brimstone religion—are not alone. I imagine there are at least a half a billion of us in the world. That's why I'm so glad Mark Karris has written this brilliant book on healing from hell-related religious trauma. If you have an "inner fundamentalist" who constantly torments you with condemnation, this book by a trained therapist (who has experienced religious trauma himself) can help you heal. Highly recommended!"

— **BRIAN D. MCLAREN**, *FAITH AFTER DOUBT*

"In *The Diabolical Trinity*, Mark Karris offers insight and care that is grounded in multiple disciplinary perspectives (psychology, religion, theology, pastoral care). The care that Karris offers readers will be essential reading for religious trauma survivors, particularly those who have been taught to think of themselves and others in terms of punishment or damnation. Karris breaks open the punitive thought systems of hell and saves us from their psychic violence."

—**MEGHAN R. HENNING**, ASSOCIATE PROFESSOR OF CHRISTIAN ORIGINS UNIVERSITY OF DAYTON, AND AUTHOR OF *HELL HATH NO FURY: GENDER, DISABILITY, AND THE INVENTION OF DAMNED BODIES IN EARLY CHRISTIAN LITERATURE*

"Many individuals today are severing ties with their conservative Christian roots and are searching for guidance in working through their religious trauma - particularly the damaging and false doctrine of hell. The process of unraveling deep-seated religious beliefs and indoctrination acquired over decades can be a long and painful journey. Karris presents a vitally crucial work, drawing from his clinical counseling experience, to provide a pathway of healing and relief for those who have been injured by their religious upbringing."

—**JULIE FERWERDA**, *RAISING HELL: CHRISTIANITY'S MOST CONTROVERSIAL DOCTRINE PUT UNDER FIRE*

"In *The Diabolical Trinity*, Karris asks a profound question, "Are some theological concepts actually damaging to our mental health?" His answer is an unequivocal "Yes!' Karris weaves together psychological research, clinical narrative and first-person accounts convincingly arguing that the theological concept of hell may be taught in ways leading to complex PTSD and loss of faith. While not a theological treatise, this book is psychologically sound and theologically sophisticated. It is also immediately accessible and practical for clinician and client. I can't wait to recommend it!"

— **BRAD D. STRAWN**, PHD, EVELYN AND FRANK
FREED CHIEF OF SPIRITUAL FORMATION &
INTEGRATION, PROFESSOR AND CHAIR OF THE
INTEGRATION OF PSYCHOLOGY & THEOLOGY,
FULLER THEOLOGICAL SEMINARY

"Karris' *The Diabolical Trinity* uses solid research and clinical concepts explained in easy-to-understand language and practical exercises so that the reader can understand the potential negative and long-lasting impacts of the idea of Hell and experience relief, healing, and hope."

— **DR. LAURA ANDERSON**, LICENSED THERAPIST,
AND CO-FOUNDER OF THE RELIGIOUS TRAUMA
INSTITUTE

"This research-based trauma informed book is a must-read for anyone who lives in fear of burning in Hell eternally and for professionals who work with them."

— **DR. GILL HARVEY**, THERAPEUTIC
PSYCHOTHERAPIST, SUPERVISOR, RESEARCHER, &
TRAINER, UK

"I know all too well the hold that hell-based theology can have on a person. In *The Diabolical Trinity,* Dr. Karris not only provides explanations for why beliefs about hell can feel so hard to shake, but he also shares practical guidance and powerful tools. I kept saying, "He gets it! He understands what this feels like!" Reading this book filled me with hope knowing I now have a resource to pass along to folks still in the clutches of these beliefs who are looking to escape. I cannot wait to recommend it to friends and clients alike."

— **MATTHIAS ROBERTS**, PSYCHOTHERAPIST AND AUTHOR OF *HOLY RUNAWAYS* AND *BEYOND SHAME*

"As a Trauma Recovery Coach specializing in Religious Trauma, I often work with clients struggling with life after deconstruction. They often find it easier to deconstruct the belief in Hell than to untangle the psychological impact it continues to have on their daily lives, even after leaving the faith. "The Diabolical Trinity" beautifully unpacks Hell indoctrination, helping readers understand its negative impact on their lives. This is a must read for anyone undergoing faith deconstruction and I am excited to recommend it to my clients in the future."

— **LACI BEAN**, CERTIFIED TRAUMA RECOVERY COACH @LACI_BEAN

THE DIABOLICAL TRINITY

HEALING RELIGIOUS TRAUMA FROM A WRATHFUL GOD, TORMENTING HELL, AND A SINFUL SELF

DR. MARK GREGORY KARRIS

CONTENTS

PART III
UNHINGING HELL FROM OUR NERVOUS SYSTEMS

Print: 978-1-948609-88-3

E-book: 978-1-948609-89-0

Printed in the United States of America

Library of Congress Cataloguing-in-Publication Data

The Diabolical Trinity: Healing Religious From a Wrathful God, Tormenting Hell, and Sinful Self/ Mark Karris

INTRODUCTION

HELL. It's just a four-letter word and a small one compared to most words in the English language. However, for many religious believers —and indeed some unbelievers—it's a word packed with explosive imagery and fear-inducing meaning. It certainly was for *me*.

Thinking about my early years as a Christian— four years in a Pentecostal church, another four at a church with a conservative charismatic tradition (before a few *more* hangin' with Southern Baptists)—makes me shudder. The perpetual outward drama fed a roiling internal volatility that left no room for a sense of safety, balance, and peace.

In those days, I constantly took it upon myself to fight the demons lurking around every corner. Like some sort of warrior magician going into battle, my prayers for myself and others included mysterious spells, such as, "I bind you in the name of Jesus!" or, "I loose you in the name of Jesus." I would plead the blood of Jesus around every doorway I entered so that demons could not follow me inside. I often sounded like Gandalf in *The Lord of the Rings*, echoing those powerful words: "You shall not pass!"

I felt the perpetual threat of being sent to Hell by a frightening and all-powerful God—along with the constant internalization of my sinfulness and depravity, which were being pounded, *no*, pulverized into me by my furious, disapproving preachers and Bible teachers. Each of my prayers had to be loud and repetitive, as if God were hard of hearing and, most importantly, because my very salvation was at stake. So, every Wednesday at Bible study and every Sunday at church, I was at the altar pleading with God to have mercy on me. *Me*—a pathetic, evil worm of a human being who continually needed to be saved from eternal conscious torment!

Being on my knees before the congregation was a chance to prove my worthiness to God by declaring how desperately unworthy I was. Somehow *that* made sense to me, as did my religion's rules, always under the threatening veil of punishment. I was so tightly bound up in fear around those rules that I sincerely thought drinking a soda would somehow defile the temple of the Holy Spirit! I believed then that "impure products" could not enter God's sacred vessel, the container of the Holy Spirit, and that if they did, punishment would swiftly result. Over time, the combination of rules, regulations, and hypocrisy, along with the constant fear of being tormented in Hell, took its toll on me until, eventually, I was done with the toxic religious bullshit.

Yet even after I stopped believing in Hell, it took me almost a decade to fully flush the fear out of my mind and nervous system, where it continued to exist as a "phantom theology." You may have heard of *phantom limb syndrome*, a condition wherein, after an amputation, people experience sensations of a limb that is no longer there. Similarly, despite no longer believing in Hell and that I was evil and depraved, at times, those phantom ideas snuck up on me and caused much suffering. Knowing how challenging being healed from Hell indoctrination is, as a licensed therapist, I am now committed to helping those seeking to heal from this religious trauma.

Hell, and its associated *eternal conscious torment* (ECT) is viewed by many as a theological treasure that glorifies God. For them, the concept of Hell makes perfect sense, given God's holiness and perfect justice. As one contemporary theologian puts it, "To sin against an infinitely glorious being is an infinitely heinous offense that is worthy of an infinitely heinous punishment."[1] Author and minister Mark Ballenger writes that, "Hell is a terrifying place, but Hell glorifies God immensely, because it makes so many of his qualities visible and knowable."[2] For these authors, Hell makes sense. God's holiness demands a verdict on human behavior, and punishment must follow for those who sin. All that God creates and decrees is good and praise-worthy. This belief necessarily includes Hell and the punishment of eternal conscious torment. Within this theological framework, trust in God's sovereignty and providence, combined with the supposed desig-nation of His followers as the "elect," mitigates any feelings of anxiety or impending doom.

However, one person's theological treasure is often another person's noxious trash. Many who dissent from this understanding of God and the afterlife, deeming it a horrific version of a wrathful, punishing Creator. For these individuals, the idea of Hell generates terrifying images of an angry preacher frothing at the mouth, loudly proclaiming a horrible place created by God and filled with hideous and duplicitous demons, unceasing fire, unquenchable thirst, and never-ending torture.

And some, with unveiled eyes, make a decision of the will, moving on from what they consider a primitive view of God and religion. They tire of *fear and shame-based* religious propositions and decrees, as well as the metaphysical niceties that don't resemble the realities of everyday life. They abhor the vision of an ill-tempered and punitive God who is some sort of grotesque composite of Hitler, Stalin, and Mao Zedong fostered by venom-filled Christian communities casting judg-ment every which way. They walk away and move forward, letting the past be the past and feel more alive than ever!

Others who walk away from this toxic religious matrix can find themselves stuck. There is a sense that, although their core self has escaped the religious trauma they experienced, they cannot move forward. It's like a frustrating sludge holds them back, keeping them from living the life of freedom they desire. It's true...they need no longer deny, suppress, or repress their doubts and troublesome questions regarding toxic beliefs. Nevertheless, they continue to feel emotionally shaken, unable to experience themselves as an integrated, whole self. They have been traumatized by toxic religion, especially by having internalized destructive teachings.

This book is a compassionate guide for those who wish to heal from religious trauma caused by Hell indoctrination. You cannot have a torturous Hell without a God who created it. And you cannot have a Hell without evil and sinful people to be put there. So, I also discuss the doctrine of human depravity and the view of God as wrathful, punitive, and violent.

I do not argue theology with a litany of Bible verses. As a matter of fact, there will be barely any mention of Bible verses. Instead, I have written this guide through a psychological, philosophical, and sociological framework. I'll let the biblical scholars and armchair theologians squabble over the questions that interest them: Who is God, according to the Bible? Who has the God's-eye view on the afterlife? What constitutes "biblical" anthropology?

This book examines the numerous potentially traumatizing aspects of religion. Part I of this book focuses on the *psychological* terrain and trauma associated with an unholy trinity: the traumatizing doctrines of a harrowing Hell, a primarily wrathful and angry God, and a view of human beings as essentially sinful and depraved. My interest and focus are on the psychological implications and ramifications of these beliefs. To capture the three interrelated doctrines that can fall under the umbrella of Hell indoctrination, I use the label *Hell-Bound People* throughout this text.

Part I pays special attention to the harmful repercussions of this type of trauma: debilitating anxiety, trauma's effects on the body, toxic shame, nagging self-criticism, betrayal trauma, and painful rejection. To best highlight these repercussions, I have incorporated the lived experiences of many who have suffered from these hellish theological teachings. Their voices are the clearest expression of this trauma and deserve to be heard.

In Part II, I share a few ideas that have helped me and others loosen Hell's iron-clad grip on our minds. I unpack my thesis that an eternal place of torment called Hell does not originate from God but is rather a result of creative human ponderings about the afterlife, morphing into a narrative of violent projections that binds communities together. The Hell narrative also feeds human pride and is used by people in power to subjugate dissenters for the sake of homogeneity. Further, I deconstruct the notion of a violence-prone God and an eternal Hell by exploring the absurd notion that our intuitions about compassion, goodness, and wise discipline could be more loving and healthier than God's.

In Part III, I explore psychological insights and therapeutic practices that have been shown to foster profound healing deep down at the level of the nervous system. A person cannot be talked or lectured out of religious trauma. Information alone doesn't produce transformation, not where trauma is concerned. Effective trauma work calls for us to travel deep within ourselves, go beyond our defenses, and move into the tender and vulnerable arena of our bodies and nervous systems. This section examines memory reconsolidation, installing internal resources, self-compassion, taming our inner critics, working through parent wounds, and identifying and living in alignment with our chosen values. In addition, there are also audio meditations based on the exercises in Part III available for download at: https://markgregorykarris.com/meditations (password: HEAL). The overarching goal is to facilitate living a life that is true to ourselves rather than a version that has been projected upon us.

PART 1

MAPPING THE PSYCHOLOGICAL TERRAIN OF HELL TRAUMA

In Part I, I will focus on the devastating impact of trauma resulting from Hell indoctrination, including debilitating anxiety, trauma's effects on the body, toxic shame, nagging self-criticism, betrayal trauma, and painful rejection. By incorporating the lived experiences of those who have suffered from these teachings, I aim to highlight the far-reaching repercussions of this type of trauma and create a space where their pain is acknowledged. It is crucial to recognize the gravity of this trauma and the toll it takes on individuals' mental and physical well-being.

CHAPTER I
WHAT IS TRAUMA?

"Trauma is a psychic injury,
lodged in our nervous system, mind, and body,
lasting long past the originating incident(s),
triggerable at any moment."

—Gabor Maté, *The Myth of Normal*

Trauma is like a violent sucker punch to your mind and body that leaves you reeling and wondering, "What the heck just happened?!" It's the kind of lasting negative experience that makes your nervous system go haywire and drastically messes with your beliefs about yourself and the world around you.

The word "trauma" derives from the Greek word for *wound* or *injury*, and "psyche" is the Latin word for *soul*. Therefore, we can accurately rephrase the clinical term "psychological trauma" to "soul wound," a more poignant, poetic phrase.[1] Events likely to inflict soul wounds include trauma of various kinds: war, mass shootings, domestic violence, and natural disasters. Soul wounds often involve actual or feared death or severe emotional or physical injury.

Who among us has not experienced trauma? We live in a culture of trauma within a traumatized world. Both trauma and *vicarious trauma* —being negatively affected by witnessing the trauma of others—are part of the air we breathe. Each of us carries soul wounds that deeply affect our minds, bodies, and nervous systems. Of course, the magnitude of people's soul wounds varies, as do their origins. While a soul wound often results from a single event, it has a variant labeled "complex trauma." This variant surpasses one-time incidents and involves more pervasive exposure to traumatic experiences.

Let's break this down in the form of an analogy. Take physical trauma. A simple trauma is analogous to my wife breaking her wrist while catching herself from a fall playing tennis. Complex trauma is like my wife's coworker developing carpal tunnel syndrome. Both incidents create excruciatingly painful wrists and prevent normal activity. What can make complex trauma particularly insidious is that the seemingly minor impacts on the joint from typing seem inconsequential in isolation. But the sustained repetition is often devastating in a more pernicious and permanent way. That's not to say that complex trauma always involves minor traumatic events. Extreme and persistent events like domestic childhood sexual abuse and war are paradigmatic cases of complex trauma where the repeated events are anything but minor. Therefore, the type of religious trauma you may have experienced parallels carpal tunnel syndrome much more than a single incident of a tragic fall and a broken bone.

On the more psychological front, neglect is a common complex trauma. If I leave my kids with my aging parents so my wife and I can get away for the weekend, and they forget bath time for the kids, they may realize it and feel bad afterwards. Then we'll joke about how frustrating getting old is with our failing memories; no real harm done. But the strung-out, drug-addicted couple in the suburbs who fail to bathe their child for weeks creates problems on a whole different level.

Religious trauma frequently falls into the arena of complex trauma.

Because it is supported by a seemingly innocuous pattern of incidents and experiences rather than a single dramatic event (e.g., hearing hundreds of sermons about Hell in a lifetime versus a one-time incident of sexual abuse by a priest), others may brush it off or try to invalidate it. They often fail to understand the contextual pattern and dismiss the individual events and experiences as inconsequential. We've all likely minimized our own trauma at one time and may still struggle to understand how religious trauma's cumulative effects can be just as consequential as more obvious and disturbing one-time incidents.

Whether single-incident or complex events, traumatic experiences can devastate our physiology, spirituality, and relationality. In both forms of trauma, the consequences an individual will experience depend on individual differences. For example, a person's perception of the trauma may determine the trauma's impact. One could see, for instance, that getting into a car accident was traumatic, and yet experience it as God's grace. They believe the event was orchestrated by the hand of God and interpret it as a wake-up call to live their life differently. In that case, their belief regarding the event could minimize their post-accident psychological symptoms. However, another person might perceive the same event as traumatic. They might see the accident as just another event in their typical series of unfortunate events because they're unlucky, and terrible things always happen to them. This person might also be angry at God for allowing such an adverse event to occur, further exacerbating their mental and emotional distress.

Sometimes genetic factors impact the effects of a traumatic event. When my wife talked with her coworker about his carpal tunnel, he explained that his wrist bones were set at a slightly deeper angle at birth than most others. Also, he was an avid gamer. The repetitive typing at work may have been the trauma's primary cause, but his unique genetic wrist bones and frequent gaming were secondary variables that reinforced the trauma.

Secondary causes or characteristics of trauma impacting our hearts and minds can be profoundly impactful and more difficult to unearth. One's reaction to potentially traumatic events is determined by many complex, interrelated factors, including upbringing, genetics, temperament, coping strategies, support network, home environment, and current life stressors. That's why the same event or series of events can be traumatic for one person yet not another.

When people lack sufficient internal or external resources to help them adequately cope with traumatic events, psychological and physiological responses to trauma can develop into post-traumatic stress disorder (PTSD). PTSD is usually related to the type of standard trauma we just looked at—distinct traumatic events—while Complex PTSD (C-PTSD) arises from complex trauma—a series of traumatic events experienced repeatedly over a long period. Typically, C-PTSD is believed to begin with physical, sexual, or emotional abuse or neglect in childhood, which is then added to by traumas later in life.

The consequences of religious trauma can be categorized as C-PTSD. Clinicians commonly group C-PTSD's symptoms into three broad categories: 1) re-experiencing the traumatic event through intrusive memories, nightmares, or flashbacks; 2) avoiding experiences related to the trauma; and 3) feeling hypervigilant as a default state where one's nervous system is on alert, expecting peril at any moment. Additionally, as C-PTSD frequently results from longer-term relational trauma rather than single or short-term events, its effects are typically longer-lasting on a person's sense of self and identity. As a result, it can profoundly compromise their sense of trust and safety in the world.

Individuals who developed a secure attachment style in early childhood, characterized by a positive and trusting relationship with a primary caregiver, tend to be more resilient in the face of trauma. Secure attachment often leads to healthy patterns of relating to others in adulthood, including the ability to cope with life stressors, regulate emotions, and bounce back quickly from difficulties. Securely attached individuals are also more likely to seek support from loved ones during hardship while embracing life's ups and downs.

This set of characteristics and behavior patterns is not just a matter of upbringing and learned behavior. I won't burden you with specific neurobiological factors involved, but these components are directly related to neurochemicals released in the brain. Due to nature, nurture, and environmental factors, individuals are quite literally wired differently. Being secure in your relationship with your parents, being financially stable, and having close relationships with a consistent group of friends are all factors that produce a resilient neurochemical balance. This balance helps regulate stress responses in the body, mind, and heart.

Complex trauma and soul wounds eat away at an individual's neurochemical balance. And those neurochemical alterations often lead to overwhelmingly negative outcomes in the face of difficult life events. Those failing to develop a secure attachment style struggle with a less integrated sense of self that is experienced as fractured and incoherent. As a result, even minor difficulties can become overwhelming. These individuals are challenged with feeling comfortable in their own bodies and may struggle to convey core wants, needs, and desires. The world feels less safe, and they likely feel a chronic urge to remain on guard for possible ways they could be hurt again. Trauma may permeate every aspect of these individuals' lives. Since early trauma strips their neurochemical balance, i.e., they can't relax and just roll with the punches, their life experience is a significant struggle. My decades-long personal and clinical experience has convinced me that religious propositions, policies, structures, and people can all contribute to complex trauma and its long-lasting detrimental effects.

Before moving on, I want to underscore that understanding trauma's physiological components does two things for those who have suffered trauma: it offers hope and legitimacy. People who have experienced trauma tend to dismiss or minimize their trauma and its impact on their lives. But knowing there's a biochemical component to a traumatic experience can lend legitimacy to the unique challenges we face. This fact also offers hope. Just like my wife understood that wearing a cast and taking it easy for a while meant a healed wrist, understanding the impact of trauma helps us realize that healing from trauma is also possible. Specific prescribed therapeutic actions (laid out in Part III) enable religious trauma wounds to heal and encourage neurochemical rebalancing. For some people, these steps may allow them to reach neurological equilibrium for the first time in their lives, which will help them roll with life's punches and live life on their terms.

CHAPTER 2
RELIGIOUS TRAUMA, ADVERSE RELIGIOUS EXPERIENCES, AND DISORIENTATION

"Traumatized people feel utterly abandoned, utterly alone, cast out of the human and divine systems of care and protection that sustain life. . . When trust is lost, traumatized people feel that they belong more to the dead than to the living."

—Judith Herman, *Trauma and Recovery*

Now that we have an operating framework from which to talk and think about trauma in general, we can turn to the more specific phenomenon of religious trauma.

One day, while sitting in the bleachers watching my son's soccer practice, I started talking with the mother of my son's favorite teammate. Making small talk, I asked her how her son was doing, and she opened up to me.

Our kids were about five at the time. She explained that her husband tucked their son into bed each night, talked with him about his day, and read a story to him before turning out the light and saying good night. Half an hour later, their son would run into their bedroom screaming about a monster under his bed. She bought a nightlight, and she and her husband tried various techniques to reassure their son there was nothing to fear so that he could relax his mind and sleep peacefully. When I followed up months later, asking how things were going, she explained that things were much better now. That period had only lasted about six months or so before it passed.

Now imagine what would have happened if, as parents, rather than trying to reassure their son there was nothing to fear, they chose to stoke and amplify those fears. What if they told him, yes, there's a monster under your bed; in fact, you would have had an older brother, but when he was your age, the monster got him? What if the entire neighborhood and school joined in on stoking those fears?

I bet a child raised like that would exhibit the telltale signs of C-PTSD outlined in the previous chapter. As he got older, I bet he'd have nightmares or flashbacks about those dreadful nights as an adult. And to help him cope and avoid any under-the-bed monsters, he'd develop a strange sleeping strategy. These strategies could be as simple as insisting on a solid bed frame with no space under the bed or sleeping directly on the floor. His hypervigilant state would likely make sleeping difficult for him as an adult.

I'd like to point out that medical and scientific communities have only recently recognized that religious beliefs can and do cause trauma. We're all familiar with how fringe religious cults and their negative social environments can inflict deep psychological trauma on their members.[1] The focus of these discussions tended to center on the overt manipulation, coercion, and brainwashing techniques used by such charismatic leaders.

In 2011, when Dr. Marlene Winell coined the term "Religious Trauma Syndrome" to describe the aftereffects of toxic religious experiences, the academic psychological community tried very hard to call "bullshit." She began talking publicly about this phenomenon as early as 2006 in her popular book, *Leaving the Fold: A Guide to Former Funda-*

mentalists and Others Leaving Their Religion. Still, convincing academics was an entirely separate hurdle.

When mainstream religion becomes the focus of trauma, religion is generally treated as a benign social environment where more standard trauma occurs. So, those discussions around religious trauma were limited to how individuals in power abused their authority and traumatized vulnerable people. The focus was on Catholic priests molesting altar boys, Baptist ministers abusing female congregants, or pastors demanding a "happy ending" from their massage therapists because of their sickened minds and warped sense of entitlement. Historically, these transgressions were viewed as the extent of what passed for religious trauma, with the religious aspects of these situations dismissed as incidental.

We now know that religious trauma is not just about big, egregious events. People can be traumatized by a wide array of *adverse religious experiences* (AREs). An ARE is "any experience of a religious belief, practice, or structure that undermines an individual's sense of safety or autonomy and/or negatively impacts their physical, social, emotional, relational, or psychological well-being."[2] These adverse religious experiences can be major or minor and can, but do not necessarily, cause trauma. Adverse religious experiences are unique to each individual, and many members of religious groups may never experience them.

Researcher Dan Koch created the "Spiritual Harm & Abuse Scale" (SHAS), a 27-item self-report inventory capturing both exposures to potentially spiritually abusive experiences in Christian churches or group settings and common internal responses to those adverse experiences.[3] The scale consists of sixteen statements referring to potentially harmful experiences, and respondents indicate the extent to which they have experienced these situations. There are eleven internal states that individuals may have experienced because of the harmful events they endured (e.g., feeling isolated, having a lack of self-worth, feeling betrayed by God, feeling self-hatred, or experiencing self-loathing). The scale perfectly captures possible adverse religious experiences. For example, one statement is, "Behavior being excessively monitored by my pastor or group members." Another is, "Vivid descriptions of Hell, Satan, Demons, or the end of the world being taught to young children." Yet another is, "Being denied opportunities to serve because of my gender." Lastly, another is "Being pressured to forgive an abuser while the abuse was ongoing."

Many technical definitions of religious trauma have been countered through the arguments of skeptics and critics, who typically belong to the offending religious traditions themselves. Using broad definitions, these defenders can blithely dismiss the "religious" element in "religious trauma" as the chance social location (wrong place, wrong time) of otherwise well-defined and accepted trauma.

Unfortunately, these broad definitions gave teeth to the common dismissive refrain that "a religion, faith or book cannot be abuse, but the people interpreting can make anything abusive."[4] One of this book's central themes is that religious beliefs, in and of themselves, can and do cause considerable harm that manifests as trauma after the fact.

The point is that trauma is not confined to abusive behaviors and disturbing events. Indoctrinated beliefs can be traumatizing. Religious trauma experts define religious trauma as "the physical, emotional, or psychological response to religious beliefs, practices, or structures that overwhelm an individual's ability to cope and return to a sense of safety."[5] Religious beliefs carry tremendous power to either heal or harm. Toxic and traumatizing theologies have consequences and lasting effects. The marginalization, domestication, and traumatization of others through dominance and ideological rhetoric, in the garbs of pseudo-liberative religion, is precisely what we are exploring in this book.

The threat of Eternal Conscious Torment by an angry, wrathful Deity, would certainly seem to qualify as a monster-under-the-bed-style belief that could cause considerable trauma. Note that in this case, religion is not simply the environment within which the trauma happens to take place. Rather, religion is the chief orchestrator and cause of the trauma. Therapists have noted that various teachings on sexuality and sexual purity also cause clear psychological damage. Religious teachings on the end times, female submission in abusive relationships, mental illness, and demons have also been categorized as traumatizing for some. My field has only recently begun to recognize and legitimize this type of trauma in the literature amid strong pushback, unsurprisingly from conservative religious groups.

Marlene Winell's very first example of the types of toxic religious experiences that might qualify as traumatic was "toxic teachings like eternal damnation and original sin." Winell describes the broader PTSD experience of leaving one's religious tradition due to toxic or traumatizing teachings as follows: "Leaving a religion after total immersion can cause a complete upheaval of a person's construction of reality, including the self, other people, life, and the future. People unfamiliar with this situation, including therapists, have trouble appreciating the sheer terror it can create."[6] Popular author Reba Riley coined the term "Post-Traumatic Church Syndrome" to describe this same experience.[7] Riley identifies the following destructive side effects of religious trauma: "...anger, grief, despair, depression, failure to believe in anything, moral confusion, loss of gravity, and emptiness."[8]

Since trauma is subjective, it's important we don't get bogged down by requiring a precise cluster of symptoms or a pristine academic definition of religious trauma. They are undoubtedly helpful and necessary for the wider academic psychological community to take religious trauma seriously. However, what is paramount is the lived experiences of those who painfully shout, "This was traumatic to me!" We are invited into people's stories of trauma. We are encouraged to listen carefully to the intricate ways their trauma intersects with their view of self, others, and the world around them.

Consider Elizabeth Baker's story. Elizabeth is a suburban mom from Texas who has written extensively about her journey away from the conservative Christian tradition within which she was raised while still wanting to follow the life and teachings of Jesus.[9] She grew up believing "I was born with my sinful nature" and, "according to the church, I deserve death simply for existing." This and other foundational tenets her parents and church taught her throughout childhood caused bitter distress.

Despite Elizabeth having documented her spiritual journey out of the religious tradition that caused significant emotional pain, she remains haunted by her religious past. Virtually all of Elizabeth's social networks—her family, friends, neighbors, and other soccer moms—are firmly embedded within this religious tradition. She continually wrote publicly about the incongruence she observed between self-proclaimed Christians and the way they led their lives. So, it wasn't a surprise when their responses to her critiques were not exactly affirming her journey. Elizabeth, writing about her trauma, shares:

> I don't sleep through the night anymore. I suffer from near daily panic attacks and almost constant anxiety. The source of my joy, my security, and my identity has vanished, leaving me with an angry grief that almost no one in my immediate circle understands. I have relationships that were once life-giving but have turned toxic. I feel manipulated, deceived, and abused. And why? The church that raised me is gaslighting me.[10]

Anxiety attacks specifically tied to Elizabeth's former religious beliefs destroyed her sleep. Lack of sleep then caused her nervous system to pump her full of the stress hormone cortisol, keeping her on edge. Anxiety was a constant companion; grief and anger were her ever-present sparring partners. Discovering her true identity or conjuring up any sense of joy disoriented her. However, one thing was clear: Elizabeth realized she was in an abusive relationship with a toxic religious system. Sounds like religious trauma to me.

It's fascinating that current members of Elizabeth's church cannot grasp that the trauma Elizabeth describes is related to their shared beliefs. Many of her blog posts focused on the new dynamics of her interactions with her former faith community. Many individuals expressed experiencing the church quite differently than Elizabeth, perhaps even relishing their time there. Others may have encountered similar negative religious experiences as Elizabeth, without the consequent symptoms of trauma. This suggests that we must always appreciate the individual's subjective experience and be sensitive to people's unique interpretations of traumatic events. Complex trauma is cumulative and multi-layered rather than one-dimensional.

RELIGIOUS DISORIENTATION GROWTH SYNDROME

I also find it necessary to distinguish religious trauma from what I coined Religious Disorientation Growth Syndrome (RDGS) in a previous publication, *Religious Refugees*.[11] While the term *syndrome* is out of vogue among many contemporary researchers, my initial aim in developing this term was to describe a cluster of signs and symptoms I frequently observed in my clinical work with people actively decon-structing and reconstructing their faith. In creating the term, I attempted to normalize the experiences of these individuals in an effort to help them feel more sane and less alone.

RDGS is characterized by six indicators: 1) doubting or denying one's once strongly maintained religious beliefs; 2) subtle or intense anxiety about one's relationship with God; 3) an increase in painful emotions such as anger, loneliness, shame, guilt, sadness, and despair; 4) isolation and criticism (feared or realized) from members of one's family and/or religious community; 5) existential angst concerning one's identity and future self; and 6) disorientation arising from these experiences becoming a powerful catalyst for colossal emotional, mental, and spiritual growth.

I have found that those who suffer Religious Trauma in response to a series of Adverse Religious Experiences that occur over prolonged periods also often exhibit profound C-PTSD symptoms. Acute symp-toms of Religious Disorientation Growth Syndrome can be highly disorienting, though this condition generally seems to represent a spiritual metamorphosis or *faith shift*, shorter in duration than Reli-gious Trauma[12]. In my clinical experience, Religious Disorientation

Growth Syndrome requires less intense trauma work than Religious Trauma.

PRACTICAL DISTINCTIONS

To better clarify the distinction between Adverse Religious Experiences, Religious Disorientation Growth Syndrome, and Religious Trauma (RT), let's consider Serena, Shawn, and Sarah. Serena grew up Christian and often attended a youth group. She remembers experiencing a few AREs. She recalls enjoying rap music but also that some kids in her youth group told her it was "the Devil's music." She remembers feeling hurt and rejected, sometimes feeling like an outcast. Serena got older, went to college, and eventually left the faith, saying, "When I went to college, I just left Christianity altogether. Now, being older, I have no regrets. Christianity had its good and bad moments. Life goes on." Serena experienced AREs but was able to move on and live her life confidently after rejecting Christianity.

Shawn grew up Christian and was very involved in his church. As an adult, he experienced a spiritual metamorphosis that involved deconstructing and reconstructing his faith. Shawn experienced AREs in the form of verbal abuse, harmful and oppressive doctrines such as eternal conscious torment, and being isolated from and rejected by members of his religious community. He experienced the disorientation of RDGS and had to wrestle with doubt, acute anxiety, feelings of anger and sadness, and experiences of isolation. Despite these difficult feelings, Shawn does not experience RT or suffer from C-PTSD. After a few months of talking with others, reading books, and listening to podcasts, Shawn indicates feeling great and content with his spiritual journey.

Sarah grew up in a very conservative evangelical family. They went to church weekly, including the midweek Bible study. She encountered many AREs over the years, including those experienced by her parents. Her parents often used scriptures and the threat of Hell to guilt her into good behavior. In her late twenties, Sarah realized that religion was doing her more harm than good. Eventually, after much wrestling and internal anguish, she developed the courage to leave her family's church. After leaving, she realized that she was struggling with depression, chronic anxiety, and shame. These feelings were accompanied by occasional nightmares about going to Hell. While she experienced many of these symptoms before leaving her church, Sarah's symptoms intensified afterwards, lasting for over three months. Sarah had a severe case of RT and C-PTSD, which has taken her years to overcome.

As mentioned, RT's clinical symptoms are usually more severe than RDGS. Clearly delineating these terms can be helpful for those who are processing their own spiritual concerns, and for those working to support others struggling with religious trauma.

Now that we have an improved understanding of the basics related to religious trauma, let's explore the negative consequences of C-PTSD symptoms that follow the religious trauma of Hell indoctrination.

CHAPTER 3
HELL ANXIETY

"I could do nothing to change my fate if God had chosen me for Hell—but my mother understood my need for comfort. "It's a good sign that you're afraid," she said. "It means that you care what God requires of you."

—Megan Phelps-Roper, *Unfollow*

Mason had spent much of his life confined by the rules set by his conservative church. His parents and religious leaders made it clear: anyone who dared question God's word would be met with an angry God. Apostates—those who chose to leave the church—would burn in Hell.

However, as an adult, he moved away from his strict religious upbringing. Mason felt like he didn't fit into any one label or group. He definitely didn't want to be a fundamentalist Christian. At the same time, he wasn't comfortable with the label "progressive" either, although he felt more comfortable with those who considered themselves progressive.

Despite his belief that Hell and eternal conscious torment were not real, Mason still experienced significant anxiety about the possibility of Hell. Despite his rational beliefs, he couldn't shake the feeling that it could still be true.

One day as Mason scrolled through Facebook, he saw an article that made his heart skip a beat: "Franklin Graham: The Eternal Peril of Progressive Christianity."[1] Though he knew better, curiosity won out, and he clicked on the article. Before long, Mason found himself reading every word with dread deepening by the second. And then there it was —words no person terrified of going to Hell wants to read: "Progressive Christianity can send a person to hell."[2]

"Yikes!" he said to himself. "This is *Billy Graham's* son speaking, the son of God's most famous preacher. Surely, he's got the inside scoop of God's truth."

Mason immediately spiraled into panic mode; all sorts of questions flooded his mind at once: *Was this true? Would God really condemn someone who practiced progressive Christianity? What did this mean for my own beliefs?*

Mason's heart pounded in his ears. He felt light-headed like he'd lost his center of gravity. His stomach contracted in knots. He couldn't quite catch his breath. He couldn't keep up with his racing thoughts. He feared that he really was on a wayward path drifting toward eternal conscious torment.

Why was Mason having this reaction?

Because he was massively triggered. Hell anxiety was kicking his ass!

HELL ANXIETY

To date, scientific research into Hell-related trauma has been sparse. Researchers have, however, coined the term *Hell anxiety* to encapsulate the apprehension many people experience regarding the concept of Hell. They've also created the "Hell Anxiety Scale," a questionnaire to measure this anxiety.[3] The scale is comprised of nine statements.

Respondents are asked to indicate how much each statement applies to them. Some example statements are: "Sometimes it's difficult to control my worry about Hell," "I feel an intense fear of Hell when I do something I'm not supposed to do," and "I am fearful when ministers and other religious authorities talk about Hell."

Baylor University conducted a study that concluded: "people who fear Hell are some of the most anxious Americans".[4] Another showed that priming, or having participants think about Hell elicited by relevant prompts, "leads to lower levels of positive emotion and higher levels of negative emotion, compared to controls."[5] These conclusions are straightforward enough. Anticipating a punishment causes anxiety —think of the kid in the 1950s waiting to receive a spanking when their father comes home. Worrying about meeting someone else's high standards causes anxiety. So, it's little wonder that thinking about a God who can cause extreme torment in one's afterlife for failure to live up to His standards in this life can cause profound psychological responses, including negative feelings and overwhelming anxiety.

While this research helps to sketch the big picture, we must hear people's lived experiences regarding religious trauma and the effects of Hell anxiety to get a clear sense of what is happening here. In her book, *Leaving the Fold,* mentioned in the previous chapter, Marlene Winell talked about a woman named Charlotte, who described her Hell anxiety in some detail:

> They quoted the scripture about the camel that can't get through the eye of a needle, so even one little sin can't get into heaven. So even though I was a real good kid, every time that I thought anything bad or felt anything that I thought was bad or did anything that somebody else thought was bad, I automatically thought that if I died at that moment, I'd go to Hell. Even though I had already accepted Jesus and went to church and did everything I was supposed to do, I had nightmares and was always anxious. I went up to the altar all the time to ask forgiveness.[6]

Another author, Dennis Gunnarson, describes similar experiences in his book on faith deconstruction: "Growing up in the church, the message of eternal punishment was vividly presented. I responded to the altar call for salvation almost every week. I was afraid I would go to Hell if I didn't."[7]

I remember one of my own experiences of Hell anxiety at a United Pentecostal Church (UPC) conference. The UPC was a strict, no-nonsense, Holy Ghost–stammering Christian group I was connected to for a while. We took our faith and the Bible extremely seriously. So seriously, in fact, that it was a sin for women to cut their hair. I couldn't have facial hair or grow long hair because that's how our church interpreted passages in the Bible that mentioned beards and the long hair of men as sinful. Only those who spoke in tongues were considered saved, and, according to our church, Trinitarians were going to Hell. By the way, as of 2020, 70% of Americans said they believe in the Trinity,[8] so the number of so-called Christians we thought were going to Hell was a lot.

During the conference, I had a conversation with a well-known preacher. I felt like I was in the presence of royalty. I was so nervous I could barely speak. After some small talk, I briefly mentioned to the preacher that I drank wine at a wedding, which, being a fairly new Christian, I didn't think was much of an issue. He clearly disagreed. His eyes widened and took on a fierce sternness while his cheeks reddened. His eyes pierced through me as he pronounced that I was in danger of hellfire. I was shocked. My heart raced, and I immediately feared for my life. It was as if God himself had spoken to me. The thought of going to Hell terrified me. Talk about an adverse religious experience. That experience, along with dozens like it, created a level of Hell Anxiety within me that eventually became unbearable and took me years to overcome.

It turns out that the experiences that Charlotte, Dennis, and I had are not uncommon. Margaret Steel Farrell grew up in the Catholic church. She writes about Hell anxiety in the book *Leaving Fundamentalism,* "But I never quite knew my status with God because I never knew if I was repentant enough for Him. . . I always had this fear that when I died, I'd get to Heaven, and God would say, 'Ah-ha! Remember that time you did such and such? Well, you thought you were forgiven, but you weren't. You're going to Hell!'"[9] An anonymous young woman interviewed in a 2009 research study treating this topic shared her anxiety about whether to date a non-Christian. She recalls thinking, *You're not gonna be happy; you're gonna live a life of evil; Satan will have a hold of you; and you'll basically burn in Hell in the afterlife.*[10] Krispin Mayfield expressed this same theme, writing about his own experiences in his book, *Attached to God*:

> I've always been terrified of Hell. I could never quite relax with God because I always worried . . . that in the end it'd turn out I was a goat, not a sheep. This fear has always hung over my head, causing me to white-knuckle my spiritual life. What if I didn't have true faith? What if, between now and my death, I made some terrible decisions or ended up renouncing my faith? As much as I wanted to feel safe in the everlasting arms, I knew that I wasn't. If anyone could go to Hell, then I could go to Hell, which meant I could never relax.[11]

Thus far, research into Hell anxiety has typically focused on the individual's anxious feelings about their own future state. But the insidious way this belief is constructed means that, even if I jumped through all the hoops and managed the fear of my future, there was always the same concern about others. Since the actions, beliefs, and motives of others were entirely out of my control, relief from this Hell anxiety loop was never possible. There's plenty of evidence to suggest that my intense Hell anxiety was not restricted to the fate of my soul but that I was also perpetually anxious over others' eternal conscious torment. As one participant in a study detailed in the research paper *The Resurrection of Self* put it:

> You wake up in the night screaming because you're afraid your mama's going to Hell. Or *I'm going to Hell*, or that even though I was

baptized, what if I don't really believe, or I've committed this sin... does *that* mean I'm not really a Christian and I've gotta go find uncle so and so who doesn't go to church because he might die, and he will go to Hell?[12]

I certainly carried that anxious burden as well. As a 21-year-old, I carried with me a terrible dread that each of my family members and every person I met on the street was destined to spend eternity in Hell unless they became "born again." But since a "born again" experience clearly wasn't enough, this dread kept sending me back to the altar at every church meeting. Nothing could ever assuage my doubts. Everyone around me, even those I knew were "Christian" and born again, might not actually be "saved." My Oneness Pentecostal church taught that only those baptized in Jesus' name *and* who didn't believe in the Trinity were truly saved or, at the very least, more likely to be saved. I can't tell you how many times I was told, "Their blood is on your hands if you don't tell them about Jesus," in reference to everyone I met. I was wracked with fear and shed many tears, agonizing in prayer, begging God to save other people from Hell. The weight of the world rested on my shoulders in a very real psychological sense. The anxiety about my eternal fate, which extended to the fate of everyone I knew, was crippling.

All of this, of course, was wasted energy. The sad realization is that the energy I expended on Hell anxiety could have been better used to love people more freely. It could have been used to consider ways to bring more beauty and goodness into the world, to learn a new hobby, or just to have more fun and enjoy life. This energy could have been directed toward effecting change in the *here* and *now* instead of the future *then* and eternal *there*. I, like others, wasted my time worrying about a projection called Hell borne out of humanity's violent proclivities and existential fears, being concerned with a tyrannical ruler called *God*, and fretting about a make-believe place of eternal torment called Hell.

SCRUPULOSITY

Hell anxiety manifests along a mild-to-severe spectrum. At the more severe end is *scrupulosity*, a topic I'll discuss briefly here as it's a brutal form of psychological suffering that deserves attention.

Obsessive-compulsive disorder (OCD) is typically composed of *obsessions*, which can take the form of undesirable and intrusive urges, desires, doubts, and thoughts. OCD also entails *compulsions*, which are actions an individual performs in an attempt to relieve the anxiety caused by their obsessions.

Religious Scrupulosity Obsessive Compulsive Disorder is a subtype of OCD that literally means *fearing sin where there is none.*[13] Scrupulosity involves obsessions and compulsions that revolve around religion and morality. Jonathan Abramowitz and Samantha Hellberg, researchers and experts on this subject, provide examples of common religious obsessions. These can include:

> Recurrent doubts that one has committed sins or moral transgressions by mistake or without realizing it (e.g., "Did I swallow too much saliva and violate the religious fast?"); intrusive sacrilegious or blasphemous thoughts and images (e.g., "God doesn't exist"); doubts that one is not faithful, moral, or pious enough (e.g.,"What if I enjoyed watching a movie that portrayed homosexuality?"); fears that one did not perform a religious prayer or ceremony properly (e.g., "What if my mind wandered while I was praying?"); and persistent fears of eternal damnation and punishment from God (e.g., "What if I go to Hell when I die?").[14]

While OCD compulsions can be triggered by guilt or disgust, the most common triggers are anxieties and fears. Religious compulsive behaviors or rituals are performed to ease anxiety and reduce the fears associated with religious obsessions. Common rituals include repeating Bible verses, writing verses down again and again, anxiously praying to God, frequenting every single church service offered by the community, and constantly seeking reassurance, to name a few. One notable feature of scrupulosity is the tendency for individuals to manage their anxieties by avoiding anything that might trigger obsessions and compulsions. This can be challenging when people consider themselves religious and are expected to attend religious functions.[15]

Abramowitz and Hellberg write that oftentimes "scrupulosity involves the perception of sin, fear of violating religious doctrine, and fear of divine punishment."[16] That reminds me of one meeting with a friend struggling with scrupulosity. He was a disheveled mess, consumed by worry, struggling to sleep, and in a semi-permanent state of panic. Plagued by thoughts of blasphemy against the Holy Spirit, he feared he was doomed to Hell because he couldn't stop his lustful thoughts. My friend hid his turmoil from his devout parents, seeking salvation through the reassurances of church members and the assistant pastor. The reassurance they offered provided momentary relief, but the panic would soon build up again. Then, after the anxieties built up, he would again begin the compulsive activity of trying to secure assurance from those around him.

Debra Peck, author of *The Hijacked Conscience*, writes about her journey with Religious Scrupulosity Obsessive Compulsive Disorder.[17] She discovered her diagnosis after forty years of suffering from it. She was a conscientious child with an anxious predisposition who always sought to do the right thing. Unfortunately, her church experiences at the time were not helpful to her.

She grew up in a conservative holiness church and frequently attended revival services. She often heard guilt-inducing statements at those revivals like, "If you don't feel God's presence, there's something wrong with you!" Even raising her hands in worship was a dilemma for her. She could feel the preacher's disapproval when folks in the congregation didn't raise their hands in worship. To not raise your hands was a sign that you were not saved and genuinely loving Jesus. However, not raising her hands would incur the preacher's and congregation's judgmental gaze. This caused her to feel tremendous anxiety and continual self-doubt in Christian gatherings.

Debra's conscience was perpetually in overdrive. She was constantly obsessing about doing the right thing before God and always fretted that she'd committed an unpardonable sin. She read in the Bible that Old Testament priests of the Old Testament had to be clean before serving in the Temple. Her obsessions about cleanliness and being covered caused her to engage in constant compulsions. She writes, "I would wash before devotional times or religious services. I could not pray unless my body was appropriately clothed—my most personal parts completely covered. No praying in the shower for me! In fact, being naked at all became nearly intolerable for fear that I would accidentally pray while uncovered." She read about the Apostle Paul taking sin seriously and encouraging Christians to beat their bodies into submission. Because of her anxiety and wanting to follow the letter of the law, she writes, "I would beat myself to show God I was sorry for my sins and serious about serving God." Questioning the rules and rigidity of the church would cause her immense anxiety. She writes about the challenges of questioning the status quo: "It is difficult to convey what a challenge this was with the Scrupulosity OCD always screaming in the background. I was terrified I would be deceived and go to hell!"

OCD is a pervasive human condition and has even been observed in animals.[18] How a person develops this form of mental and emotional anguish is not yet fully understood. The current evidence indicates an amalgamation of genetic, biological, familial, and environmental factors. As a form of OCD, scrupulosity appears across cultures. Interestingly, there seems to be a higher prevalence of religious obsessions in OCD patients that follow more traditional or orthodox religions.[19] I am convinced that scrupulosity would be reduced if there were fewer religious teachings that set out to scare followers with thoughts of a wrathful God, evil and sinful humans, and an afterlife where eternal torture is possible.

CHAPTER 4
SHAME AND SELF-CRITICISM

"This faith I was living in nurtured my shame. I believed there was inherently something wrong with me, irredeemable even... Sure, he loved me in a "you're my kid, I have to love you" sort of way. Deep down, however, he was so displeased with me that he couldn't stand to look in my direction. His sense of purity would not allow him to."

—Ben DeLong, *There's a God in My Closet*

S teven was raised by strict, religious parents who taught him about a God of wrath and judgment. Despite his best efforts, he could never seem to live up to their expectations or the expectations of this God they spoke so highly of. He was constantly told that if he ever strayed from the path of righteousness, then Hell would be his punishment for eternity.

So, when it finally came time for him to make an independent decision about religion as an adult, he felt a heavy burden on his shoulders. Steven thought about the loving, kind, and generous church members.

However, being surrounded by such goodness wasn't enough for him to fully commit to faith-based living. Deep down inside, Steven was afraid that he wasn't good enough to turn his back on what he'd been taught since childhood. So, instead of acting on what really made sense in his heart and soul, he reverted to his habit of attending church services every Sunday morning just like before.

Sitting alone during church service one day, Steven's internal turmoil erupted. The brim of his hat veiled the tears spilling down his face. He'd decided that enough was enough. This life wasn't meant for him anymore. Over time, slowly but steadily, he started walking away until no one saw or heard from him again.

However, after leaving religion behind altogether, it seemed like no matter how far removed he was physically or mentally, the shame and guilt always lingered like an invisible chain around his neck, dragging and weighing down any chance at true freedom and joy. So, Steven turned to drugs to help momentarily numb the pain. But they only created more issues that drove him deeper into isolation and depression. Outwardly, nothing prevented him from moving forward, but internally, he was full of potent, unrelenting shame and fear. These feelings were rooted in past teachings about an angry God who punished sinners by sending them to Hell. Even after leaving church behind, Steven believed wholeheartedly that he was a wretched sinner deserving eternal punishment.

The doctrine of Hell is deeply connected to the doctrine of Original Sin and a view that all human beings from the moment of their birth are unclean and repulsive to a holy and perfect God. As Hell-Bound People, we humans have zero worth in and of ourselves. We are objects deserving of wrath, and there is nothing good within us or about us. Taking this theology to its logical conclusion, even eternal conscious torment proponents that wax poetic about God loving us must admit that it cannot be *us* whom God loves. According to Hell-Bound People theology, God cannot even look at us without wanting to send us into the pit of Hell because we are evil (a common belief that even Jesus alluded to in Matthew 7:11). This narrative proposes that because we are so repugnant before God, He can only see us through the prism of Jesus. God's disgust and wrath toward us are absorbed by Christ. So, humans are nothing, and Christ is everything.

For those who consider that description overly dramatic, note the following outline of this theology by Jonathan Edwards, a revered revivalist preacher in the 18th century, with a narrative adhered to by many today:

> The God that holds you over the pit of Hell, much as one holds a spider, or some other loathsome insect, over the fire, abhors you, and is dreadfully provoked; his wrath toward you burns like fire; he looks upon you as worthy of nothing else, but to be cast into the fire; he is of purer eyes than to bear to have you in his sight; you are ten thousand times so abominable in his eyes as the most hateful venomous serpent is in ours.[1]

Unfortunately, such theology has consequences, and in this case, not particularly pleasant ones! The pathological ramifications of indoctrinating willing followers and children who can't even consent to follow a religious path with Hell indoctrination are grievous. These toxic theologies can potentially create monumental soul wounds with such insidious and destructive reverberations that their effects may take many years to overcome. That was certainly the case for Steven. Two of the most harmful aspects of C-PTSD following the religious trauma of Hell indoctrination are shame and its common bedfellow, self-criticism.

SHAME AND SELF-CRITICISM

Although most researchers differentiate between guilt and shame, there is surprisingly no consensus concerning their exact definitions. *Guilt* is commonly understood as an aversive experience that individuals feel after they perceive they've done something wrong. It is focused on behavior and the negative implications of that behavior.

Those who feel guilty typically experience remorse. If the guilt is due to one's actions toward others, the person is often motivated to repair the harmed relationship. *Shame*, on the other hand, is focused almost exclusively on the self. Moreover, toxic shame causes individuals to believe that they *are* something wrong or that they are flawed, inferior, or tainted in some way.

Lewis Smedes describes shame as "a vague, undefined heaviness that presses on our spirit, dampens our gratitude for the goodness of life, and slackens the free flow of joy. Shame. . . [not only] seeps into and discolors all our other feelings, primarily about ourselves, but about almost everyone and everything else in our life as well."[2] Unhealed shame is a body and soul-poisoning emotion, draining our vitality and painfully chaining us to an internal cave of sheer darkness. Therefore, it is a formidable obstacle that prevents others from recognizing the light and beauty within us.

Paul Gilbert, a well-known researcher on shame, differentiates between internal and external shame.[3] Internal shame involves a hyper-acute awareness of how one feels flawed and inadequate. This shame-oriented awareness of the self is usually accompanied by negative self-evaluation. For example, due to internal shame, Lyndsay could have shame-based thoughts, such as, *I am broken and too emotional. Something is really wrong with me.* Those are thoughts she is having about herself. In contrast, if she felt external shame she would be "sensitive to negative feelings and thoughts about the self in the minds of others."[4] In this case, due to external shame, Lyndsay could have the thought, *Others think I am broken and that I am too emotional.*

I define religious shame as *an intense and lasting neurobiological imprint that was formed in a religious context that perpetually affects a person's core identity (i.e., worthlessness, unlovability, etc.) and decreases their overall quality of life.* For some, when a pastor harshly warned them a powerful God will throw them into the pit of Hell because of their sin, they may have perpetuated feelings of religious guilt and shame. When parents admonish their children, "Don't do that; God is watching and doesn't like disobedience," they inflict religious guilt and shame on their children. When youth pastors use the Bible to condemn and harshly judge those working through and integrating their sexuality, they inject them with poisonous religious guilt and shame. Internal and external religious shame arising from Hell trauma can be potent contributors to intense emotional suffering and may catapult individuals into addiction, self-harm, or harming others.

Shame often leads to paralyzing self-criticism. While a degree of self-criticism can be useful and even beneficial, too much can quickly become harmful. Self-criticism is strongly related to a host of psychopathologies, including anxiety, anger and aggression, depression, perfectionism, and self-harm.

One popular view of self-criticism has been detailed by Gilbert, who describes it as the tendency to engage in self-judgment directed toward different aspects of the self, including behaviors, emotions, thoughts, and performance.[5] Gilbert notes that there are different forms of self-criticism. For some, it involves feeling small, incapable, and inferior, while for others it may be connected to self-hatred due to past trauma.

I define religious self-criticism as *the negative evaluation of the self, based on repeated contact with past religious propositions, practices, policies, and persons.* Here are some shame-based, self-critical statements from people I've worked with on their Hell trauma:

- "I feel tainted. I deserve to be alone."
- "I feel horrible about myself. People don't want me. God doesn't even want me."
- "I feel like I did something wrong for this to happen. Truth is, there were a lot of sinful things I did in my life. God is probably right to punish me."
- "I deserve to go to Hell."
- "God hates me for being gay. I don't want to burn in Hell."
- "God loves everyone else but me."
- "I cannot trust my core self because it is wicked."

- "I am sinful and no good. Any goodness that I have is like a filthy rag to Him."
- "I am unloved. God is mad at me. What is the point of living?"
- "I am terrible for deconstructing my faith. I am nervous that I will bring my family along with me on the road to destruction."

Personal testimony provides sharp perspective on how the trauma of Hell and its related doctrines lead to shame, self-criticism, and other adverse effects. One participant in a 2022 research study shared this about his anxiety over himself, God, and Hell:

I learned that He [God] couldn't be around me because I was permanently unholy. I learned that anyone who wasn't straight was an abomination destined for hell, and that even if I was saved and would go to heaven, I would still be separated from God because I was unholy. God couldn't have me near Him even in heaven.[6]

David, a friend of mine, shared with me his own experiences of Hell trauma, relaying to me, "Mark, I was raised as a Pentecostal Christian. I constantly heard how my righteousness was as filthy rags. I was constantly made to feel that with each lustful look, every thought about myself in a really positive way, and each prideful glance, God can send me to Hell in an instant." Alison Downie, associate professor in the Department of Religious Studies at Indiana University of Pennsylvania, writes about her religious shame due to Hell indoctrination at an early age:

I remember sermons about the indisputable proof of total depravity being children, who are bad in all natural inclinations and behaviors. I specifically remember the congregation's knowing chuckle in response to the minister's quip that " No one needs to teach a child how to lie." I also vividly recall a time of private prayer in which I tried with all my might to cry, to show God how sorry I was for being such a horrible sinner. I could not think of anything particularly bad I had done recently, but I knew without doubt I deserved hell. I was ten years old.[7]

A study exploring the underlying mechanisms of religious trauma among young LGBTQIA+ people detailed their accounts of feeling intense shame and constant dread about the fires of Hell. The researchers wrote, "The intensity of rhetoric directed against them imbues a deep fear of the sexual dimensions of their identity, perpetuating cycles of shame and self-loathing that frame their whole sense of self."[8] Matthew Distefano, in his book *Learning to Float*, writes about his confusion about the prospects of a violent God and disappointment in a God who could not love him for who he really was:

And then there were the questions about God's nature. Why was his solution to my sin so archaic? Hell? *Really?* Eternal torment? Violence to the nth degree? Abandonment times a trillion? I had a dad who left me when I was at my most vulnerable, so why did I need a heavenly father who was the exact same? He is the one who made me, *right?* Then why was he going to hold my ineptitude against me for all eternity?[9]

Kevin Miguel Garcia, author of *Bad Theology Kills*, discusses the "internal shame narrative in Queer Folks" due to the Hell-Bound People teachings they have been taught. He writes about the messages he internalized, "It's very clear logic. Who I am is sinful. God hates sin. So, God hates me. Because I am an abomination."[10] He continues:

When you hear your whole life that your sexuality is displeasing to the God of the Universe, to your Heavenly Father (whom you already see as pretty punitive because you grew up in a very narrow religious space), and being that your sexuality is deeply interwoven with your body, your spirit, and your essence, you can imagine how easy it is to fall into the belief that you, at your core, are bad.[11]

Unhealed shame can be one of the most harmful emotions a human can experience, especially if it's left to fester and darken one's view of self and others. It's unthinkable that the debilitating feeling that one is unlovable, tainted, dirty, and no good, and the toxic fuel this provides to the Inner Critic, is often perpetuated by religion that preaches freedom and abundance. It's mind-boggling that parents can teach their kids they're sinful and deserving of hell only to create a hellish view of themselves. But unfortunately, we see it all too often in our daily lives.

CHAPTER 5
"I FEEL BETRAYED."

"When we're injured by betrayal, we can suffer high levels of anxiety,
depression, anger, sadness, jealousy, decreased self-worth,
embarrassment, humiliation, shame,
and even trauma symptoms."

—Brené Brown, *Atlas of the Heart*

Darius is a man in his mid-30s who spent much of his early childhood immersed in religious activities. His parents were very religious and went to church often, sometimes three times a week. He has been a worship leader in a Baptist church for the past five years. During our conversation he shared that he loves God but has always felt a little distant from Him. Darius is highly skilled and people hold him in high esteem for his musicianship and ability to lead the congregation in heartfelt worship. However, he said that while on one level he believed God loved him, on another he felt that he was hiding a theological secret. Darius struggled with the idea of a God who could be so punishing, and he constantly feared that if was not perfect, without blemish, he could lose his salvation and spend eternity in Hell.

Fearing that God was continually angry at him, Darius struggled with anxiety and depression and experienced intrusive thoughts about having sinned. He started reading books on deconstruction and listening to podcasts that were considered "progressive." At this point, he didn't know what he really believed. He started to feel angry and didn't know why. After some time working together, Darius revealed to me that he felt "betrayed by God." It was as if the dam of cognitive dissonance broke—and the rushing waters of angry thoughts and feelings about God he had thus far managed to keep at bay suddenly came crashing through.

After confronting the version of God he had been taught his whole life, Darius felt angry that he was in relationship with what he called a "schizophrenic" God, and blamed God for the anxiety and depression he developed in response to all the "legalistic" doctrines he had been taught.[1] He was also angry that God could send people to Hell. He felt "gaslighted" by God and talked about wanting to extract himself from a relationship with an abusive Deity. He was experiencing something highly reminiscent of what psychologists refer to as "betrayal trauma."

According to researchers, "betrayal trauma occurs when the people or institutions on which a person depends for survival violate that person in a significant way."[2] Betrayal trauma is most often examined in reference to childhood physical, emotional, or sexual abuse. A core principle of betrayal trauma is that "the way in which events are processed and remembered will be related to the degree to which a negative event represents a betrayal by a trusted, needed other."[3]

In other words, the more dependent we are on someone and the more we trust them, the more severe the trauma will be if we are betrayed. Researchers have shown that "traumas high in betrayal are linked with greater severity of PTSD, anxiety, dissociation, alexithymia [inability to describe or express one's feelings], and depression symptoms relative to traumas low in betrayal."[4]

Within the betrayal trauma concept is the term *betrayal blindness*, which relates to how victims may be blind to trauma out of a desire to keep a relationship intact. An example would be a woman in an abusive relationship who denies how badly she is being abused so as not to lose the relationship. This blindness stems from a need to maintain the attachment relationship at all costs, and may involve denial, suppression, repression, and dissociation. Another strategy victims of betrayal use to avoid fully acknowledging the perpetrator's betrayal and abuse is to unconsciously, and tragically, blame and shame themselves: "The reason why he belittled me was because I deserved it. If I was not so dumb, then he would not have yelled at me like that."

Returning to Darius, there seems to be a strong resemblance between the experiences identified in betrayal trauma theory and Darius's thoughts and actions in his relationship with God. We could place Darius as the victim in this relationship and God as the perpetrator. When I discuss *God as the perpetrator*, I do not mean *God* in an objective, metaphysical sense. I mean the version of God that Darius has been taught. The brain does not care if the images and ideas of God that are presented to it are objectively or metaphysically true. The brain acts on what it believes to be true, regardless of how this corresponds to reality. The psychological and physiological consequences of these images and ideas will follow, whether beneficial or harmful. For Darius, the outcome was an idea of a God that was cruel, punitive, harsh, and controlling, yet also loving, kind, and gracious. This picture maps quite neatly onto the pictures we generally see in victims with an abusive partner.

Darius was in a relationship with a cruel deity, yet as soon as his betrayal blindness abated to a certain level he was better able to see his God for who He really was. While his God may have been loving and gracious at times, He could also be unpredictably harsh and judgmental. Previously, Darius would criticize himself and believe he was a horrible sinner, rather than see God for who He was—a temperamental God prone to gaslighting and abuse. Darius would see his struggle with mental and emotional problems as something he deserved. Because God is just, Darius' sins warranted the punishment of decreased joy. As Darius trusted his God immensely, the level of betrayal he felt was deep. Darius stated, "I just can't believe I fell in love with that kind of God."

Christians who believe in eternal torment and original sin might emphatically state, "Yes, you are a wretched sinner deserving of eternal torment. But God loves you so much that he sent his Son to die for you so you can go to heaven!" In my work with domestic abuse victims, I have often heard similar presentations from abusive partners. "You are a piece of garbage," the abuser would exclaim. "You ain't worth nothing. Nobody would ever love you. You are nothing without me." Then, moments later, the abuser would say, "I love you. I will do anything for you. Things can be different. Just listen to what I say, will you? If you would just listen and do what I say, I wouldn't have to hurt you and we can be happy together forever."

Under Hell-Bound People theology, God is perhaps the ultimate gaslighter. He is a powerful figure who, through manipulation and abuse, makes us question our own reality, our judgment, and our sanity. Hell-bound people theology tells us that we are nothing, or worse than nothing. We are intrinsically evil and there is nothing good within us. Yet, at the same time, we are somehow valuable, and God loves us. Can you imagine the impact on a child's mental and emotional health from a parent giving the child such contradictory messages?

If we are so absolutely dispensable that we could be thrown into eternal fire by a wrathful God, we must be exponentially more evil and despicable than we are valuable or precious. Such a God seemingly wants to save us only out of pity, and *not* because we are intrinsically lovable.

And this is where the real gaslighting kicks in. After being told such confusing and upsetting messages, we are then ordered to ignore our cognitive dissonance and to pretend it does not exist (i.e., "Don't question God's Word!"). We are manipulated into burying the dissonance deep down in the caverns of our psyches and forced, like Darius, to believe, "...that's just who we are and how God is." The emotional and spiritual consequences of this kind of religious gaslighting are profound, and seem to be particularly devastating for those with a sensitive temperament and propensity toward feeling shame. It is no surprise, then, that Christians who are regularly bombarded with these indigestible messages, are prone to C-PTSD and its consequences: shame, self-hatred, and self-criticism.

CHURCH FACTITIOUS DISORDER IMPOSED ON ANOTHER (CFDIA)

Last year, my wife and I finally had some downtime and the rare opportunity to watch a movie together. We settled on the psychological thriller, *Run*, which came out in 2020. The screenwriters introduce us to the main character, Chloe, and her mother, Diane. Chloe is paralyzed from the waist down and must take medications constantly, including for asthma. Diane appears as a loving mom, thoroughly attuned to her daughter's needs. Her interactions with her daughter are warm, showing Diane doing everything she can to take care of Chloe.

As a high school senior eager to seek out new adventure at college, Chloe has been excitedly anticipating university acceptance letters in the mail. As time goes on, however, there appears to be an unusual delay with Chloe constantly being disappointed that she has not heard from any of the schools she applied to. Her mom lovingly reassures her that when such a letter arrives, Chloe will be the first to know.

One day, searching for some yummy chocolates in a bag of groceries that her mom has just placed on the kitchen counter, Chloe finds a bottle of green pills with her mom's name on it. She is alarmed because these are the same pills that she takes for issues her mother does not have. Confused, she puts them back quickly when her mom comes back with the second load of grocery bags from the car. When Chloe asks her mom about the pills, her mom says that the pharmacy just put the receipt over the bottle with her name on it, and to not worry about it.

Something about her mom's response doesn't sit right with Chloe. She soon becomes obsessed with finding out what is going on with those pills. Through frantic twists and turns, and a display of her incredible will and strength, she is able to travel to a pharmacy. Meanwhile, her mom, Diane, has become suspicious of Chloe's intuitions and intentions and tries to stop her at every turn.

At the pharmacy, Chloe shows the pharmacist the bottle, asking about the uses and purpose of this medication. The pharmacist is leery of sharing such information, citing confidentiality concerns, but Chloe's ingenuity and quick thinking allow her to disarm the pharmacist under the guise of a scavenger hunt–type game. Discovering the answer to the simple question is the key to winning the game. At the height of the suspense, with Chloe knowing her mom is on her heels, the pharmacist finally reveals that the pills she has been taking religiously are muscle relaxants for dogs.

Shocked and processing the information as quickly as she can, Chloe follows up by asking what would happen if humans took them. At that moment, the mom runs into the pharmacy, frantically calling Chloe's name. The pharmacist, distracted for a moment by the commotion, answers Chloe with, "I suppose your legs could go numb."

The sheer look of shock and brutal betrayal on Chloe's face is tragic and terrifying (she also realizes her mom has been hiding her acceptance letters). She begins to have an asthma attack. Then, when the pharmacist goes away, Diane shoves a needle in her daughter's leg, and Chloe begins to slowly fall asleep.

The type of appalling behavior Diane exhibited in the movie would be diagnosed as *Factitious Disorder Imposed on Another (FDIA)*, which you might know by its older name *Munchausen by proxy*. Another cinematic portrayal of this condition appears in the movie *The Sixth Sense*, where the ghost Kyra gives Cole, the boy who sees dead people, a videotape. The video shows Kyra's own mother poisoning her, keeping her perpetually sick. *Church Factitious Disorder Imposed on Another (CFDIA)* is a term that I have coined that I think aptly explains the religious betrayal trauma that some people experience leaving the church.

There are many religious trauma survivors who feel much like Chloe. The pain and anguish they regularly experienced in their fears about Hell was just matter-of-fact. Like other tough things in life, they just sucked it up and had to grin and bear it as a normal part of life. They thought they were lovingly being taken care of by the church, which was the only one to really address these fears. They thought it was a safe space where the church was nurturing them with the medications of sermons, worship music, Bible studies, and altar calls. It wasn't until they made new mental connections between the pain (the fear of Hell, an angry, wrathful God, and a despicable view of self) and the medications the church was feeding them that the wheels came off and they had their WTF moment. Unfortunately, making that mental connection is never as easy as Chloe's interaction with the pharmacist. They had to first stop denying, suppressing, and repressing their doubts. They had to allow themselves to ask the troublesome questions and let the resulting piercing cognitive splinters do their thing. Only then could they realize the madness of what was going on. They were experiencing the consequences of CFDIA.

Through the teachings of the church they, like Chloe, were fed constant poison. While the church fed them medication, supposedly directed at the pain, shame, and fear, it would only make them sicker. They were told they were paralyzed by sin. They were told that they were sick inside; so sick they could do nothing good at all. They were told that their feelings were instruments of the Devil. They were told that their bodies were not to be trusted and their desires were fleshly and ungodly. They were told that their hearts and minds were desperately wicked. The sicker they felt, the more they desired the "saving" medication the church offered. That is until they realized what was going on.

The betrayal Chloe felt in the movie *Run* is similar to the feelings that many awakened people feel toward the church. Many victims of CFDIA move from shock and disbelief to the feelings of betrayal, disgust, and rage.

The defining feature of FDIA, what makes it what it is, and why it so captures our imagination that filmmakers return to it over and over, is that the perpetrator knows they are making their victim sick. I do not believe the majority of religious pastors and teachers are as nefarious as Chloe's mom. Some, like Chloe's mom, are sick themselves and do not realize the full ramifications of their actions. One cannot be in their right mind to choose to harm their children in such a terrible manner. I have also met some pastors who *are* manipulative and know they are trying to make people feel guilty and shameful, while in another breath offering them *the good medicine of the gospel*. What fits the most in this diagnosis is the experience of those who feel betrayed like Chloe.

Sophia, a woman I met who was suffering from religious trauma, after coming to grips with what the church was doing to her, said:

> I can't believe they told me who I was in my core was rotten. I can't get over the fact that they had me believing in a God who despised me yet loved me and would punish me if I didn't follow the path He set out before me. There was so much fear. So much shame. For what? I wasn't even sick to begin with. They were the ones who were sick to feed me that shit. Yeah, I make mistakes, but I am not evil in my core. Loving my body, my sexual desires, and just loving myself, is not bad, it is good. And, now that I am not going to church and listening to that nonsense, I feel freer than ever.

Just like Chloe began to feel better and was able to walk and run after she stopped taking those pills, a lot of people who stop taking the medication their churches were giving them feel the same. After either leaving the institutional church altogether, or leaving certain fundamentalist expressions of the church, many people feel freer than ever. As one person told me, "It is like I am born again, again." Researcher Amy Phillips summarized the sense of freedom many of her respondents described as their experiences after leaving their church:

The respondents' sense of liberation stemmed from no longer carrying shame around their "sinful" or "demonic" self. They no longer believed the scriptures and religious teachings from which those labels originated. They were able to research, gain knowledge, and determine for themselves what they held to be true and what they valued, and what their morality would be.[5]

For many affected by religious trauma, the struggle of betrayal trauma is real. For some, in hindsight, it felt like being in an abusive relationship. For others, it felt like being in a relationship with someone with factitious disorder. The traumatic aftereffects are something they all struggle with. Thankfully, trauma does not have to have the last word. Many do heal and recover. They can walk and run with a sense of freedom that they never had before (Part II and III will explore principles and practices to help you on your healing journey).

CHAPTER 6
COMMUNAL REJECTION

"Another wave of rejection surfaced when people either shamed us for not being in church, or just stopped talking altogether. It left me wondering whether I truly was accepted by God—his people surely weren't making me feel that way, except when I did what they wanted me to."

—Karl Forehand, *Out Into The Desert*

For those in the liminal space of deciphering what to believe about Hell, one of the most painful experiences you may have had to endure is rejection from members of your family and religious community. The sense of loneliness and isolation this causes can wreak havoc on a person's sense of stability in the world.

Religious trauma not only causes us to struggle internally with anxiety, fear, shame, self-criticism, maladaptive avoidance strategies, and a host of other C-PTSD symptoms, but also forces us to face continual rejection from people whose support we desperately need. The *fear* of rejection from God and from others, and *actual* rejection from others, can feel suffocating, as negative emotions become all-consuming. The feeling of aloneness when working through one's doubts, questions, and the decision to move away from harmful religious teachings can feel unbearable. Consequences of this prismatic array of emotions can include sleepless nights, hiding, pretending, unhealthy addictions, isolating, ruminating, and engaging in a variety of other coping behaviors.

Famous Christian artist Lisa Gungor, author of *The Most Beautiful Thing I've Seen: Opening Your Eyes to Wonder,* writes about how her internalized fears of judgment spawned out of her intense questioning of things she once held dear. Such fears usually originate from outside sources before being taken in and accepted as if they are a person's own ideas. Gungor writes, "Me, the good girl once on the 'straight and narrow,' with Grammy-nominated songs and singing about God all over the world, now blinded by evil, or her evil husband, and forever to burn in the eternal pit of despair because I was doubting."[1]

Gungor's experience involved the internalization of her community's criticisms, such that she began to believe them about herself. Why did they perceive her to be blinded by evil and no longer a good girl? She had not even moved away from her faith. The criticism and rejection were merely because she had raised questions and expressed doubts. It is sad that rejection by family or community can result from such genuine concerns and uncertainties. But more than sad, it is another example of gaslighting. When doubters question ideas that should indeed be questioned, they are made to feel at fault for daring to query. But they are absolutely right to question. It is normal to question these dastardly doctrines. They *should* be deconstructed and discarded.

In her book *Pure*, Linda Kay Klein relays a heartbreaking experience she had with her conservative Christian mother, who had grown suspicious about Klein giving a voice to traumatized women in the aftermath of their ordeals with purity culture. Her mother was uneasy that Klein was deconstructing the status quo. Klein recalls a difficult conversation one day in which her mother told her, "Just be sure you don't wreck your salvation, Linda. Even if your intentions are good, if people misconstrue what you say and get bad feelings about God, that isn't good for you. For your salvation."[2]

Her mother continued, "Linda, Satan is the Prince of Lies," and, "I don't want him using you. What if people turn away from God because of what you say the church did? Those people will go to Hell. Which is a lot worse than whatever is happening to you and your friends."[3]

There is a simple equation underlying this difficult interaction: doubt + questions + resisting the status quo = HELL!

I try to look at everything through a lens of compassion. Reading this extract, I do believe that Klein's mother genuinely cares about her, authentically believes what she is saying, and is trying to keep her daughter from harm, eternal harm. The same can be said for so many of our conservatively religious family and friends. However, we should all be mindful of our power. We must be aware of our capacity to attune ourselves to the hearts and minds of those in our sphere of influence and encourage them rather than tear them down. Klein's mother, because of her conditioning and beliefs, chose to shame her daughter rather than empower her. She sought to instill fear as a form of her power so that she could manipulate the outcome of her daughter's path. She caused Klein to fear for her salvation, implying that she, her own daughter, would face eternal torment in Hell if she continued to be a rabble-rouser. She alluded to Klein possibly being in cahoots with Satan, and placed others' eternal destinies in her daughter's hands and words. No pressure, of course.

Do you know what is sad? Think about what Klein was trying to do. She saw people who were hurting, abused, and suffering from long-term emotional pain and wanted to help. She was coming from a place of love and care and was simply trying to give voice to the oppressed and marginalized. She was offering them compassion and being a witness to their pain.

Isn't it ironic that those who are so vilified and judged by religious communities can look and sound more like Jesus than his self-proclaimed "true" followers?

WHY DOES IT HURT SO MUCH?

Following rejection from disavowing doctrines like eternal conscious torment, people can, of course, feel extremely angry at critical family members and dismissive church communities. They may express that in terms like, "I have been *hurt* by the church." But what do they mean by "hurt"? Most describe a cocktail of feelings such as anger, sadness, and fear, all of which they can feel pulsating through their entire body. This is both a physical and emotional pain, which, as we shall see, are neurobiologically entangled. For those who struggle to relate to "de-churched" people, and since few of us are trained neurologists, here is an example that might help to make sense of their experience. The emotional pain they feel when they experience judgment and rejection by other Christians is equivalent to the physical pain that comes from getting hit in the back of the head with a huge brick.

This intense feeling of pain makes complete sense in light of recent work by cognitive researchers, who found evidence that physical and emotional pain are located in the same part of the brain. They hypothesized that if it was true that both physical and emotional pain were processed in the same brain region, then acetaminophen (Tylenol) should help to reduce emotional pain. For three consecutive weeks, the researchers administered acetaminophen to one group of participants and gave a placebo (a fake pill) to another. In the middle of the three-week period, the researchers intentionally made the participants feel rejection by excluding them from an activity. Afterwards, they hooked them up to an fMRI machine to examine their brain activity. The conclusion was that those who received the acetaminophen reported "hurt feelings" less frequently than did the placebo group, demonstrating significant overlap between emotional and physical pain as registered by the brain.[4]

The emotional pain and visceral hurt we experience, even long after our negative experiences with family or church members, are real. But unlike a badly bruised arm that people can clearly see, it is not possible to see the bruises on our hearts and understand how much they hurt. Being rejected from, or indeed having to reject, our family or faith community due to personal growth or a response to spiritual abuse cuts to the deepest core of our emotional, physical, and spiritual being. It hurts our brains, our hearts, and our bodies. It just hurts.

And it hurts for a very good reason. We are neurobiologically wired to belong to a tribe and connect intimately with others. It makes sense, then, why choosing to leave our fold, our religious tribe, and the belief systems of our religious relatives is filled with anguish and turmoil. Contemporary neuroscience tells us that humans have an innate need to belong, feel safe, and be loved, and that these feelings are processed by very primitive parts of the human brain. In fact, we need these things so desperately that our nervous system encodes loneliness, isolation, and rejection as primal threats.[5] Loneliness can cause anxiety and produce considerable amounts of stress hormones, which ripple through our brains and bodies with devastating consequences to our immune system and well-being. So next time you're feeling the sting of rejection, remember that it's not just in your head - it's in your brain and body's wiring, and you're not alone in feeling that way.

Our tribally wired brains evolved at a time when our distant ancestors belonged to small and very tight-knit groups. Our early relatives sang the songs, followed the rules, and engaged in the rites and rituals that helped bond their group and maintain social order. Novelty was accepted, as long as it was sanctioned by the group. However, no one dared to deviate too greatly, firstly because this could make the tribe vulnerable to attack, and secondly because non-conformity, especially against the tribal leader, could end in banishment, which was essentially a death sentence. Our brains and bodies evolved to accept the fact that people could not survive alone. So, for thousands of years, most human beings fell in line with the status quo, and there was little chance for the brain to evolve away from its tribal roots.

Because of our tribal brains, it is now almost impossible, without intense anxiety, to stop singing those songs, to break the rules, to disobey our religious leaders, or try to become anything other than the docile followers we are used to being. But while straying from our group causes enormous apprehension due to our tribal history, this is massively exacerbated once we add a punishing and angry God into the mix. No wonder voluntarily leaving our tribal beliefs and community can be one of the most confusing, anxiety-provoking, and Herculean tasks in which we could ever engage!

When we leave elements of our faith behind, we may not realize initially just how primitive and deep these fears run. We are left utterly confused and may feel like we don't know what is going on inside our own heads. Chaos is the perfect word to describe this sense, the feeling that we are not okay, and we don't know why. The logical, rational parts of our brain seem not to be in sync with the more primitive, emotion-laden parts. As a result, we can end up listening to the voice of our fearful, tribal-wired unconscious nervous system, which might tell us all kinds of lies as we attempt to deconstruct our faith. Lies like:

- *I am going to be all alone.*
- *I am going to die in the wilderness.*
- *I will be a lost soul and won't know who I am anymore.*
- *God will hate me forever.*
- *I won't be successful without other Christians liking me.*
- *I will cause other members of my family to fall away.*
- *I will be vulnerable to demonic attack.*
- *I will never recover from this.*
- *I will be miserable for the rest of my life.*
- *If God doesn't exist, then what is the point of living?*

But don't worry. If you start hearing phrases like these, it is not a sign that you have been possessed by crafty demons. You do not have "evil spirits of confusion, anger, and pain" that need to be cast out. Instead, there are under-the-hood brain processes that produce such fear-based messages. These are, initially at least, beyond your control. Thankfully, there are therapeutic ways to deal with these inner critical thoughts, which we will explore in detail in a later chapter.

THE HURT IS REAL AND WON'T LAST FOREVER

If you went hiking, tripped over a rock, and broke your leg, it would of course be normal to experience immense physical pain. It is just as normal to experience emotional pain and disorientation when a community or family member you love rejects you, or as you choose to stray from your tribe's beliefs and rituals. So, if you're deconstructing your belief in Hell and its ideologies, be prepared for some discomfort along the way. Understand that it is part of a natural process as you explore what feels true for you. In the beginning of one's awakening, it can be scary and painful for anyone. Yet the disorientation and hurt you feel will not last forever. It just may be the dawning of a new understanding about yourself. It may also mean that liberating paths lie ahead, including the potential to form a new community with people like you who are open, expansive, inclusive, creative, and love-centered.

CHAPTER 7
RELIGIOUS TRAUMA'S EFFECTS ON THE BODY

"Many trauma survivors can't begin to imagine their bodies as safe, let alone sacred, thereby denying themselves the experience of living a safely embodied life. A trauma survivor might easily describe their body not as a temple but instead as a desecrated, scorched earth."

—Deirdre Fay, *Becoming Safely Embodied*

Ryan's belief in Hell riddled him with severe anxiety. No matter what he did, he couldn't shake the all-consuming fear. At times, the anxiety was so intense that it felt like his heart would burst out of his chest.

The religious trauma inflicted by Ryan's belief in Hell manifested in pain and suffering throughout his body: chronic headaches, shortness of breath, chronic fatigue, insomnia, and, at times, a racing heartbeat. The emotional toll was also significant. Whenever friends or family discussed religion, Ryan would succumb to depression's grip because it reignited his biggest fear: losing himself entirely to the hell-bound belief system.

If you've never experienced religious trauma, it may be difficult to wrap your head around its ripple effects on the bodies and nervous systems of those who carry soul wounds. This trauma is not just a struggle with beliefs or an intellectual problem to solve. It can set into motion a cascade of adverse effects throughout the body that develop into a profoundly physiological and emotional dilemma. Bessel van der Kolk, a contemporary expert on trauma, writes:

> Traumatized people chronically feel unsafe inside their bodies. The past is alive in the form of gnawing interior discomfort. Their bodies are constantly bombarded by visceral warning signs, and, in an attempt to control these processes, they often become expert at ignoring their gut feelings and in numbing awareness of what is played out inside. They learn to hide from their selves.[1]

A deep dive into the neurobiology of the trauma of Hell is unnecessary here because the sufferer's experience can be described in simple terms. Whether the trauma occurred during the first encounter with the doctrine of Hell or at some later point, it produced fear that sent stress hormones surging through the victim's body and nervous system. These encounters were fueled by the idea of a mighty God who believes the individual is a depraved sinner deserving of Hell's torture for eternity. The question is, how could that not leave a traumatic imprint on their brains and bodies?

But why is that? Because the brain's primary purpose is to keep us alive and free from pain. Think of this imprint in terms of what happens when a child touches a hot stove. The shock of the scorching heat's aftermath is a constant reminder: "Fear the stove! DO NOT TOUCH!" Likewise, the imprint of Hell would say: "Fear God! DO NOT SIN!"

One of the consequences of religious C-PTSD is that, after experiencing it, we never truly feel at home in our bodies. We know that our brains are already geared toward self-protection, and then you add an incessant need to be on high alert about ourselves and our loved ones' eternal fate. That leads to inactivity of our brains' *tend and befriend* or *care circuit*, which diminishes our capacity to experience feelings of warmth, positivity, and comfort. That's because the *fight-or-flight* system is constantly activated, putting us into a state of hyperarousal with associated physical reactions, such as muscle tension, upset stomach, fatigue, dizziness, rapid heart rate, teeth grinding, and chronic pain.

THE TRAUMATIC EFFECTS OF PURITY CULTURE

Unfortunately, the spectrum of Hell indoctrination may include the traumatizing effects of purity culture. Purity culture inflicts violence not just on our minds but on our bodies. Desires from natural bodily drives and longings are held up as sinful. Harsh and coercive teachings and sermons on purity shame men and women about their sexual thoughts, feelings, and desires. And the message, whether implicit or explicit, is that feeling and acting upon those natural yearnings typically means you'll be sent to Hell.

I remember attending a picnic organized by a few United Pentecostal Churches—picnics being a type of social gathering surprisingly *not* on the "demonic activities to stay away from" list. At the event, a young man told me one of the local churches kicked him out because of his continual masturbation. As a new Christian, I was shocked. This person was not an exhibitionist and did not do anything sordid in public. He was a young, single guy who occasionally masturbated for release and pleasure. Yet, due to his inability to manage his evolutionarily provided hormones and his openness and honesty about this private, solitary behavior, he was not only kicked out of his church but also led to believe that his salvation was in question. He believed that he was in very real peril of hellfire.

Women experience similar purity culture scenarios, and their effects are exquisitely explored in Linda Kay Klein's *Pure: Inside the*

Evangelical Movement That Shamed a Generation of Young Women and How I Broke Free. Klein's research and interviews with women about their experiences of purity culture fuel a powerful indictment of toxic religious teachings around the body and sexuality. She writes:

> Many feel that engaging in even a "hint" of sexual immorality—such as kissing or hugging if done in a sexual way—is a slippery slope. And in the words of one interviewee, the sexual "slippery slope leads straight to Hell. It leads to flames and desecration."[2]

It is important to note that a religious emphasis on oppressive forms of purity is not universal. In some churches, there are likely healthy religious teachings around sexuality. However, countless people have been traumatized and suffer C-PTSD symptoms because of unhealthy, fear-based church teachings. This powerful passage by Linda Kay Klein has caused me immense heartache:

> Evangelical Christianity's sexual purity movement is traumatizing many girls and maturing women haunted by sexual and gender-based anxiety, fear, and physical experiences that sometimes mimic the symptoms of post-traumatic stress disorder (PTSD). Based on our nightmares, panic attacks, and paranoia, one might think that my childhood friends and I had been to war.[3]

I read that excerpt a dozen times before including it here. And rereading it has again brought tears to my eyes. Some of these tears represent my incessant shame and tiresome fears I've had to work through due to purity culture. I can't tell you how many times, after masturbating, having a wet dream, or looking at a woman lustfully, I felt God's fury. Punishment loomed around the corner. It was just a matter of time before God would strike me with blindness and doom my relationship with my future spouse. I knew in my bones that if I continued my behavior, God would send me to Hell when I died. Thankfully, I no longer believe such things, but feel deep empathy for that young man who did. My heart aches for those who dread their bodies, despise their sexuality, fear their impulses, doubt their future relationships, and believe with every fiber of their being that God is angry at them and will light the fires of Hell when their time comes. These teachings are an assault on the minds and bodies of precious people who deserve better from a religion that proclaims love as its core message.

RELIGIOUS TRAUMA CUTS US OFF FROM OUR EMOTIONS

Our emotions serve as a built-in GPS, guiding us to understand our current situation, where we want to go, and how to get there. Each primary emotion conveys essential information that leads to adaptive action. For example, sadness signals a loss and prompts us to seek comfort and support, while fear alerts us to danger and propels us to take action to protect ourselves. Disgust warns us of something harmful and drives us to avoid it, while joy signals a successful outcome and moves us to share our success with others. Anger indicates that something is unfair or unjust and compels us to take action to correct it.

While emotions may not always convey accurate, objective, truthful information, they always point to an individual's valuable subjective truth. However, emotions don't have to lead to ultimate conclusions or definitively determine one's course of action. So then, how are emotions useful? When we listen mindfully to how we feel, our emotions can help us navigate the beautifully chaotic and wondrous world with greater skill and awareness.

Many of us were taught that our bodies and emotions are inferior, untruthful, unspiritual, and fleshly. Biblical propositions and reasoning were emphasized as the primary vehicles to truth and living the Christian life. For some of us, our experiences were filled with religious leaders who believed emotions were troublesome demons that needed to be quickly cast out of hurting people. Some folks were taught that listening to their emotions and desires is a one-way ticket to Hell, so they decided to cut them off completely. But denying and splitting off aspects of ourselves is not a healthy way to live.

Not being in touch with the feelings within our body can have serious consequences for our overall well-being. Without the valuable information emotions provide, we cannot fully understand and process our experiences, leading to a disconnection from our core selves. This can manifest in various ways, such as difficulty forming healthy relationships or detaching from unhealthy ones; difficulty regulating emotions (it's hard to regulate emotions you're unaware of); struggling with trusting ourselves and our intuitions; and an increased likelihood of developing mental health issues such as anxiety and depression. Such disconnection can also lead to difficulties in setting and maintaining boundaries, as individuals may have trouble understanding what they truly want and need. Furthermore, not being in touch with our feelings can make it difficult to heal from past traumas and move on from difficult experiences. Finding ways to connect with and understand our emotions is crucial to living a harmonious, fulfilling, and healthy life.

For example, if fear is a beacon alerting us to emotional or physical threats, and anger is a beacon alerting us to injustice and unfairness, then imagine living in a world where those beacons are dimmed or non-existent. We would not only miss vital information but also find ourselves in situations that do not align with our core values. Consider religious indoctrination experienced by someone with a broken beacon. Their inability to listen to their fear and anger may trap them in a church that preaches guilt and damnation because they're unable to tap into their core impulses that inform their values. And decisions driven by their values will lead them to a place that feels both intellectually and emotionally safe and fulfilling.

In a nutshell, fear and anger, just like any other fundamental emotion, play a crucial role in helping us navigate life's challenges and in finding our paths toward genuine happiness. Without the guidance that emotions provide, we would not live a life that is true to ourselves. So, when our emotions are stripped away, what can guide us? The external. We'd rely solely on external sources for clarity and direction. Unfortunately, that's how churches that use coercive control disempower us, strip our individuality, and make us forever dependent on them. However, we can gain a fresh perspective and a newfound sense of vitality and purpose by having the courage to tune in to our inner selves and break free from the constraints of toxic religious norms and expectations.

LASTING EFFECTS OF HELL TRAUMA

Janis, a thirty-two-year-old woman, enjoys being a stay-at-home mom. She loves composing music, writing poetry, and volunteering at a local animal shelter. Janis has three beautiful children and an adoring husband. She struggles with having so many good things because a part of her can't shake the nagging fear she has about her eternal fate. And not just hers. She worries that her husband and precious kids could also spend eternity in Hell. Here's the twist: Janis stopped believing in Hell five years ago.

Many can attest that views about original sin and Hell are tenacious, lingering long after de-converting and changing one's beliefs. The main reason is that trauma becomes trapped in the body and nervous system and is not something you can merely think yourself out of. Phillips writes persuasively about this phenomenon based on the experiences of her study participants: "The fear of hell was a concern that was so hard to overcome, that respondents experienced it throughout their deconversion and even after loss of belief had occurred."[4] Such occurrences raise the question of why these dastardly doctrines are so stubborn and difficult to discard.

Beliefs linked to the trauma of Hell persist not because they are true but because they are so vile and horrific that our nervous system encodes them as perpetual possible threats. The brain, and in particular the amygdala, which is thought to form the core of a neural system for processing fearful and dangerous stimuli, carries the anxiety-producing message, "Even though I don't believe it now, I don't want to forget it, just in case it is true." This primitive part of our brain is not necessarily concerned with what is objectively accurate, as it functions only to keep us alive and protect us from pain.

Choosing to no longer believe in original sin and Hell is like trying to tell the brain, after a lion attack that happened years ago, "You remember that ferocious lion? Well, that really wasn't a lion" (even though you have scars to suggest otherwise). Sufferers of Hell trauma were told by those in authority, God's mouthpieces, that God thinks we are depraved sinners deserving to be tortured for all eternity. It is hard to simply forget those instances and the traumatic shock of fear that rushed through our nervous system.

Continually being reminded of these doctrines by Christians carrying hate-and-Hell-filled picket signs or angry preachers threatening us with fire and brimstone on the radio or television hardly helps. These can act as cues or triggers, setting off an immediate emotional reaction. While the neocortex, the brain's evolutionarily *newer* region, typically associated with rational thought, might assure us that Hell-Bound People theology is illogical nonsense, the more primitive part of the brain where fearful memories are stored (the amygdala and dorsal hippocampus) can be easily triggered to remind us that God-created nightmares are probably true. Since the amygdala does not have a sense of time, each memory can feel like the first time you experienced the terrifying shock of the original fear-based teaching.

CLOSING THOUGHTS

I hope Part I effectively illustrated the absolute devastation from religious soul wounds and how the interrelated doctrines of Hell, an angry, punitive God, and sinful, wretched human beings can inflict long-term scarring effects. Even those with expertise in this area would have to admit that we have only scratched the surface when understanding the profound consequences of such indoctrination.

Anxiety, shame, self-criticism, betrayal trauma, nervous system damage, emotional cutoff, and communal rejection are just some of the potentially devastating effects of poisonous theological ideas and religious trauma. It's easy to forget that Jesus came to preach good news to the poor, proclaim freedom for prisoners, open the eyes of the blind, release the oppressed, and proclaim the year of God's favor for all (Luke 4:18-19), among other things. Yet many people's encounters with Christianity have left them with bad news, bondage, blindness to their own beauty, and a belief in a punitive God who, at some level, abhors all humans. *That* is the true tragedy. Thankfully, there is healing even for religiously created soul wounds, and we'll look at how to treat them next.

PART 11

WIGGLING HELL BELIEFS FROM OUR MINDS

In Part II, I intend to deconstruct Hell through the lens of psychology, philosophy, and sociology. By doing so, I hope to show that the eternal torture chamber known as Hell is like an intimidating, ferocious-looking dog with long mangy fur, who, after getting wet, looks like a skinny, feeble, and downright laughable animal. My aim is to demonstrate that Hell does not originate from God but is, rather, a result of human ponderings about the afterlife, morphing into a narrative of violent projections that binds communities together. The Hell narrative also feeds human pride and is used by people in power to subjugate dissenters. Further, I seek to deconstruct the notion of a violence-prone God and an eternal Hell by exploring the absurd notion that our compassion, goodness, and wise discipline meter functions more adequately than God's.

CHAPTER 8
CONCEIVED IN CURIOSITY, BIRTHED IN CREATIVE IMAGINATION

"Curiosity is unruly. It doesn't like rules, or, at least, it assumes that all rules are provisional, subject to the laceration of a smart question nobody has yet thought to ask. It disdains the approved pathways, preferring diversions, unplanned excursions, impulsive left turns."

—Ian Leslie

My son Alex is an inquisitive little boy. He is always asking questions and seeking answers to the mysteries of life. On one particular day, he had so many questions that they were coming faster than I could answer them.

"Dad," he said, "Why is the sky blue?" I smiled at Alex's enthusiasm and replied with a patient explanation about how light from the sun scatters across molecules in the air as they pass through creating a blue hue.

But before I could finish explaining, Alex asked another question: "Where do clouds come from?". I explained that when warm air rises, it meets cooler temperatures high in the atmosphere, causing water vapor to condense into white fluffy clouds.

Alex couldn't believe what he was hearing; everything sounded so interesting! But before long, curiosity got the best of him again and he asked yet another question: "What are stars made out of?". As a non-physicist, I chuckled and unsuccessfully talked to him about hydrogen and helium, which was the best I could do.

We went on for hours discussing every possible thing under the sun - from why kites fly to why birds migrate - until finally night fell and it was time for bed. As Alex laid down in his bed, contented with all of his newfound knowledge, I bet one thought still lingered in his curious mind: What else will I discover tomorrow?

We are all wonderfully curious beings. Curiosity is not only a built-in survival strategy to motivate us to know our environment so that we can adapt to it in an effective and safe manner, but it is also an information-seeking behavior that drives us toward novelty and wonder. Each question answered leads to more curious questions. Even as adults, our curiosity drives us to do such things as check out new podcasts, watch the news, check when the latest album is coming out from our favorite artist, and to see what our friends just posted on social media. This drive to know things is why some researchers call us "informavores." Just as herbivores consume plants and carnivores consume meat, we informavores love to be curious and to search out new information.

Curiosity and wonder are the main ingredients in the origin story of Hell. Curious people were asking questions about the afterlife long before the characters in the Hebrew Bible. In ancient Mesopotamian mythology, which existed 1,000 years before the Hebrew Bible's stories, there are accounts of people wrestling with the afterlife. The writer of the *Epic of Gilgamesh*, one of the most popular Mesopotamian stories, provides a bleak account of the afterlife for the Sumerians of that time. Time is short, life is a struggle, death is awful, and once you are dead, you grovel in the dust.[1]

Who knows who the first person was to ask curious questions

about the afterlife? It must have occurred within a group of hominids, our ancient relatives, who evolved from communicating through grunts and guttural sounds to using a more complex system of language. The more consciousness evolved and the more complex the language developed, the more abstract the questions became. Perhaps the questions sounded like:

"When we dream of loved ones who have passed away, does it suggest the existence of an afterlife?"

"What happens after we die?"

"Is there nothingness after we die, or is there something?"

"Do ancestral spirits or gods exist, and do they continue to have an interest in our lives after we die?"

"How can we please the gods to gain rewards in the afterlife?"

"If we please the gods, what kind of afterlife will we experience?"

"What about the people who get away with doing evil things in this life? Will they be punished?"

"What kind of punishments will the bad people endure?"

At some point in history, curiosity moved to tentative answers, and those answers birthed creative imaginations.

THE SPARKS OF CREATIVE IMAGINATION

Here are some examples showcasing the remarkable breadth of human creativity. A quick search on Google reveals that Spotify recognizes over 1,300 unique music genres, while linguists estimate that over 31,000 languages have existed throughout human history. There are over 4,000 distinct religions worldwide, and within Christianity alone, there are roughly 39,000 different sects and denominations. From classic flavors to the most exotic, there are more than 1,000 delicious ice cream varieties to enjoy. Over time, countless individuals have created billions of paintings, and humanity has produced approximately 129,864,880 written works, filling endless pages with knowledge and imagination. These examples are a testament to our creative and imaginative nature, which is also evident in the diverse concepts we have imagined about the afterlife.

Many thousands of years ago, our ancient ancestors contemplated the question, "What happens after we die?" Seeking answers, they embarked on a journey of imaginative speculation, postulating that the afterlife might resemble... From that initial spark of curiosity, a flame was kindled, which burned for centuries, perhaps even millennia, as they wove together increasingly more complex narratives of the world beyond the veil. Over time, these creative musings evolved and multiplied, as new geographic regions birthed their own distinctive afterlife narratives, complete with local deities, ancestral spirits, or high gods to explain the mysteries of life, suffering, flourishing, seasons, and death. Curiosity, inquiry, and creative reflection fueled an ongoing evolution of richer and more imaginative narratives, producing wildly diverse beliefs about the hereafter.

When we lived and where we lived dictated what we believed about the afterlife. For example, if I had been born in ancient Egypt, I might have contemplated my posthumous fate, hoping to meet the god Osiris and praying that my good deeds outweighed my bad ones.[2] I might be anxious knowing that my heart would be weighed in the balance against a feather, which was the symbol of justice. If my deeds failed to pass the test and my heart was heavy with unrighteous deeds, I would be given to a ferocious monster who was a composite of many different fierce animals.[3]

If I were Hindu, I might have meditated on my death and thought about how my soul would leave my body and holy messengers known as yamadutas could take it to the court of Yamaraja, the king of death, to be judged.[4] Depending on the kind of Buddhist I was, I might have believed in eight different kinds of "hot hells," where people could be subjected to brutal torture due to their karmic debts.[5] If I were an Israelite drawing close to the end of my days, I might have thought about Sheol, the "Kingdom of No Shadows," a place where there are the shadows of dust, darkness, and nothingness. Fast forward to today. If I were Mormon, I would hope to be sufficiently righteous to spend eternity in the celestial kingdom, rather than the terrestrial kingdom, or experiencing endless punishment with the sons of perdition.

I am not interested in whose version is correct. I am not even interested in tracing the evolutionary steps of how the version of Hell we know today came into existence. I will let the cultural anthropologists, theologians, and Church historians have fun with that endeavor. What interests me is the sheer breadth of creativity emanating from the vast human imagination.

In this chapter, I want to deconstruct Hell not by thinking deeply theologically or philosophically but by thinking simply. I am attempting to appeal to the fundamental building blocks of all complex thought: curiosity, wonder, and imagination. By appealing to Hell's origins (and the origins of all afterlife narratives) within the curious human imagination, rather than an instant download from a Divine figure from the heavens, it becomes easier to disentangle it from our minds. The endless capacity of humans to imagine the impossible, create the once intangible, and weave narratives that serve as the fabric of our communities is what makes us stand out as a species.

A prime example of this is Dante, the Italian storyteller and poet who in 1320 published his *Divine Comedy*. He shares his journey to Hell, Purgatory, and Paradise with his guide, Virgil, a renowned poet of Roman antiquity. It is like a wild sci-fi fantasy into the eerie underworld, moving through ever-descending circles of the pit of Hell until he reaches his final destination in Paradise. His version of the afterlife, compared to the biblical version, is like 4K ultra high-definition versus a bland, black-and-white film done in the 1930s.

Dante describes in stark detail the punishments in Hell. In the Second Circle of Hell, Dante and Virgil encounter people who were consumed with lust and who were unable to find peace as they were blown violently back and forth by fierce unceasing winds. In another circle, ruled by the monster Cerberus, a monstrous hound with three worm-like heads, there resided the gluttons who were mercilessly punished by being forced to lie in a horrid sludge that was produced by a continual mysterious ice rain. Some believe that Dante's masterpiece changed the landscape of the modern world as we know it and it certainly influenced our present-day fantastical views on Hell and the afterlife.

Whether it was Dante, biblical writers, Hindu writers, Buddhist writers, Sumerian writers, or any person like them who penned views on the afterlife, what stands out is that we just love to imagine stories about places to which we have never been and then believe whole-heartedly what our minds concoct.

Sit with that for a moment. It is one thing to worry about whose version of the afterlife is correct. But, if we take a big picture view, much of the discussion consists of people arguing over stuff other people made up. No religion's sacred text, and I mean none (despite adherents' claims), was given by an omnipotent being from the clouds who majestically shouted, "Here in this text lies the one true religion. Take this sacred text and let all the world know that this is the truth about all matters." That simply did not happen.

Amid a world where religious adherents constantly joust for the supremacy of their own religious ideas, one truth that no one can deconstruct, and upon which all religious people can agree, is that humans love to create. There is not one culture in the world where religion—the human-created system of narratives, rituals, propositions, and practices that bind communities together—has not been practiced. That should make us pause and reevaluate as we ponder our beliefs around Hell and the afterlife.

LOOSENING OUR HELL BELIEFS

My aim in discussing human curiosity and creativity is to attempt to loosen the grip that Hell beliefs may have on you. I am aware that having knowledge or facts does not automatically lead to change or transformation. I am aware that trauma resides in the body, deeply affecting the nervous system, and sharing ideas by themselves will not bring about lasting change. However, I am hoping that by discussing the wondrous curiosity and creative capacity of human beings, I can create a bit more space within your mind to help distance you from toxic Hell-Bound People theology, and help you embrace truths that resonate with your heart and mind.

Given the vastness of human imagination, why should we buy into what a group of people say about a deity called God, Hell, and the nature of our own selves? If we lived in another time and place, we would be watching a ceremony take place in which our mummified relative was being prepared for his or her next plane of existence with the Egyptian gods.

Stories are vital to our existence. They move us, inspire us, and unite us. However, why should we allow other people's creative imaginations to become our stories, especially if they are outdated, caustic to our souls, and make no rational sense? Why should we believe that there is a God who is so prone to offense that He becomes filled with anger and wrath and wants to punish us because of our propensity to miss the mark of the ideals of love? I can understand why folks would believe that many thousands of years ago, but why should we believe that now? For the most part, we no longer live in an age where natural disasters are viewed as signs of divine displeasure and bountiful harvests are a sign of approval. Why should we then still believe that there is a tyrant God who would want to send us into the pit of Hell to be tortured forever for not being perfect? Why should we believe that we are primarily sinful in our core? Why do we have to believe other people's awful stories? How many tens of thousands of versions of the afterlife have existed throughout time? Why, out of all the stories that have ever existed, do we have to believe in the one that is outdated, primitive, irrational, and horrific?

The answer is: "We don't have to."

"OH, HELL-BOUND PEOPLE THEOLOGY, WHERE ART THOU?"

I can deeply relate to the struggle to forget about Hell, eternal torment, and our core depravity, due to the fear of dismissing what we have been told is "God's Word." I have heard the concern many times: "Mark, I can't let go of Hell and our sinfulness, because Jesus talked about it. And my whole life I have been told that the Bible is God's Word. So, it is hard for me to just not believe it. Eternity is too long to be wrong."

I get it. These fear-inducing doctrines that form entrenched neuronal connections in our minds and nervous systems are fiercely stubborn. Hearing that these doctrines are coming from the "Word of God" adds another level of ferocity.

I can hear the mind chatter: "Who are we to question God?" "Didn't Satan question God's word and aren't we in cahoots with him if we start questioning core doctrines?"

The reality is that no one is questioning God. Rather, we are questioning other people's creative versions of who God is, what God is like, what God really feels about us, and what happens in another plane of existence after we die. Theology is "human talk about human talk about God." Theology is our beautiful and sometimes horrifying attempt to make sense of God, life, and the afterlife. Our theological fingers pointing toward the moon are not the moon itself. Our ideas about God are not God. From a philosophical perspective, it's plausible that biblical authors could be inspired by a transcendent loving Spirit. However, like us, I am sure they may have sometimes been mistaken about what constitutes reality.

My compassion runs deep for those of us who have a hard time letting old theologies go. It can feel like there is a perpetual ceiling about to collapse on our heads every moment as we move away from our ingrained religious beliefs. Some of us can have nightmares about Hell. And the guilt, shame, and doom-and-gloom radio blasting inside our heads can be piercing. Since this chapter is focused on creativity, let me briefly appeal to the creative and evolutionary nature of Hell expressed in the Bible. My hope is that it can offer some wiggle room when our minds wonder if it is okay to doubt the Hell-Bound People narrative.

Let's go back to the beginning, in the book of Genesis. The Genesis creation account is a beautiful mythological narrative that describes the beginnings of creation, life on earth, and the relationship between God and humanity. I have encountered many Jewish people who mine the account for beautiful, inspiring, and challenging truths about God and humanity. When I hear them, their interpretations feel earthy, practical, and poetic, with a bent toward wisdom and ethical living. However, some Christians' hyper-literal reading of the account, and reading into the narrative ideas of Hell, demons, and God's pristine character, seem illogical, constricting, and fear-based.

As the story goes, many Christians teach that Satan and his minions fell from Heaven to earth. Supposedly there were literally thousands, or perhaps hundreds of thousands, of demons on the earth, along with Satan in the form of a serpent, hanging out with Adam and Eve. How that is considered "good" is beyond me. Wouldn't that be like a parent allowing their children to play in a neighborhood park that was infested with murderers, drug dealers, and pedophiles? Those parents would not receive the parent of the year award.

Yes, I know the argument. God is apparently so holy, pure, and powerful, that God doesn't owe humanity anything. However, if God birthed humanity, would God not watch over and supervise his first two naïve, sinless, and very inexperienced children (Adam and Eve)? It seems reasonable to assume that God, a loving parent, would make sure they were safe. Why would God, instead of watching over them, move his kids into a neighborhood to live around godless creeps and be influenced by such bad company? God also certainly knew, just like any parent, that when you tell a young child not to do something (e.g., "Don't touch this!"), they are going to want to do that very thing! The last zinger is that according to a majority of Christians, God foreknew all of this would take place. According to some Christians, this disastrous event, and the curses that followed, were all a part of God's creative plan and purpose.

The biblical account also suggests Adam and Eve had not sinned before all of this. Therefore, they did not even know what sin was. Even if God explained it to them, we all know that it's a totally different experience to hear about something than to experience it firsthand. Did they know what death, lying, pride, coercion, and manipulation were? How would that be possible if they had never before participated in, nor been the victims of, such acts?

The sad reality is that, according to the sinful Hell-Bound People story, two very sincere and gullible people, who had never previously sinned or experienced sin, were deceived by an experienced, wise, manipulative, and savvy talking snake. Tellers of this toxic religious story say that when Adam and Eve ate of the forbidden fruit, a loving, wrath-filled, angry, and compassionate God (I know, confusing, right?), who knew it would happen and surrounded them with evil demons, harshly punished them for it. Talk about entrapment. Sure, God lovingly covered them with animal skins. But because they gave into temptation and were not perfect anymore, they were cursed, along with the rest of humanity, with eternal torment. God also threw in a few extra curses to make the journey on earth a living hell.

Wow! Plot holes aside, what creativity! What imagination!

However, there is something oddly missing in this Genesis account. It is the Hell-Bound People narrative itself. The words and concepts of "Hell" and "eternal damnation" are nowhere to be found in the Genesis account of God's punishments ("You will surely die" does not correlate to "You will spend eternity in Hell where you will be tormented forever"). If you read the story apart from preconceived bias and in the ancient genre in which it was written, you find that it is simply a mythic explanation (complete with talking animals—another common ancient mythic trope) for why there is pain and suffering in life, and why snakes and humans are at enmity. If the story about the original transgression and the curses that followed never mentions ideas such as "Hell," "eternal damnation," and "torture for eternity," then violence-prone and creative religious people must have made up that heinous and horrific punishing narrative at some point along the vast theological road.

Here is my main point: why should we believe this sick narrative about a punitive God who will torment people forever for not behaving in the right ways, when the account in the biblical text that describes the original curse for the original sin was never, ever mentioned? The Jewish people never believed in such a sick and twisted narrative, and still don't, even though the original curse for the original sin is found within *their* sacred Hebrew text. As biblical scholar Bart Ehrman states, "There is no place of eternal punishment in any passage of the entire Old Testament...nowhere in the entire Hebrew Bible is there any discussion at all of heaven and hell as places of rewards and punishments for those who have died." Julie Ferwerda, author of *Raising Hell: Christianity's Most Controversial Doctrine Put Under Fire* discerningly writes, "If hell is real, and God really doesn't want anyone to go there, He would have taken great pains to explain it in repetitive detail through Moses and the prophets."[6] To that I say, "Exactly!"

"But, Mark," you may say, "Jesus mentioned Hell, and he mentioned it way more times than he did Heaven."

I promised myself I would not go into theological debate mode in this book. However, I will interject just a small point here. Jesus did indeed mention a place called Hell (*Gehenna* and *Hades*, to be precise). However, Jesus talked about Heaven, the future kingdom, and eternal life far more than he did about Hell.

Further, Jesus' use of the concept of Hell, in creative dialogue with people of his day, doesn't legitimize it as the official destination of the damned in the afterlife. It is widely known that Hell in Jesus' day, or more properly *Gehenna*, was a God-forsaken place where heathens sacrificed children to pagan gods.[7] Jesus regularly used parables and metaphors to discuss spiritual truths with folks, but that *doesn't* mean every one of his illustrations is meant to be taken hyper-literally. While Jesus was an apocalyptic preacher, with concerns about the afterlife, he often used familiar places or situations that would evoke strong emotions among his listeners to illustrate spiritual truths that were relevant to their present-day realities. Contrary to popular belief, Jesus cared more about healing the Hell out of people's hearts, minds, and bodies than he did about obtaining for people get-out-of-Hell-free cards.

CREATIVE IMAGINATIONS BASED ON THE BIBLICAL TEXT

The typical view of God likens him to an immortal human-hating vampire needing pure blood to be satiated and content, and who would only be happy with despicable human beings and be willing to remit their sins if He received a perfect meal of pure blood coming from a sinless person, so that he can look upon perfect people without spot or blemish. This is not the only creative, imaginative view of Hell in town.

There are Christians who take the Bible seriously and who have come to very different imaginative conclusions than the *Infernalists* described above. *Universalists* are those who believe that Love Wins, and that all human beings will be saved and come to know the beauty of God in the afterlife.[8] *Annihilationists* believe that God would not want anyone to be tortured for eternity, so the repentant go to Heaven and God annihilates the wicked; the weeping and gnashing of teeth described in the Bible refers to the trauma of the unrepentant realizing they will cease to exist. Those who hold to the existence of *Purgatory* believe that while some people will spend eternity in Hell, there will be others who go to purgatory and will remain there until after they are sufficiently punished for their sins, when they will be able to go to Heaven and spend eternity with the saints in Heaven.

There is the *Relentless Love* view, espoused by Thomas Jay Oord, who believes that God's unconditional love extends into eternity. In this view, since God does not control anyone, people are free to love God or not love God in the afterlife. People can choose Heaven, which involves a close relationship with God, or choose Hell, which is a life apart from God. Oord writes, "God never stops inviting, calling, and encouraging us to love in the afterlife. Although some may resist, God never throws in the towel."[9] This contrasts with certain forms of Universalists who believe God will unilaterally save everyone, regardless of what they want.

Lastly, Sergius Bulgakov and Pavel Florensky, priests and theologians of the Russian Orthodox Church, provide a slightly different flavor of the afterlife. They neither have an angry, punitive, and wrathful God nor any version of Hell as eternal conscious torment in their view of the afterlife. They focus on the freedom of human beings in the afterlife in a similar way to Oord, although they have a different view of God's nature and power. They also emphasize that Hell is a place for education and purification. Arvydas Ramonas summarizes their views: "The existence of hell is a complement to human freedom, thus its presence is a consequence of human freedom. To deny hell would be to deprive a person of freedom of choice."[10] Ramonas goes on to state: "The suffering of hell is not eternal because it has an educational aspect, so it is not a desire for revenge, but more like a cure."[11]

According to proponents of views of the afterlife that emphasize love, such as Oord, Bulgakov, and Florensky, preachers of eternal conscious torment have distorted views of the afterlife and have marred the image of a loving God. They point out that Hell is not a created location for a wrathful God to inflict pain on people for eternity. It is to provide a place for people to be away from God if they so desired. It is a place for them to hear God's loving viewpoints on their lives, while also offering pathways toward greater experiences of goodness, beauty, and truth. The hope is that by relating to God as He is, and not the projections in which they have believed during their whole earthly lives, they would see how loving, tender, and accepting God really is. This version of hell is steeped in the worldview of a God who lovingly sustains the created other while still respecting the autonomy for which he made them, rather than an angry God punishing mistakes.

My hope is that when your mind reminds of you of the version of Hell that is terrifying, along with an authoritarian God wanting to dish out some violent physical and emotional punishment for eternity, you can remind yourself that these are someone else's stories and they do not have to be yours. If you are a Christian, and you want to take Jesus' words seriously, know that there are much saner versions of God and the afterlife that do not require a cruel vindictive God. If God is anything close to loving, I am sure that you can rest assured that God is not like the worst sadists of humanity. If you want nothing to do with Christianity, then I invite you to continue to flip the script that has been handed to you. May you courageously take your pen in hand and write a narrative that is much more appealing to your innermost being: a creative imagination that aligns with your values and honors your truth.

CHAPTER 9
HELL AS PROJECTIONS

"Whatever is God to a man, that is his heart and soul; and conversely, God is the manifested inward nature, the expressed self of a man,—religion the solemn unveiling of a man's hidden treasures, the revelation of his intimate thoughts, the open confession of his love-secrets."

—Ludwig Feuerbach, *The Essence of Christianity*

Now that we've explored curiosity and creative imagination—two ingredients necessary for afterlife beliefs—let's travel to the darker side of humanity and explore how the version of Hell with a moody, punitive God and his demonic masterminds of torture functions in people's lives. The task in this chapter is the same as the last: a fingerprint analysis of the gnarly Infernalists' Hell narrative (those who believe in eternal conscious torment). I suspect we'll find that what we believed to be God's fingerprints turned out to be those of humanity all along.

THE CANVAS OF GOD AND HELL

The painter Bob Ross was the coolest cat in town. Watching him wielding his paintbrush as a weapon of love and painting beatific and serene landscapes was mesmerizing. His colors flowed smoothly from his brush onto the canvas like they were meant to be together; blues and greens blended so naturally that it looked like Mother Nature herself had painted them.

With his calm demeanor, Bob would paint and gently whisper to himself, "Let's add some happy little trees." Then he would seemingly just tap with a brush, and, before you knew it, he had taken those happy little trees smiling and dancing in his mind and projected them onto a blank canvas. After an hour of moving his brush gracefully across the canvas like a ballerina dancing across the stage, Bob stepped away from his work and admired what he had achieved—it was perfect! God and Hell function similarly: they act as a canvas for humans upon which to project their polychromatic psychological palette.

WHAT IS PROJECTION?

Projection is a defense mechanism we learn early on to deal with our complex emotional landscape. There is a common understanding of projection. Instead of bearing what feels unbearable inside, we project it outside ourselves, usually onto other people. Let's look at some examples.

When children grow up, they experience more complex emotions, drives, urges, and wishes, especially when relating to harmful parents. A child can feel mixed feelings like rage and love toward their parents who abuse or neglect them. As the child's emotions toward their parents grow, so does their anxiety, creating an unconscious dilemma. On the one hand, they love their parents. On the other, they feel profound anger toward them. To rid themselves of the internal anguish, they split off parts of their experience and project them onto others. For example, a child may project all good onto their mother and project their rage onto a playmate or teacher. As they do that, they can momentarily rid themselves of their rage while protecting their love for their parents.

Another example of projection occurs in relationships between couples. Imagine a husband with lustful thoughts and desires for a woman at work. Because he sees himself as a good Christian man, he cannot tolerate what he considers unacceptable sexual thoughts, feelings, and desires. As the internal cauldron of those feelings boils and bubbles, his anxiety increases, although he may not be conscious of this. Once the anxiety reaches a given threshold, the husband's defenses will kick in.

One evening he sees his wife on her phone. He doesn't know to whom she is talking, but her laughing and free-spirited conversation catch his attention. After the call, she walks by, and he says, "Who was that on the phone? Are you cheating on me?" She is floored by his comment and feels hurt that he would even think something like that. Both of them get caught in a negative cycle of distress. Feeling hurt and frustrated, each withdraws from the other, and they go to bed feeling alone and angry. The husband projected his unbearable thoughts, feelings, and sexual desires for another woman onto his wife as if she, too, was having lustful thoughts for another person. His projection reduced his anxiety momentarily, so rather than him being the "cheater" in the relationship, she's the one having the same wandering thoughts. In this way, he avoids being upset with himself by becoming upset with his wife for feelings he thinks she has. However, like many defenses in adulthood, there was a cost. The connection with the person he loved most—his wife—ruptured.

Another feature of projection entails not just projecting unbearable urges, drives, feelings, and thoughts onto others but also conscious and often positive attributes, feelings, attitudes, and strivings.[1] This form of projection "involves the tendency to engage in anthropomorphic thinking," which involves perceiving others in their own image and likeness.[2] For example, someone could idealize their self-disciplined and loving self and then project that onto their new boss as if that other person fully embodied those qualities. The projection could turn out to be true, and in this case, the boss could be a loving and disciplined person. However, the projection could be wrong, with the boss being quick-tempered and lazy. The person projecting may then experience disappointment, grief, or anger as their perception of their boss is shattered and the pedestal they placed them on comes crashing down.

PROJECTION IN RELIGIOUS COMMUNITIES

SLAP! Everyone heard it. It was the slap heard around the world. Chris Rock was doing his thing at the Oscars, cracking jokes and making everyone laugh, until he made his *G.I. Jane 2* joke about Jada Pinkett Smith's bald head. Jada was embarrassed. We think Will saw his wife in distress and sought to protect her honor (as well as his own). Whatever was going on with him, it was clear he was going through a lot that night. After a few seconds, he got up and slapped Chris in the face.

Aside from the rich social discussion held in the aftermath of the slap, what struck me, particularly on our topic of projection, was Denzel Washington's response to Will Smith immediately afterwards. Denzel told him, "At your highest moment, be careful; that's when the devil comes for you." Washington also spoke to Bishop T. D. Jakes about the incident a short time later at Jakes's leadership summit: "Well, there's a saying, 'When the devil ignores you, then you know you're doing something wrong.' The devil goes, 'Oh no, leave him alone; he's my favorite.' Conversely, when the devil comes at you, maybe it's because he's trying to do something right. And for whatever reason, the devil got ahold of that circumstance that night." This is a perfect example of community projection.

I am a huge fan of Denzel. However, he projected Will Smith's humiliation, pride, rage, and dormant, tender childhood wounds onto a metaphysical entity called Satan. This may be a case of projection *for* others instead of *onto* others. Is it the case that every time someone becomes humiliated and lashes out in retaliation, it's because Satan had something to do with it? I don't think so. Sometimes anger, humiliation, pride, shame, and sadness are just that—human emotions. Even Jesus said, "For out of the heart come evil thoughts—murder, adultery, sexual immorality, theft, false testimony, slander."[3] He didn't say that they came from Satan or demons.

For me, one of the clearest forms of projection, in the broadest sense of the word, is taking what's inside and "evacuating" it on to someone or something else—the way religious people use Satan and demons to explain human phenomena.[4]

I had Christian friends who, every time they got sick, blamed it on the Devil. Another friend had a birthday party, and when he saw that it was going to rain, he said, "The Devil just wants to ruin my day, but I know God has got my back." Every mishap and experience of suffering was due to the Devil, and every good thing was attributed to God.

I will never forget one of my friends who was in the throes of grief. After weeks of being an absolute wreck, unbearably distressed because his girlfriend broke up with him, he decided to go to a weekend church service to find solace and community. After the service, perceptive church members quickly gathered around him like bees. They began to sting him with passionate and bold prayers, such as, "I bind the spirit of sadness in the name of Jesus," and "You come out of him, you spirit of depression and anger." By ridding him of those nasty varmints (emotions), he would supposedly be restored and free again.

It's absurd to "cast out" naturally occurring emotions and label them "demons." Projection, in this case, is obvious. Instead of naming them as emotions and processing them accordingly, they are evacuated and catapulted onto unseen entities. Given that my friend's relationship ended, feeling sadness, heaviness, depression, and grief over losing someone he loved was normal. The communal projection, as well as my friend's projection, was an attempt to ease their own anxiety about emotions they felt uncomfortable being present with.

I find it's nothing more than old-school superstitious projection when people blame demons and project their emotional maladies onto them. A dear Christian friend recently gave an example of a friend complaining of "hearing loss, and ringing in her ears, and pain in her legs that made her feet feel like she was carrying lead in them." Additionally, she said her friend was suffering from immense guilt. All these symptoms led her and her friend to conclude that she was suffering from a "tormenting spirit." Spirits don't need to torment the souls of people. Living our everyday lives amid this beautiful and chaotic existence provides plenty of fodder to cause severe internal struggles and tormenting unconscious conflicts, which can then wreak havoc on our minds, bodies, and relationships.

From a psychological and neurobiological perspective, such symptoms as guilt, hearing loss, ringing in the ears, and pain in the legs that make people's feet feel like they're carrying lead are in no way due to a "tormenting spirit." These are easily explained by debilitating anxiety, which, when experienced in the smooth muscles and parasympathetic pathways, including cognitive/perceptual disruption, causes people to feel the above somatic symptoms.[5] That's simply science.

As a therapist, I've had people experience the same somatic anxiety symptoms in my office. Their anxiety and its symptoms must be regulated in the here-and-now. Then we examine their guilt, underlying painful emotions, and inner conflicts. And following a corrective emotional experience, they feel calm, peaceful, and more energetic. Their symptoms and recovery had nothing whatsoever to do with demons needing to be exorcized.

Let me share another example of projection often found in religious communities. Liam had always been an upstanding member of his conservative religious community. He attended all the meetings and services and tried to live his life according to the strict guidelines set forth by his faith. But there was one thing that Liam couldn't deny: he was struggling with his own gender identity and sexual orientation.

Despite his best efforts to suppress these feelings, they'd inevitably bubble to the surface. He found himself judging and criticizing others who didn't fit into traditional gender roles, accusing them of being sinful and going against the teachings of their faith. But as Liam struggled with internal conflict, he realized that he was projecting his shame and self-hatred onto others.

A recent study explored the psychological dynamic of projection with conservative and liberal American Christians on topics of morality, such as gay marriage and abortion, and economics and generosity.[6] The researchers focused on questions asking participants to characterize the liberalism/conservatism of their own political views and the views they thought Jesus would express if he were alive today.

The conclusion was obvious. If Jesus were alive today, according to liberals, he would look like them. Jesus would prioritize what they would prioritize. In other words, Jesus would focus on issues related to compassion and fellowship. For conservatives, Jesus would also look like them, focusing mainly on issues of morality. Both groups created Jesus in their own image.

Another feature of this study was to explore whether the participants' projections represented a possible means to reduce their cognitive dissonance for not measuring up to Jesus' ideals. That appeared to be the case. For example, conservatives admitted Jesus would be more liberal than them on issues of compassion for the less fortunate. However, to reduce their dissonance, they thought of Jesus as having a "stricter morality" on abortion and gay marriage, issues they themselves championed.

In other words, to deal with their possible guilt and anxiety for not loving others the way Jesus might, they project on Jesus the qualities they consider essential in the Christian faith. If they took a truth serum, they might share, "Yeah, I know I'm not like Jesus when it comes to being kind to others, but since I focus on what Jesus really cares about, issues of morality, then I unconsciously get to deny my guilt about being less compassionate. I feel really good about myself as I look at Jesus. When I see Jesus, it's like looking in the mirror." The liberal participants are not off the hook. They engaged in the same dissonance reduction strategies as conservative participants.

PROJECTION ONTO GOD

Why would our concepts about sickness, disease, the cosmos, our bodies, mental illness, weather systems, and energy evolve over time, yet our understanding of God remain static? That doesn't make any sense. Given the innate capacities of human curiosity, creativity, and learning, and that we're projection-prone creatures, God's evolution alongside that of humanity's, seems logical.

In the Old Testament, we find a mostly tribal God who was very similar to other tribal gods in the ancient Near East. It was not uncommon for all those gods to prescribe rituals and sacrifices, not merely for their appeasement but for the formation and security of their communal identities. Like the gods of other ancient societies, the Israelites' god had its codes, laws, rules, and regulations and used violent physical punishment as a means of discipline. The Israelites' god was also one among many. Instead of being monotheists, the Israelites engaged in monolatry—they acknowledged other gods but paid allegiance to and worshipped only one.

The move from an Old Testament "God is an angry Warrior, among other gods" view, espoused by Moses who declared "The Lord is a man of war" (Exodus 15:3, KJV), to a modern-day "God is nothing but love" view, espoused by those prioritizing the verse "God is love" (1 John 4:16), seems apparent.

Admittedly, through careful inspection, this trajectory and the dichotomy that makes it possible is not as cut-and-dried in the biblical text. For example, David wrote in Psalm 103:13–14, "As a father has compassion on his children, so the Lord has compassion on those who fear him; for he knows how we are formed, he remembers that we are dust." Clearly, the writer was on a different wavelength than other Old Testament writers, as is often the case for mystics and musicians. Then, you have God in the New Testament involved with the death of Ananias and Sapphira (Acts 5:1–11). In the New Testament, God was also involved with striking Elymas blind (Acts 13:11) and bringing about King Herod Agrippa's death (Acts 12:20–23). God seems to be a

God of wrath and a God of grace in both testaments. However, just like many men, as they get older, God seems to soften a bit by the time He is described in the New Testament.

Despite the lack of a perfectly linear evolution of God, or more appropriately, the evolution of the human understanding of God in the biblical text, clearly, most modern-day Christians do not believe God needs continual sacrifices to be appeased. Most Christians today do not believe God would presently command genocide or that God wants rebellious children to be stoned. Most would agree that God would not presently declare that "if a man commits adultery with another man's wife—with the wife of his neighbor—both the adulterer and the adulteress are to be put to death" (Lev. 20:10).

For the most part, it can be shown that Ancient Israel's view of God would be vastly different from the versions of God sung about in churches today. That would make a great deal of sense if God were repeatedly projected in man's image. Reza Aslan, the author of *God: A Human History,* summarizes my point well. He writes:

> The very process through which the concept of God arose in human evolution compels us, consciously or not, to fashion God in our own image. In fact, the entire history of human spirituality can be viewed as one long, interconnected, ever-evolving, and remarkably cohesive effort to make sense of the divine by giving it our emotions and our personalities, by ascribing to it our traits and our desires, by providing it with our strengths and our weaknesses, even our own bodies—in short, by making God us.[7]

As curious and creatively imaginative people who project what's on the inside of us onto the outside, we are very adept at making God into our own image and likeness. The thousands of religions that exist today, the tens of thousands of different Christian sects and denominations, and the myriad afterlife accounts throughout history are a testament to those realities.

THE ANGRY, PUNITIVE, AND TORTURING DEITY

There is a Sufi story about an ant that left its colony to search for God. When it came back, it claimed to have seen God. Naturally, the colony of ants asked, "What does he look like?" It answered, "He looks like...a really big ant."

We know that projection takes our internal qualities and places them externally on others. So, isn't it probable that the angry, punitive, and torturing God and horrific Hell described in the Bible and taught by preachers are merely projections of the unbearable emotional feelings, wishes, desires, and urges that exist within us? I think that is the case.

I think the Hell of the Infernalists—those who believe God will torment people for eternity because of their sins—is a projection from ancient creative, imaginative, and traumatized humans. While our species can be extravagantly sacrificial and altruistic, we have always had a strong penchant for justice and violence. "An eye for an eye and a tooth for a tooth" existed long before the Hebrew scriptures, found in the Code of Hammurabi. We are also fickle and moody. We can love one minute and inflict harm the next. We can commit genocide and rob people of vital resources. We can be jealous and angrily demand loyalty. If we are betrayed, then punishment or death may be a consequence. The worst of our shadow side seems to be fully displayed by the God found in the Bible.

I have compassion for our earlier ancestors who have projected the worst onto God, the same projections many people believe in today. Think about the trauma people faced from rampant injustice, whether getting conquered by other tribes or seeing the rich flourish while many starved, along with other tragic sufferings. Our ancestors faced hardships we can't even imagine today. Such intense suffering created feelings of profound despair and rage. Out of that pulsating grief came thoughts of violence, wanting to see people harmed, even tortured, to pay for their wrongdoing.

Honor/shame societies were indeed the norm in the ancient world, where vengeance for wrongdoing was not only expected but encouraged. If you didn't get revenge or punish the offender in some way (or find someone to do it for you), you'd lose face. However, in societies based on the principles of honor and shame, such as ancient Israel, laws, rituals, and the concept of revenge may not have been sufficient to address all instances of trauma and harm. Consider a scenario wherein a young man's parents knew he was in love with one girl, yet they forced him to marry another. As a result of the parent's disregard for his desire, the son experienced betrayal and anger.

Another example is a situation wherein a family killed a young man's father along with his livestock. The family got away with it due to their influence on local leaders. The young man was overcome with feelings of rage and a desire for retaliation, but no specific legal framework or communal ritual existed that addressed his emotional distress. The young man was left with his festering rage and other intense emotions.

In a culture where openly and vulnerably expressing emotions such as hurt, fear, rage, and shame may not have been socially acceptable, it's likely that individuals internalized their mixed feelings. They may have also projected their anger and fantasies onto a divine entity. In the example above, imagine the deceased father's young son years later, traumatized and jaded, in command of an army where a hypermasculine warrior God is perceived to be their mighty general.

As an example of religious projection, when the Hebrews attempted to kill all the Canaanites and steal their land, was not God the ideal figure to unite a community and justify their genocide, thus alleviating their consciences? Is it really God who inspired Moses to command violence and call the Israelites to spare young virgins (Num. 31:17-18? Was it really God who commanded the Israelites: "go, attack the Amalekites and totally destroy all that belongs to them. Do not spare them; put to death men and women, children and infants, cattle and sheep, camels and donkeys" (1 Sam. 15:2-3)?Or are those instances of violent and selfish humans projecting onto God in order to justify such atrocities?

As an aside, since men are prone to more violence than women, and men wrote the Old and New Testament, I wonder what kind of Bible women would have written as they projected their version of God within the biblical text. Would we see a less violent God? Would there be more feminine metaphors to depict God? How would that have shaped readers' understanding of God throughout the centuries? The monotheistic faiths like Christianity, Islam, and Judaism could have benefited from a more diverse range of voices in their texts. I suspect such diversity would have also had a more positive impact on the wider world.

Let's return to the topic of projection. Imagine fast-forwarding thousands of years to a time when curiosity gave way to more imaginative thinking, and intricate narratives of Hell began to emerge. A time when the inner trauma became a lens through which to project that creativity. A time when there was a desire to see wrongs made right and for those in power to control individual morality. At that time, what better projections could one fathom than an angry, punitive, and violent God who created a place called Hell? For those who suffered evils or witnessed loved ones suffer without taking vengeance or imposing justice, at least the projection of Hell in the afterlife offered them some solace, knowing their unjust and evil perpetrators would be tortured. Alan Bernstein, bolstering my views, author of *The Formation of Hell*, writes "Belief in future punishment is a manifestation of the sublimated desire for vengeance. Belief in punishment after death becomes necessary when no sign of restoration is visible in life."[8] In the afterlife, the harrowed and haunted victims would finally see the justice denied them in this life.

God has become a mirror reflecting the image of the one peeking into it. God is man; man is God, and the two have become one flesh. From where does the wrathful and punitive God come, along with His torture chamber called Hell? They derive from the hellish wounds that oozed out from traumatized humans who could no longer bear their internal anguish of rage, guilt, fear, and desire for vengeance (the same inner turmoil that propelled people to nail the scapegoat Jesus to a cross). They needed those feelings to be exorcized, and the canvas of God and Hell obliged. The consequences of violent and vengeful projections ultimately cause destruction and harm to society, negatively impacting human flourishing.

CRITIQUE OF RELIGIOUS PROJECTION

The proposal that much of religion can be distilled down to creative and imaginary projections is not a novel idea. Sigmund Freud was a proponent of the idea that religion was mere wish fulfillment. Freud is famous for saying: "Religious ideas are illusions, fulfillments of man's urgent wish in the terrifying impression of helplessness in childhood which aroused the need for protection through love by the father...later represented by the benevolent rule of a divine Providence."[9] He even wrote an entire book entitled *The Future of an Illusion*, arguing this point in some detail.

While I disagree with Freud's reductionistic statement about the need for a loving father, as many traditions have strong female deities, I believe his thoughts about projection are correct. However, I want to address a common critique of religious projection and psychological wish fulfillment, which sounds like a reaction by kids being teased on the playground, "I know I am, but what are you?" The Christian apologetic response is to turn the argument around on ourselves. Denise Ostermann's chapter "Is Christian Belief Just Psychological Wish Fulfillment?" summarizes the critique well. She states:

> If Freud was arguing that religion (God) is simply the psychological creation of an illusory father figure to avoid the feeling of helplessness, what do we make of his atheism that sought to deny a heavenly Father? By the same logic employed by Freud against Christianity (i.e., in its "myth" of a longed-for benevolent and protective Father God), one could say that his denial of this Father is a psychologically competitive, murderous desire to eliminate one's father. The motive here would be to avoid deserved punishment.[10]

Roger E. Olson, who wrote *Against Liberal Theology*, offers the same argument. In response to Bishop John Shelby Spong's critique of a faith that posits a supernatural being in the sky waiting to intervene in human affairs, he writes, "Ironically, Spong's critique of supernatural theism as projection can easily be turned around; it may be Spong's and other liberals' ideas of God that are projections of the human need for self-esteem onto ultimate reality, calling that God."[11]

Lastly, Paul Vitz, who wrote *Faith of the Fatherless*, explores how the most biting critics of religion, such as Freud, Voltaire, Nietzsche, and Camus, did so because of their own projections based on their fractured and/or non-existent relationships with their fathers. For example, Vitz believed that Freud didn't have a satisfying relationship with his father and, at times, hated him. Freud's emphasis on the Oedipus complex was evidence that he had an unconscious desire not only to hate his father but to project that hatred onto God and wish for God's death.[12]

My response to biblically conservative-minded folks is that we are guilty as charged. It would be intellectually dishonest to suggest that everyone except ourselves engages in projection. Of course, Freud engaged in projection, but we have no idea to what extent. We can barely understand our own projections being thrown out into the world. We all unconsciously project what is unbearable onto others at times or, at the very least, project our fantasies, wishes, and ideals onto them. It would be helpful for everyone if we were all honest about that. We could all benefit from more truth and less falsehood in our lives.

It is also vital that we honor our own subjectivity, conscience, and intuitions. For too long, many of us have accepted the projections of others as if they were God-given. It's okay to finally say, "Enough!"

What many of us thought were God-given truths were shadow puppets performed by human storytellers. It is time to stop following everyone else's illusions, intuitions, and truths while denigrating our own. If we're repelled by the idea of an angry, wrathful God who needs perfect blood to be content toward humans and to forgive them, then we should trust that intuition. I also think that if people trust their intuitions and believe in Hell, then great. I believe in non-coercive love. Everyone should have the freedom to follow their own intuitions, while also striving to avoid causing harm to others in the process.

I understand trusting our *intuitions* can be suspect. Throughout history, people trusting their intuitions has led to cruel and harmful actions. However, all we've come to know as truth originates from others' struggles, intuitions, curiosities, reflections, revelations, and creativity. Think of any concept; someone else likely thought of it first. All the symbols that we know were assigned meaning by other people. Most of what we've come to believe was constructed and believed by others well before our understanding. Think of the style of clothes you like and the music you listen to. They were all created by others. We are born into a world not of our own making.

It may be time to create a world of *our* own making. It may be time to start trusting ourselves and create our own version of our lives that feels congruent instead of living in a religious and social matrix created by others.

Sometimes we'll get it right. Sometimes we'll get it wrong. And oftentimes, it will be a mix of both. All of us will have truths likened to wood, hay, and straw that will eventually burn in the refining fire of life's experiences. Our truths will translate into behaviors and will be tested by our relationships and society. It's wise to discover our truths in a community with trusted others. It's also helpful to learn from those who have come before us, whether in books or in real life. I trust that we'll receive the necessary feedback that will help us savor the good, spit out the bad, and become who we are meant to be.

Despite the chaotic unknown, we must take risks. And we need to accept where we are right now in our spiritual and emotional journey. If we wait for our truths to be seen perfectly through shiny, transparent glass, peering into the heavens with a Divine figure smiling and giving us a thumbs-up on our perspectives, we'll be waiting a very long time.

Will our truth be perfect? Definitely not. Whose is? Will our truth be revised? I'm sure it will change over time. Until then, we should have permission to be congruent and authentic and to share *our* embodied truth, through *our* unique hearts, with the world.

If our gut tells us that Hell, God's designation of eternal torment because, as humans, we can be both our best and worst selves, feels monstrous, then we should trust that instinct. We certainly join a great cloud of witnesses who believe likewise. If our heart tells us that it's wrong to deem ourselves sinful and too wicked to be considered by a Creator whose main attribute is supposed to be love, we should trust that feeling. If there is a God who has anything to do with grace, love, and forgiveness, and we're being true to ourselves—especially if we're elevating love and healthy relationality—then I'm sure we'd all be okay in the mystery called eternity. If not, it would seem hellish to spend eternity with a cosmic tormentor whose callous heart would be glorified in others' eternal sufferings.

GOD HAS NO VOCAL CORDS

Before this chapter ends, I want to respond to those readers who still believe in God, remain Christian, and hold to a grander and saner version of Hell. I acknowledge this chapter may have been challenging. You may be left with, "Is everything just made up?" "Is there no such thing as truth?" "Does God really exist?" "Is everything just a bunch of human projections?"

While this book is not intended to answer these big questions, allow me to share a few imperfect thoughts.

If there is a God, then God, like most religious traditions suggest, is a Spirit, Force, Energetic Being, or something else that defies human categories. However we label God, He/She/They does not appear to exist in material or fleshly form. If God is not walking around in the Bahamas somewhere, it's because God has no feet. The same could be said of God's speech. In other words, since God doesn't have vocal cords, then God doesn't communicate via sound waves through vocal cords.

If there is a God, and that God is Spirit, then it would make logical sense that God could only speak through an interface or some kind of medium. If that's true, then it's possible that God as Spirit can only communicate through humans' inner knowers—their conscience, mind, and core intuitive self. Therefore, it is possible that Divinity as a creative Lurer can *prompt*, *nudge*, and *impress* upon us truths. The problem is that if God is love, and love doesn't force its will and way within humans' minds, then God's non-audible communication will not always be clear. The vast number of groups within the Christian tradition, many claiming to have capital "T" Truth, would bolster that point.

If there is a God, the truth remains: While our understandings of God may not all be projections in the psychoanalytic sense, all we know about God is filtered through human cognitive and emotional processes. If the Spirit exists without vocal cords and does not clearly communicate to us, "You got it. That is the definitive truth for all people and for all times," then that reality should give us pause. It should invite us to humility regarding knowledge, non-coercive prudence when sharing our perspectives with others, and freedom to trust our wild and wacky intuitions, doing our best with the data presented to us.

CHAPTER 10
COMMUNAL GLUE, TOXIC PRIDE, AND OPPRESSIVE POWER

*"I like your Christ, I do not like your Christians.
Your Christians are so unlike your Christ."*

—Mahatma Gandhi

GOD AND HELL ARE BINDING AGENTS

Hell has survived this long because of the evolutionary value it has provided human beings and the communities in which they are embedded. Value? Yes, absolutely. Hell, along with its counterpart, Heaven, became creative narratives born out of curiosity and funneled through projections that have promoted cohesiveness to communities throughout the ages. All the diverse tribes' religious codes, rituals, creative myths, and projections bound their respective communities together like sacred glue. As a result, unique communal identities were forged that allowed them to stand out from others. Those narratives help create *in-groups* and *out-groups*, *us* and *them*, all toward the value of communal sustainability.

We discussed one important psychological benefit of Hell; it serves as a canvas to deal with the grief of suffering and injustice one experiences in this world. Bart Ehrman writes, "It is also not hard to grasp why heaven's antipode, a place of everlasting punishment, arose. People have always wanted justice, and if it is not to be found in the present world, possibly it will come in the life beyond."[1] Our beliefs about Heaven and Hell reduce our anxiety and diminish internal suffering. They provide hope that this whole messy and wonderful life in the midst of this chaotic world has some kind of purpose and that justice will prevail in the end. Such beliefs also reduce the negative energy and emotional pollution that is propelled out into the world. Instead of projecting the internal despair, rage, and grief onto those around them, some are able to project it out onto God or future afterlife realities.

Another important value of a punitive God and the threat of eternal punishment in Hell was to promote cooperation among its members. If I were a member of a tribe and I knew that if I stole food, harmed a member of the community, or challenged foundational beliefs of that community, I could be punished by the most powerful figure in the known universe as well as the tribe, I would definitely think twice about doing so. While we have not discussed the concept of Heaven, the same logic applies. If I believed that by keeping the community's moral codes I could attain an eternal reward, that would certainly help increase my motivation to being in the deity's good graces.

I can speak firsthand of the power of a punitive God and Hell motivating me to conform to communal morals. I will never forget reading Jesus' words in Matthew 5:29: "If your right eye causes you to stumble, gouge it out and throw it away. It is better for you to lose one part of your body than for your whole body to be thrown into hell." At the time, I took it very seriously. The Bible was my set of **B**asic **I**nstructions **B**efore **L**eaving **E**arth. In my experience in the Pentecostal tradition, I was told when I opened the Scriptures and saw Jesus' words in red, they were the exact, unaltered words of God. I really did believe that God would want me to gouge my eyes out if I were to continue to sin. That is how seriously God took sin. To avoid burning in Hell, I tried really, really hard not to transgress God's commands.

During the days of my passionate love for God, and my extreme fear of His ever-ready hands of punishment, I was working in a psychiatric center. I met a gentleman who struggled with schizophrenia. He also had a physical feature that I always wondered about: a glass eye. One day I was talking to a nurse who had known him for quite a while, and I asked about his eye. Shockingly, she told me that he plucked out his own eye because of a verse he read in the Bible. I knew exactly what verse she was talking about. Matthew 5:29 was a verse constantly in the back of my mind, always coming to the forefront when I looked at a woman lustfully or looked at others with envy.

Despite our location in a mental hospital, I couldn't help but wonder if he was more of a Christian than I was. I was amazed that he actually listened to Jesus' words. Maybe I was not being as obedient as I once thought. That experience definitely horrified me. If I was anxious about that verse before meeting him, you had better believe that I was terrified afterwards.

Matthew 5:29 is one verse among many that preachers and teachers have often used to cause congregants to fear God's punishment and, in turn, coerce them to engage in communal standards of morality. In this case, Matthew 5:29 has been and is still used to combat male lust. The message is clear, "If you look at a woman lustfully, you can burn in a literal Hell for a literal eternity." That interpretation has caused considerable anxiety and fear for many clients I work with. Of course, there are different interpretations. Jesus may have been a wise spiritual teacher trying to elevate love and use hyperbole to encourage folks not to dehumanize others through lust and maintain purity in one's heart to protect the sacred bonds they may have with their partners. However, when it is interpreted in a literal sense, while it may encourage community members to bind together through homogenous standards of sexual morality, it can reinforce fear of punishment by an angry God and Hell trauma.

I want to make it clear that while I am suggesting that the narrative of Hell has held some value throughout history, I obviously do not condone it. I am trying to point out the function of Hell, which points to its very human origins. The concept of Hell has been historically utilized to enforce religious doctrines and practices and to maintain social cohesion within religious communities. The fear of eternal punishment in Hell has served as a powerful motivator for individuals to adhere to religious teachings and norms while encouraging them to be loyal to their community. However, as many of us know, the use of fear and coercion through Hell-Bound People theology to enforce religious beliefs has led to negative consequences, such as the suppression of critical thinking, psychological harm to individuals who are unable to reconcile their own beliefs with the fear of eternal punishment, and the perpetuation of prideful intolerance and discrimination towards those who hold different beliefs.

HELL, AN ELIXIR FOR TOXIC PRIDE

There I was, at a men's conference with hundreds of people in attendance. The famous Pentecostal preacher and author T. F. Tenney was the guest speaker. All the speakers' messages were very similar: fear-based rants seeking to instill terror into us so that we would shape up our morality to make God happy with us and to escape the fires of Hell.

As T. F. Tenney railed about the need for holiness codes for the Church, he shouted a line I will never forget. Talking about Christians smoking cigarettes, screaming at the top of his lungs, he proclaimed, "If they are smokin' now, they will be smokin' later!" The whole crowd was cheering and yelling, "Amen! Praise God! Praise the Lord!" I was thoroughly confused, and I just started weeping. I thought to myself, *How could these people celebrate because Christians who smoke cigarettes will be going to Hell?* The dissonance in that moment was something I have never forgotten.

One of the tragic elements of the punishing God and eternal conscious torment narrative is that while they can be glue that binds communities together, too often they can create toxic pride, feed animosity toward those in the out-groups, and encourage active hatred and judgment toward them. The example of the men's conference demonstrates that well. I am sure that many of the men there felt a true brotherhood, united in their stand for Christ and against those they deemed to be on the outside.

And, unfortunately, for anyone at that conference who smoked, or who knew anyone else who smoked, it probably triggered immediate panic and fear. The neurochemicals of endorphins were creating their feelings of ecstasy. Oxytocin, which is known as the "cuddle hormone," was increasing their feelings of joyful connectedness. There is a dark side to oxytocin, however; while it can increase social bonding, it can also unite people to increase aggression and help facilitate well-coordinated attacks on those in the out-groups.[2] Their collective praise and elation toward those who were going to Hell was at the same time a form of aggression and a demonstration of sadistic delight in their enemies' future torment, even if for many that dark hue was unconscious. The narratives and neurochemicals created rigid *us* and *them* mentalities that can lead to a lot of hurt and trauma for those not in step with the in-crowd.

Another example of tribal mentality and toxic pride can be seen in the story of Marty Sampson, who was a well-known Christian worship leader and avid songwriter for Hillsong and other renowned worship bands. If you were in an evangelical church for a bit, chances are you sang a few of his songs. In August of 2019, he shocked the Christian community by stating, "I'm genuinely losing my faith." He went on to describe some of his questions and doubts. One of his biggest struggles was with the doctrine of Hell and eternal conscious torment. He stated, "How can God be love yet send four billion people to a place, all 'coz they don't believe? No one talks about it." He continued by saying, "Christians can be the most judgmental people on the planet—they can also be some of the most beautiful and loving people. But it's not for me."[3] Sampson, like many people, couldn't wrap his head around a God who is the greatest of all possible lovers, yet can torment people in Hell for eternity.

There was much love, grace, and overwhelming positive support for Marty. But the brutal judgment, so indicative of what many of us receive for just doubting and questioning, was downright awful. The toxic pride and judgment oozed out from folks. I jotted down just a few Facebook posts:

- He brought it on himself for not being rooted and grounded in love and God's word.
- He should have taken that to his pastor and started a praying session to get himself back in order.
- APOSTASY is an end times sign ... That's what's happening to Christianity. It's just that simple.
- He was never saved to begin with. Just another hell-bound hipster.
- He is just an artist and a singer ... but never a true worshipper!
- Whatever demon has taken over his mind won't let him listen obviously.
- Go away, sort your head/heart out, come off your self-made pedestal and maybe you'll find God again. Don't lead other snowflakes into the abyss.
- Wonder why Marty Sampson is so upset. He shows he wants to be used by the devil.

Here we have another example of members of a religious community coming together to attack a member moving to what they considered to be the out-group. The ridicule, judgment, and threat of Hell for simply having doubts and asking hard questions is a clear sign for me that something is amiss. How important and special they must have felt to be a part of the in-group with a unique knowledge about God and the afterlife. If humans can't be mightier than God, they will do whatever they can to feel more powerful than others. If those prideful responses demonstrate the fruit of the Spirit, then sign me up for another kind of fruit tree.

HELL, A WEAPON FOR THOSE IN POWER

Samuel Morse was an artist and inventor in the 1800s. He and some others invented the electrical telegraph system. He was also a co-developer of Morse Code and an avid spokesperson on the divine purposes and benefits of slavery. As a Christian, his faith informed him to believe that slavery was ordained by God and was a positive force for good in the world. Samuel stated:

> Are there not in this relation [of master to slave], when faithfully carried out according to Divine directions, some of the most beautiful examples of domestic happiness and contentment that this fallen world knows? Protection and judicious guidance and careful provision on the one part; cheerful obedience, affection and confidence on the other. Christianity has been most successfully propagated among a barbarous race, when they have been enslaved to a Christian race. Slavery to them has been Salvation, and Freedom, ruin.[4]

There are countless examples of this atrocious thinking and behavior throughout history. Christians and missionaries who set out to convert societies with swords, guns, and Bibles blazing—often with the tragic results of enslaving, oppressing, stealing, and pillaging—did so because they believed that it was the godly thing to do. Part of their rationale was an inner mandate to reach with the Gospel whom they deemed to be ungodly barbarians and sub-human folks with the Gospel. It was the *us* and *them* mentalities in full force. Under the guise of some form of noble godly love they thought they could save and could make Christian those they thought of as "heathens" and "barbarians." They also too often believed, rather conveniently, that God's will was not only to save them from eternal damnation, but to make them their slaves. Frederick Douglass, an American abolitionist, orator, and social reformer in the 1800s, commented on the treacherous entanglement of faith and slavery. He stated:

> I have heard sermon after sermon, when a slave, intended to make me satisfied with my condition, telling me that it is the position God intended me to occupy; that if I offend against my master, I offend against God; that my happiness in time and eternity depends on my entire obedience to my master. Those are the doctrines taught among slaves, and the slave-holders themselves have become conscious about holding slaves in bondage, and their consciences have been lulled to sleep by the preaching and teaching of the Southern American pulpits.[5]

Another function of Hell narratives, and their interrelated doctrines of human depravity and a punitive, terrifying God, is their power to legitimize oppressive structures and maintain the status quo. The narratives have been and continue to be used by those in power to maintain control and reduce their anxiety, all at the cost of subjugating and oppressing others. In extreme cases, Hell narratives have contributed, and continue to contribute, to people's deaths.

There are many ways that Hell has functioned as a weapon in the hands of the powerful. It certainly has been used by some folks to oppress those of different races, cultures, and ethnicities. It also has been a weapon to instill fear in those who are LGBTQIA+. Preachers, teachers, and religious people have used dehumanizing language, as well as narratives around Hell, sin, and a wrathful and punitive God, to force homogeneity and quash identities while increasing their sense of pride as someone in the in-group. The result has been nothing short of disastrous. The level of trauma left in its wake is maddening. It is reprehensible that there have been precious people who have taken their lives because they were repeatedly told how sinful and abhorrent they were to God, and their eternal destiny consisted of torture and torment.

As I am writing this book, there has been another mass shooting at an LGBTQIA+ nightclub. I can't help but think that Christian churches who uphold Hell-Bound People theology are partially complicit in the beliefs, both on a conscious and an unconscious level within individuals, that drive them to murder members of the LGBTQIA+ community (other religions and societal ideologies and structures are complicit as well).

Every Christian fundamentalist on the streets with a bullhorn angrily condemning queer people to Hell; every hellfire and brimstone preacher shouting at the top of their lungs how queer people are condemned to eternal conscious torment; every leadership team making queer people feel less than or sub-Christian; every Christian's silence (including my own) when witnessing the oppression and marginalization of another—all of this has contributed to rage-filled energy that becomes internalized by individuals and propels them to want to annihilate LGBTQIA+ people.

Hell beliefs, contribute to hellish actions. If people's all-powerful and all-knowing God, filled with anger and wrath, thinks these folks are trash and are especially worthy of eternal punishment in the future, it is not a leap to wonder why they are treated in a hellish way by this God's followers and those they influence in the present.

There are many other ways people in power have wielded the weapon of Hell narratives. Because of those narratives women have stayed in abusive marriages; victims of sexual abuse have been silenced; the environment has been neglected; relationships have been dissolved; creative minds have been stifled; children have been terrified into obedience; and books have been banned. These types of leaders are in the business of creating clones. There is no room for messy dialogue, discussion, and dialogical encounters with people of differing theologies or ways of being in the world. They use their toxic religious narratives as whips to get people in line. Thankfully, we are becoming savvy to their wily ways.

HUMAN FINGERPRINTS

The evolutionary value of a Hell narrative, that includes an angry God and good-for-nothing humans, is apparent. Like other doctrines and rituals, they promote cohesiveness and bind communities together. Why? Because similar beliefs facilitate a sense of belonging. To belong to a tribe is a primal need. The experience of belonging provides us the felt sense of safety. When we feel safe and belong and are part of that in-group, we will do whatever it takes to protect that communal system. In a tribe, I am you, and you are me, and we will not let anyone or anything affect or infect us. To protect members of our group is to protect ourselves.

If we are members of a tribe centered on a punishing and intermittently gracious God, we will be more inclined to keep ourselves in line with the hive mind. The fear of punishment, especially of eternal torture, can be an effective means to keep our morality in check. I have heard the sentiment often: "Mark, if Hell didn't exist, then people, including myself, would sin all they want." Fear is a powerful motivator and a tragic taskmaster.

Sadly, this unholy and destructive Hell narrative has been used throughout the ages to fuel toxic pride. One of the consequences of an in-group mentality is cruelty toward those in the out-group. The cruelty is also expressed toward those they fear are veering off to out-group sensibilities and practices. The trifold narrative of a punitive God, tormenting Hell, and wicked humans has often been used to oppress and marginalize others. Like a seed, leadership reproduces after its own kind. Those in power set the parameters as to who is in and out. They decide what beliefs and practices are good and what are evil.

I hope that by waking up to how Hell beliefs function, you can see the harrowing hound of hell narrative for what it is—a functional and effectual human-made story. The destructive Trinitarian narrative is meant to foster cohesive in-groups; reduce those in-groups' existential angst and future fears; increase their feelings of connectedness, belongingness, and specialness; and excavate their repressed violent proclivities toward others. It is beautiful to want to belong. It is healthy to want to have a healthy spirituality with like-minded others. However, rigid tribalism immersed in fear-based beliefs devoid of relationality and lack of awareness of our collective interconnectedness is destructive.

CHAPTER 11

OUR COMPASSION, GOODNESS, AND WISE DISCIPLINE METER IS NOT OUT OF WHACK

"The intuitive mind is a sacred gift and the rational mind is a faithful servant. We have created a society that honors the servant and has forgotten the gift."

—Albert Einstein

Years ago, amazingly, I wouldn't even have cringed at the idea of God commanding genocide (Joshua 1:12); flooding the planet and giving sharks a smorgasbord of human entrees (Genesis 6–9); killing precious Egyptian babies (Exodus 11:5); burning people to a crisp (Numbers 11:1); striking down seventy people for being curious and peeking into the Ark of the Covenant (1 Sam. 16:19); ordering someone to be stoned to death by an entire community for working on the Sabbath (Numbers 15:32); being prejudiced against people with disabilities and those who looked different (Leviticus 21:17–24); or committing a host of other Hitleresque monstrosities. I suppose I was just going with the Christian flow.

There were moments when the belief that *every passage of Scripture must be taken literally and, therefore, a holy and just God does use violence to punish disobedience* would feel uncomfortable, but I had to push those feelings down. Why? Because the text clearly and unequivocally quoted God commanding violence. It was staring at me from the page. The biblical text clearly depicted God, angry and wrathful at their sin, violently punishing and killing human beings. It would have been heretical to many people in my Christian circle to question the veracity of passages in the Bible describing divine violence. I was told that to suggest God did *not* call the religious community to enact divine violence because of sinful disobedience—when passages of Scripture clearly showed God doing so—would be the same as questioning God himself. That was a problem for me. After all, you know who else questioned God's truth? You got it! Satan.

In essence, I was told that questioning whether God really did violently kill babies (or had God's angelic hit-creatures do it), or created an eternal torture chamber, was tantamount to being inspired by Satan. I heard responses to my doubts, such as:

"How dare you question God!"
"Mark, I am praying for you! I know God will lead you to His truth"
"Pride comes before a fall!"
"You will go to Hell if you keep that up and take others with you."
"Don't let Satan deceive you."
"God is not just loving, but God is just and holy! Sin demands punishment!
"Mark, just trust in God's word."

I was in a bind. I knew God hated Satan. And in my naive mind, it was not a stretch to assume that God would abhor me for listening to that sly, slithering snake. To entertain the idea that biblical writers were merely culturally conditioned to describe portrayals of God would have been irreligious. It was not a giant leap to think that my fellow Christians, some of whom were pastors and leaders, would deem me a heretic for doing so. Not to mention I would be out of a job for questioning the Word of God, seeing that I was working full time in a conservative-minded church. You better believe I shoved that splinter down as far and as fast as I could!

Church folks also brought up the slippery slope argument, one that sounded very scary to me at the time. They hinted to me that if I started questioning God's Word (which is really theology and people's interpretations of people's interpretations of God's word), then I would be led swiftly down a demonic slope, swiftly into a life of miserable debauchery, with my final destination being Hell.

"Don't go down the Devil's path, Mark!" they warned.

"Without God, you can do no good. Leave the truth of God's word and curses will follow," said one confident preacher.

After all of these subtle, and not so subtle messages, it was apparent that I didn't need people to scare me. My inner critic, on its own, would have a field day providing me with apocalyptic, doom-and-gloom messages of what would happen if I didn't trust God and His word. I believed that a consequence of my doubts would be suffering a horrible and unrecoverable depression. Perhaps I would find myself homeless, roaming the streets with a debilitating addiction, unable to break free. Why? God's blessing and favor on my life would instantly dissipate because I was rebelliously doubting Him and His word. It would be a life without God and a life without goodness, or so I falsely imagined. So, I continually engaged in the fine art of suppression, pushing the doubts I harbored about the biblical text down further and further. That is, until a spiritual metamorphosis started happening within me.

SPIRITUAL METAMORPHOSIS

Can you imagine if a caterpillar had an astute mind, intense feelings, and the ability to voice its concerns like we do? I expect that, in the mayhem of metamorphosis from a crawling insect to a majestic butterfly, it would totally freak out! It would fear the absolute worst and drop some serious F-bombs. Its rasping groans would be heard by many around it, as it called its sanity into question. All this before the butterfly could even realize what had just taken place—complete transformation!

No one wakes up and excitedly tells themselves: "Today I want to start unraveling my faith, throwing myself into the throes of social rejection and one of the most despairing seasons of my life." But sometimes, before we know it, spiritual metamorphosis throws us onto the deconstruction and reconstruction journey. At one point we are fine, crawling our way around snugly and smugly in a comfortably familiar world. Then, by what mechanism we know not, we step into new territory, become painfully disoriented, and appear "unrecognizable" to those around us. Still, we keep moving forward and, before we know it, we are soaring on a beautiful tapestry of new wings, laced with the vibrant colors of our newfound beliefs—ones more congruent with who we really are. Suddenly we understand it: we've grown. Still, the process of growing is certainly chaotic and confusing!

On my spiritual metamorphosis journey, I realized that a violent and punitive God, along with Hell and the idea of eternal conscious torment, was no longer tenable to believe in. When I brought my questions to people, questions about some biblical writer's violent portrayal of God, assuming these writers were culturally conditioned and simply viewed God as any other tribal deity from that time period, they would say: "Well, God is just. God is holy. God hates sin. And there are consequences to disobedience. God is just in his discipline." If those people were right, then I needed to take my compassion, goodness, and wise discipline meter immediately to the repair shop.

It boggles my mind that our notions of what constitutes love, goodness, compassion, and healthy discipline could be considered so marred by sin that, in actuality, our views are deviant and ungodly. What appears to be loving and just from our standpoint (a belief that a lovingly just God would use wise, health-promoting, non-violent discipline) to others is just a satanic mirage. But could that *really* be? Has sin so poisoned our hearts and twisted our minds so greatly that what we call that which is good and just (God's violent and retributive punishment of sin) evil?

For example, when confronted with the reality that throughout the Old Testament, God caused or commanded the deaths of over 2 million people, it's difficult to feel inspired with joyful praise.[1] For most of us, commanding violence—including stoning, burning, maiming, and killing, which God is said to have done plenty of in the Bible—is inhumane, ungodlike, and missing an invaluable and moral sense of restorative justice. The same can be said of eternal conscious torment. Clearly, those acts are retributive and not restorative.

Restorative justice is completely contrary to seeking the brutal and violent cessation of life, which God is guilty of doing plenty of in the biblical text. It is also contrary to eternal conscious torment, where there is no learning and opportunity for growth and redemption. Restorative justice is creative and forward-thinking. It leads with fierce compassion and seeks to restore wounded and wayward human beings to a right relationship with self and others. Doesn't that type of justice make sense? After all, if you're a mangled corpse due to the mob of angry folks with stones in their hands who think they are following God's orders, the only transformation that's going to happen is metamorphosing from a human being to nutritious bird, bug, and bacteria food. Dead people don't learn valuable lessons that help them become ethical members of society. Eternally tortured human beings do not learn anything valuable either.

Based on what religious people are telling us, if we had the good, wise, and compassionate mind of God, we would value the killing of disobedient people. Why? We would value what God values. We would have a proper picture of a glorious, righteous, and holy God who always does what is good and just. Right? Then, instead of cringing when we read about God killing babies, we should boldly say—in humility, perhaps with a faint tear coming down our cheek—"Praise God, the mighty Egyptian baby killer, for His just acts!" Instead of questioning why God's wrath comes upon the disobedient and sends people to Hell for eternity, we should proclaim, "All of God's punitive commands are praiseworthy, just, and good!"

No. We cannot offer such praises. We simply cannot muster up enough faith to believe a loving and wise God could do the violent things written about in the Bible. We cannot put our conscience and intuitions away. A God could not look like humans at their worst.

HELL OFFICIALLY DIED WHEN I BECAME A PARENT

The final death stroke to the image of a wrathful God who commanded violence as punishment for sin and who, in the Bible, decreed eternal conscious torment for sinners in the afterlife hit me when I became a father. I imagine a conversation with my young son while sitting at a table outside Baskin-Robbins as both of us enjoyed a mint chocolate chip ice cream cone. It would have gone like this when I was just beginning to be struck by my metamorphosis:

Son: Daddy, my Sunday school teacher told us we should try to be like God. I want to grow up to be just like God. Do you think I can do that?

[Ice cream was now covering the sides of his mouth]

Me: Of course, that is what God wants from us. I'm so proud of you.

Son: Well, when I talked with you about wanting to play basketball like Stephen Curry, you showed me some things I could practice learning to play like him. What are some things that are true about God that are definitely not true about me right now?

Me: Oh...well, you are certainly loving and kind like God—except to your brother.

Son: Yeah...I can be kind of mean to him.

Me: God is honest and trustworthy, and you are honest and you do what you promise to do—except when we ask who ate the cookies.

Son: You got me there, Daddy.

Me: God is also just and holy, but you don't need to worry about that right now.

Son: What do you mean? If God is holy and just, I want to be those things too. But I don't really know what they mean.

Me: Well, for the most part, God being just and holy means that he punishes people when they do bad things, when they sin.

Son: Oh. How does he punish people? When I do something wrong and disobey you or my teachers at school, you go into teaching mode and ask me to try again (or not do it again) and then you give me a great big hug to let me know you still love me. Does God do something like that?

Me: (shuffling my feet nervously) Well, no. For the most part, in the Bible, God violently hurts people for disobeying him. Because he is so pure and cannot stand sin, he must teach them a lesson. In most cases that meant God used horrific violence in punishing people. Remember when we read about God killing everyone but Noah and his family? Or when God struck those priests dead for just touching the Ark of the Covenant? I'm pretty sure you remember God killing all those Egyptian babies because I seem to remember you cried at that one.

Son: Yeah, that was a sad story. And I didn't understand it. So, if I want to be more like God, when people hurt me or don't do what I ask, I should beat them up? Do you need to start beating me up when I punch my brother or don't tell you or Mommy that I was the one that ate the cookies? I want you to be more like God too Daddy, but I don't want you to start beating me up.

Me: Well, that's why I said you shouldn't worry about being just and holy. That's one way that we shouldn't be like God. We should forgive other people. Like you forgave your brother for ripping the head off of your favorite Transformer.

Son: I'm sorry, Daddy, but I don't think I have forgiven him yet for that. But anyway, why was my Sunday school teacher telling us we should be like God if he is not really someone we should be like?

Me: She didn't mean...well, it's just that...look, it's kind of complicated theology stuff, but when you get older, you'll understand. For now, just focus on loving and forgiving other people. If they hurt you, don't punish them, but pray for them.

Son: Isn't that something God should be doing rather than punishing people?

Me: Just eat your ice cream.

It wasn't until I played that scenario out in my head that my eyes were really opened to just how broken this system is. God, at least the God of the Bible, is certainly not someone I want my children to emulate.

When I was working this out for myself, I told this hypothetical story to a dear friend of mine (one of the few who wasn't judging me at the time). After hearing it he said to me, "But Mark, your son is just a child. The scenario you just laid out involving punishing people requires authority. I think the reason the story sounds so absurd is that it is not an apples-to-apples comparison. A ruler or a judge or maybe law enforcement have authority to do the things you are talking about, but not a child." It was an interesting point, and I thought about it for a while before responding. "So, if your son, Tommy, were to become president, would you be proud of him for ordering the death of a group of babies in another country because that country was treating our expatriates harshly? If he became a judge, would you want him to sentence a group of criminals, each of whom had committed a different crime, to drown together regardless of which crime each committed? If he..." "Stop, stop..." he interrupted. "I get the point."

As a father, I simply could not imagine violently punishing my child (or giving someone else permission to do so) because of his disobedience. I could never kill my child for not listening to me. I could never use violent and gratuitous physical force to discipline him. I could never allow demonic creatures to torment him for his wrongdoings for one second, let alone eternity. Karl Forehand, author of *Apparent Faith,* puts it succinctly: "The Scriptures [particularly those in the NT] were written by people who often portrayed God as a parent using the term Father. If God is Father and if He is love, then His love for His children must at least be better than the love I have for my children."[2]

I also realized that I would never instill shame and fear messages into his precious mind and heart. Identity is everything. Out of that fountain of identity within us is how we relate to others around us. I can acknowledge the wonders and wickedness, selflessness and selfishness, that can spring from the complex hearts of humanity. But you can be sure I will never, ever tell my young son that he has a wicked, sick, and evil heart—messages I repeatedly heard as a Christian. He has a good heart because he is my son. He is lovable simply because he exists. No matter what he does, *that* is his core identity. And I will remind him of that many times throughout his life, especially when he chooses to not always live out of the truth of who he is.

Are we supposed to believe that a God who is vastly more loving and just than we are, would be less loving and just than ourselves? No matter where you are on the liberal/conservative divide, I am sure we can agree that maiming, burning alive, stoning, threatening eternal punishment, toxic shaming, or drowning our children, when they selfishly go against our wishes (even if they were our adult children), is not the most compassionate, just, wise, and loving thing to do. Right?

"God is not just a God of love; God is holy and just!" some people shout.

Okay. Let's say that God's righteousness necessitates a desire for justice, a need to make things right. Certainly, justice seems to be a need for us. When something unjust happens to us, when someone hurts or offends us, we usually demand that wrong to be made right. We usually demand payment of some kind. We demand justice! When that pained part of us wants and demands justice, what is it that God requires of us? And does that requirement provide a glimpse into what God's true impulse is in the face of injustice?

Here is my concern with the "God demands justice for sin" motif. It seems to me that in the New Testament, when people act unjustly toward us, God asks us to forgive without first requiring the violent physical punishment of the perpetrator. So, how is it that God demands justice in the form of violent physical punishment if people sin against Him, but God calls us to extend love, mercy, and forgiveness when people sin against us? Something is amiss here. Why is our primitive impulse toward justice—"an eye for an eye,"—to be superseded by love, mercy, and forgiveness, while God's impulse to violently punish for all eternity every last offense is to be applauded as holy and righteous? Wouldn't that make us more lovingly just than God?

And further, doesn't it seem God's knowledge of discipline should be vastly superior to that of the researchers, parenting professionals, healthy development strategists, and transformation gurus of today? From these experts, we know a long-term pattern of spanking is cruel, harmful, and negatively impacts the brains of developing children.

For example, a recent study examining the effects of spanking young children concluded that "parents should be aware that, in fact, spanking may hinder their children's development of self-control and interpersonal skills and increase externalizing behaviors, even if used infrequently."[3] Another study by the same researcher showed that "children who were recently spanked at the age of 5 showed significantly lower reading and math scores at ages 6 and 7 compared with those who were spanked but not recently."[4]

It is true that some research shows that spanking may not screw kids up for life. However, maybe it is not really a fair comparison. I suppose we would have to look, not at the research on spanking, but at the literature on violent punishment. God's interventions seem to be on the spectrum of violent physical abuse. And one thing is clear from the research, physical violent abuse as a disciplinary measure for children is not healthy and is not effective for long-term growth and development. Do present-day researchers have something to teach God?

When I think of Hell, I think of Norway's Halden Prison. Why? Because they are complete opposites of each other. Hell, at least the Infernalists' version, is for sinners who were chosen by God before the foundation of the world who will never have a chance to be restored and live a normal life again. For them, it is just torment, night and day, without ceasing. Five years. Ten years. One thousand years. One million years. One billion years. Eternal torment forever, and ever. All because God's pure holiness could not stand to be around sin. Even one sin apparently would have warranted the just eternal torment. God's justice is all about retribution, adequate payment, and just punishment.

Then you have Halden Prison. It exists because people have committed crimes, yet it is meant to be restorative. Drug dealers, murderers, and rapists enter the prison greeted by a handshake by one of the guards. They have a private bathroom, a TV, kitchen, and amenities. The point of the prison is to turn criminals into good neighbors. The prison focuses on rehabilitation and restoration through education, job training, and therapy. They also see relationships as vital for them and that includes with the staff.

Ragnar Kristoffersen, an anthropologist who teaches at the Correctional Service of Norway Staff Academy, trains the correction officers. When interviewed by *The New York Times*, he was asked about whether the prison system works. He acknowledges that treating people nicely doesn't always work. Yet, he stated, "If you treat people badly, it's a reflection on yourself."[5]

How are those in power at the Halden prison more just than the cruel version of God presented to us by some religious folk? How is it that they could have a heart for restoration and God be bent on vengeance and eternal torment? How is it that the prison can offer the inmates cold water to drink, yet God sends people to Hell to have a thirst that is never quenched? It is just not rationally possible. God, who by definition must be the greatest of all possible beings, must also be preeminent in love and the wisest of all disciplinarians. Based on that definition, God cannot be a worse disciplinarian than the authorities at Halden prison. Logically, it simply cannot be the case.

We know that the healthy carrot is better for all of us—including adults—than the Negan-like stick. And we've been taught by cutting-edge researchers a plethora of non-violent techniques to discipline children and adults that promote compassion, equity, and overall morality. If God existed, could God really use primitive violence, killing, and torture as the primary methods of loving discipline and justice? I think not.

It took quite a long time to have a shift in perspective from "Every passage of Scripture must be taken literally, and, therefore, a holy and just God does use violence to punish disobedience" to "God cannot be less loving and less wise than we are. Love does not perpetrate gratuitous violence and could eternally punish anyone; therefore, the God of the Infernalists cannot exist."

It took many separate experiences over many years, and many conversations with like-minded peers, to finally come to a place where I could not believe a Divine Creator, *the* role model for compassion, wisdom, love, holiness, and justice, would use horrific violence to punish His children (in this life and the life to come). There came a point when I could not believe, with a clear conscience, that God acted like every other tribal god of the Ancient Near East. I could not believe the worst, that a Divine sense of discipline and justice most resembled a twisted composite of the evilest authoritarian dictators that have ever lived.

So, I made a confession to my Christian friends: "I cannot praise God for killing children. I cannot praise God for commanding genocide. I cannot praise God for commanding people to be stoned, maimed, and burned alive for missing the mark of His ideal. I cannot validate God's goodness in people not being restored in the afterlife but only experiencing His retributive punishment. If that is good, then it seems that my justice, goodness, and compassionate discipline meter is broken and can never be fixed. And, in truth, I don't want it fixed if it means that I would have to confidently believe the very things I detest."

This far into our journey together, dear readers, I am sure you have come to a place where you could be honest with yourself and ask, "Is my meter really broken?" And over time, if you haven't already, I hope you realize on a profound experiential level that it is working just fine. I think your growing understanding of compassion and loving justice is perfectly on point. It is okay to not believe that the Divine's loving justice encompasses brutal and violent displays of punitive power. From a philosophical perspective, if there is a God, and this God epitomizes wise and loving discipline, this God must be far more loving than we could ever think or imagine. God cannot be less loving and less wise than we are. Perhaps it is true, that if there is a God, and this God *is* love, then love does not perpetrate violence and send people to Hell to be tormented for eternity.

THOUGHTS FROM A FELLOW BUTTERFLY

We no longer need to be afraid of the feeble narratives of an angry, punitive God and a place called Hell where people are eternally tormented due to their sins are thin, feeble projections of which we no longer need to be afraid. They are merely a result of creative human ponderings morphing into violent projections that became religious narratives. Those narratives lasted because they served as a cohesive glue that bound communities together. Unfortunately, they also fueled toxic pride, and were used by people in power to control the in-group's morality and maintain the hierarchical status quo. It is also absolutely absurd to think that our compassion, goodness, and wise discipline meters functions more adequately than God's. To Hell with Hell and a version of God that is cruel and punitive. Humanity deserves better.

PART III

UNHINGING HELL FROM OUR NERVOUS SYSTEMS

In Part II, we journeyed through the origin and function of Hell and its interrelated narratives. We also examined the Infernalists' image of God as one who commits violence, commands violence, and punishes with eternal torment. We found that image emotionally and mentally indigestible. While simply gaining knowledge does not necessarily lead to transformative healing, especially in the healing of trauma, my hope is that those chapters shook loose some strands of the web of Hell indoctrination.

This section will explore specific, down-to-earth pathways, practices, and principles from the field of psychology. I have selected, designed, and shaped them to help you heal from religious trauma and, more specifically, from Hell indoctrination.

I don't believe in quick-fix, snake-oil healing. It is more of a journey than an absolute destination. However, I hope this next section will help you travel the healing journey with beneficial knowledge and resources to move at a quicker pace.

Each individual who has gone through trauma undergoes a distinctive healing process. Everyone's journey is unique, and what works for one person may not work for another. The key is to find the practices and perspectives that feel like a warm hug for your nervous system, and leave the ones that feel like a scratchy wool sweater in the donation bin. This is your story to write, your healing journey to embark upon. You have the power to determine what nourishes you and what does not.

CHAPTER 12
HEALING RELIGIOUS TRAUMA WITH MEMORY RECONSOLIDATION

*"Reconsolidation research has revealed—for perhaps
the first time in human history—the process
that commutes the life sentence of problematic
emotional learning."*

—Bruce Ecker

There are two aphorisms I mention frequently in trauma work: "Facts will not heal the tracts" and "Information does not necessitate transformation." The trauma of Hell indoctrination is lodged in the tracts of the sub-cortical nervous system. Since trauma's imprint is on the mind and body, knowledge alone is insufficient to heal it. It is impossible to talk or lecture a victim out of chronic shame, unrelenting inner criticism, unworthiness, helplessness, insomnia, rumination, flashbacks, nightmares, and disturbing feelings. Effective trauma work calls for us to travel deep within ourselves. We must go beyond the defense systems to enter the tender and vulnerable arena of our bodies and nervous systems.

Listening to podcasts on healing the trauma of Hell indoctrination, venting on social media, reading books, and telling our stories are all important actions we can take on the healing journey. These, however, may not adequately reach the recesses of trauma in our body. This is why a person can sit through a thousand sermons without experiencing transformational change. It is also why preachers can preach a thousand sermons without healing the exiles that reside within themselves—the wounded, traumatized parts of them that are in pain—to the detriment of those they serve. Healing trauma requires putting on scuba gear and diving into the muddy waters of our complex internal systems.

Effective healing from trauma also requires going into the memories of the traumatic events. This includes dredging up much of the material associated with the memory—the imagery, emotions, beliefs, and somatic sensations. It is there, in those memories and the neural networks associated with them, located deep within our bodies, where we find the sources of so much terror and shame. These need processing, revising, and updating. By processing traumatic memories, we unlock and release energy in the body that has been trapped and blocked. Once it is released it can move elsewhere, helping us live more authentic lives.

Religious trauma, like all trauma, is a shock to our nervous system and affects the brain's ability to regulate emotions and process information in an integrative and healthy way. Our bodies then store the trauma where it remains unprocessed, frozen in time in memory networks. Much of the emotional pain we experience signals that our trauma yearns for us to integrate it and work it through to completion. Until we adequately process and integrate the trauma, experiences in the present can trigger the unprocessed and unintegrated information stored in those neural memory networks. A trigger can consist of any internal or external event that activates a painful memory network. Once it's activated, we once again experience emotions, beliefs, and somatic sensations as if the original trauma had just taken place. The explosion of energy and emotions being released from the core wound trapped in a memory can become so overwhelming that we do all sorts of things to cope with its aftermath. Unfortunately, the defenses and strategies we use to deal—or not deal—with the emotional pain often brings further suffering.

Take Sarah, for instance, a six-year-old, who has a very sensitive temperament. Sarah's parents were strict conservative Christians within the Pentecostal tradition. Sarah often found that expressing what she wanted to do, or how she felt about little things throughout the day, was often met with harshness from both parents. If Sarah whined about anything, her father would immediately yell and threaten her with the belt. Sometimes, he used that belt.

Her stern parents would tell Sarah that God loves her very much. Then, as time progresses, however, they begin to explain that this same supernatural being can punish her if she sins. They also mention a terrible place called Hell where God sends people for not listening to Him. When Sarah is out of line, it is common for her parents to say things like, "God is watching you, so shape up, missy." Her young brain encodes this image as a significant threat. Yet, because mommy and daddy say they love this Being, it doesn't seem right to voice her fears to her parents.

Sarah is terrified of a God who can punish her for doing bad things but upsetting her parents risks jeopardizing their love, and that would only make things worse—so she says nothing. Unable to fully comprehend that data, Sarah is left with a traumatic imprint on her nervous system. Then, repeat those messages over a hundred times through her parents or church, and now it is an entrenched memory linked with other memories that have similar fear-based themes.

As an adult, Sarah is now left with a vast array of neural networks that have been encoded with the terror of an all-seeing and all-knowing God. The God she envisions can harm her if she does the wrong thing. He could also send her to Hell if she doesn't stay on the straight and narrow path. Along with those memory networks, she also has repeated experiences with an angry, distant, and punitive dad and a controlling mom. There is no adaptive resolution to her trauma. She grows up with stuck, unprocessed, unintegrated emotionally laden information within her memory networks. She tells no one of the mixed feelings she has inside. On the one hand, she loves her parents and wants to please them, and on the other, she fears that her parents and especially God will punish her. The effects of her trauma are not fully realized until her young adult years.

As an adult, Sarah notices she becomes very triggered when her boss, her friends, and her fiancé are not happy with her. When they do things that hurt her, she becomes too anxious to speak her mind. It causes her debilitating anxiety. She also still worries about her relationship with God and if she is doing enough to please Him. She is kind to others but struggles to be kind to herself. Over time, the cognitive dissonance—the contradictory beliefs she holds that cause tension within herself—becomes overwhelming. Sarah eventually realizes how much she is suffering due to a belief in a primarily wrathful God who created a place called Hell to send people who do not obey Him. She also realizes that her parents' ways of relating to her caused her significant harm. She comes to therapy being at a loss as to what to do. Thankfully, there is a brain mechanism that allows healing to take place for Sarah and all of us affected by trauma generally, including religious trauma: memory reconsolidation.

MEMORY RECONSOLIDATION

Is our memory of an event permanent, or can it be "updated" in the course of time? *Memory reconsolidation* is a remarkable new discovery within the field of neuroscience. It seems that memories are not, as had been previously thought, static, fixed, or entrenched for a lifetime.[1] In fact, every time we bring a memory to mind, we have the potential to alter it. Memory reconsolidation is the brain's natural mechanism for transforming the cerebral baggage that comes with painful experiences and traumatic memories. More specifically, the memory persists, but the beliefs and meanings associated with the memory, along with the feelings that are part of the memory system, are likewise positively altered. This means that even memories of childhood wounding or religious trauma *can* be reactivated, reshaped, and recast to bring about lasting change in our lives!

Scientists now know that whenever we retrieve a memory, we can engage a mechanism that makes it malleable again for a short period of time. Like a document on a computer screen, we can "edit" or infuse the memory with new information and emotion, thus fundamentally altering it in some way—especially in the way the memory makes us think, feel, act, and interact with others and ourselves. In some cases, the memory itself might change as new details emerge and combine with fresh information or emotional sensations through this brief, mutational reconsolidation process. The details and events of a memory may remain the same, but the emotions and thoughts associated with them are transformed!

Memory reconsolidation allows us the possibility of erasing negative feelings and thoughts surrounding difficult past events by recalling, updating, and rewriting them with a deeper understanding of the wider truths that time has revealed about an event. Before we return to the neuroscience of memory reconsolidation, consider one practical example of this principle.

SARAH AND MEMORY RECONSOLIDATION

Let's return to Sarah. In therapy, I experience her as a woman who is shy, anxious, and is cautious to speak her mind. Sarah acknowledges those behaviors. She has many goals in therapy. One of her goals is to speak up more in relationships and be involved in conversations with her friends. Unfortunately, her anxiety gets the best of her. During conversations, she is usually frozen with fear and keeps quiet.

Through our work together, especially exploring her childhood memories, we believe we have discovered the subconscious emotional belief that is generating her symptoms: *If my parents got angry with me when I wanted to express myself, then expressing myself with others will make them angry, too. I am deficient and my voice is not worth listening to. Therefore, it is better to keep my mouth shut.* There is also a young part of Sarah that believes that *I must be obedient and not share anything that contradicts my parents, or I could go to Hell.* And so, she often stays silent and maintains the status quo, despite her desire to speak up.

Sometimes these faulty beliefs sound strange and unbelievable when said aloud and they only ring true because, when believed, they explain a clear pattern of otherwise irrational behavior. Sarah's emotionally laden beliefs may have been useful for survival in childhood, but they are severely limiting her now.

Sarah shared a key memory with me. When she was younger, she had tried to talk to her parents about how she couldn't believe God would send people to hell. Her parents immediately yelled at her. Dismissing her thoughts, they told her that she was being argumentative. Not only this, but that she must also be listening to Satan, who likes to question God's Word. Her parents then sent Sarah to her room. That was a pivotal moment for her. The event formed a life-changing *emotional learning* moment that continuously told her that her voice was not worth listening to and if she did speak, it could lead to an aversive outcome. It became the basis of a distorted lens through which she viewed talking with others in every subsequent conversation. It constituted a "no disagreeing with others rule" that imprisoned her voice in a falsehood.

Psychologists call that lens a *schema*.[2] Schemas are mental frameworks that help us interpret and make sense of the world around us. For example, someone can have a shame schema, in which they believe they are fundamentally unlovable. Another can have a mistrust schema, where they have a pattern of believing they will be abused, neglected, or hurt by others. Someone could have an entitlement schema, where they believe they deserve special privileges in the context of their relationships. In any case, the schemas that shape our view of the world and ourselves operating within it often exist outside the realm of (or deeply hidden from) our own awareness. For

Sarah, that unconscious emotional truth of being subservient and quiet prevented her from sharing her voice and opinions with confidence.

THE SCIENCE

Bruce Ecker, student of neuroscientific research, therapist, and author of *Unlocking the Emotional Brain,* has brought the practical applications of memory reconsolidation to communities all over the world via workshops and publications. Ecker notes that the *transformational change sequence,* which is at the root of healing clinical symptoms, is a "theory-independent, universal metaprocess" (a process I will explain, shortly).[3] In his understanding of the research, he demonstrates just how, if transformational and lasting change has taken place, whether inside the therapy room or through a coaching session via Zoom, memory reconsolidation has occurred. If a person is in therapy and after an incredible session, the person no longer suffers from anxiety, depression, or debilitating self-doubt, memory reconsolidation has taken place. If a person did a coaching session with someone working through their Hell trauma, and they had a "breakthrough," no longer fearing Hell, then the brain mechanism of memory reconsolidation had occurred.

Based on the synthesis of memory reconsolidation research to date, Ecker has identified a three-step erasure sequence, as follows, that can bring about the transformational process.

THE "THREE-STEP MEMORY RECONSOLIDATION TRANSFORMATION SEQUENCE"

How does memory reconsolidation become the key to unlocking memories at the synaptic level and bring about healing and transformation? There are three preparatory steps, but for simplicity, I will describe only the three main steps of memory reconsolidation. These steps allow your brain to unearth and erase targeted emotional learning, beliefs which were once adaptive but cause present-day difficulties.

Step 1: Evoke and reactivate the problematic memory. It is *this* memory, which formed a belief, that is continually generating negative symptoms and keeping you stuck. In a therapy context, the therapist would guide the client into the specific memory they believed to be the source of the distorted "rule" that has the client tied up with painful emotions.

Step 2: Reactivate and relive (in a deeply experiential manner) a completely different memory that contradicts the conclusions that you have been drawing from the painful memory. This step is the key to unlocking the synapses of the original memory and emotional learning.

According to Ecker, retrieving the original memory renders it pliable and changeable for about five hours. Within that timeframe, not only the memory but the entire unhelpful emotional schema that used to flow from it can be altered. It is this crucial step of *entering into and experiencing* a contradictory memory, with the experiential juxtaposition of both the old memory and the new current view of reality, that supplies new evidence our brains can use to transform the original memory.

In Sarah's case, she shared with me a recent example of progress where she had actually taken a risk and spoken up in a book study with her friends. By being an empathic listener and speaker, Sarah was then able to help a friend and fellow attendee find a solution to a difficult problem she was facing. With a smile on her face, Sarah related to me how her friend was extremely grateful and gave her a hug. Sarah reported feeling excited, loved, and special after this event. This is precisely the type of "mismatch to belief and simultaneous contradictory experience" we are looking for in Step 2.

Step 3: There is a repetition of experiencing the original memory— most importantly the *feelings* and *thoughts* that come from the original memory—alongside a vivid experiencing of the mismatched and contradictory, new experience. The third step is where the magic finally happens, with the erasing or revising of the lie-based memory and negative emotional learning. The task is to go back and forth between the old memory and the new experience that entails contradictory information. It is a side-by-side experiencing of the two incompatible truths that allows for the transformation of the original memory. Basically, you are trying to embed and encode the information contained in the present, fuller, "more truthful" experience into the original memory, with its damaging negative emotional truths. What was once adaptive is no longer adaptive to present-day circumstances. And sometimes we must experience the original memory multiple times, alongside facts and feelings from the new, contradictory memory, for transformative truth to stick.

Returning to Sarah: I began by reminding her of the painful memory she had relived about sharing her thoughts with her parents and the problematic conclusion her mind drew from that experience (*I am deficient, and my voice is not worth listening to*). With this fresh in Sarah's mind, she could then bring up her more recent joy-filled and empowering memory of the time when she shared her voice with her friend in a helpful way—an experience that contradicted her previous false conclusion.

It is important that both memories be recalled side-by-side, in a deeply experiential manner, with all the feelings, thoughts, and bodily sensations that accompany both of them. Remember, it is the *juxtaposition* of both memories simultaneously that causes the synapses to unlock and become open to lasting change. In Sarah's case, doing so served to weaken the absolute authority of her parents on a deep neuronal level.

It was natural for Sarah, a child at the time, to assign unquestionable authority to her parents. And with new life experiences, Sarah could now recognize that her parents do not have to have the last word in her psyche. She could understand and question the unconscious "rule" her younger self had put in place at that time. She could see that the connection her mind drew from that experience didn't have to have the last word, either. The reaction of her parents and the lie she believed because of it—*which she had thought was the truth*—was not true. The truth was that her voice was valuable and that she could share with confidence in a way that could demonstrably help those she cared about. In this way, the original memory, and the false emotional learning buried in her unconscious, lost much of its power to control her behavior. This revelation of truth had, indeed, made her free!

The test of whether this process worked long-term or not is revealed in Sarah's own life. Is Sarah still anxious about sharing her voice and unable to express herself freely with her friends? The extent to which she can or not reveals whether she still believes *I am deficient, and my voice is not worth listening to*. If Sarah is still fearful in group situations and cannot muster up enough courage to share, there is no reason to despair. There may be other earlier life experiences and associated beliefs that need to be unearthed and processed, via memory reconsolidation, for deep, lasting change to occur.

Sometimes there is a collection of memories that work in concert to produce the distorted lens that we look through. With each problematic and painful memory we can recall, process, and reconsolidate, we move that much closer to freedom from the chains that have bound us.

MEMORY RECONSOLIDATION IN PRACTICE

The *transformational change sequence of memory reconsolidation* can help us deconstruct traumatizing images of God and reconstruct new, life-giving images. We don't have to be held hostage to a traumatized brain that cannot rid itself of haunting images of God. Practices that can bring healing and transformation are now at our fingertips! Tim Desmond, a well-known speaker and therapist who uses memory reconsolidation in his work, writes:

> This [memory reconsolidation] is the neurological recipe for emotional healing. In other words, you get in touch with your suffering from the past and connect with compassion at the same

time. You embrace your pain with loving presence. If we try to process pain from the past without compassion, we end up ruminating and reinforcing our old stories. However, once we learn how to hold our suffering the way we'd hold a crying baby, real transformation becomes possible.[4]

One of the most difficult images to delete from our minds is the judgmental God who is ready to pounce on us for doing something wrong. It could be an image of a God who is cruel, judgmental, harsh, critical, and always displeased. It could be an image of a God who is ready to send us to Hell if we continue to sin or if we don't have all of our theology correct. Thankfully, we can take advantage of memory reconsolidation to help transform old, toxic images of God. Set some time aside in a safe, nurturing environment to try this out yourself.

This is an exercise with its own unique steps that takes advantage of the memory reconsolidation process. An audio file of this activity can be found at https://markgregorykarris.com/meditations (password: HEAL). Some readers may not be able to do this exercise without a trusted guide or therapist. If it becomes too difficult, then be kind to yourself and move on to something that feels life-giving.

Step 1: Think about the old, traumatic image of God that still causes you some mental and emotional pain. For some, it could be an angry old man in the sky with a white beard and a harsh scowl who is bent on criticizing and punishing mankind. Perhaps a memory of when that frightening image first appeared comes to mind. Hold it in your thoughts.

Step 2: When the disturbing image of God is clear, become aware of tension or uncomfortable sensations in your body. Notice where you feel them. Stay with those sensations without trying to change them. Also notice your feelings. *Do you feel sad? Angry? Fearful?* If you get distracted, bring your attention back to the image and your experience. What *emotional meanings* do you have when you think of this image? For example, *"God is angry at me. I'm sinful. I'm unlovable. I am unsafe."*

Step 3: Now move to an image of someone you find truthful, wise, comforting, and protective. You can recall a loving and accepting pet animal, relative, deity, or friend. Whatever image you use, notice the initial sensations of warmth and love you may feel when bringing this image to mind.

Step 4: For those who have found a comforting image of a strong, nurturing, and protective figure, picture them sending you love. Imagine that figure approaching you with compassion. Imagine them holding you tenderly and lovingly accepting you as you are. Picture them saying kind words to you like "The image of a punishing God, waiting to send people to Hell, is someone else's projection. You don't have to believe that. You are okay just as you are and no longer need to live a life of fear." Use whatever expression of love that is meaningful to you. Better yet, allow those powerful and positive figures to tell you their healing truth. Close your eyes, listen, and allow them to speak. Then, scan your body and feel what it is like to receive this love from this person.

As humans, we all have a primal *fight-or-flight* response. We also have a "tend and befriend," system, or *care-circuit*. The care-circuit is that part of our nervous system that gives us the warm fuzzies and feel-good feelings. The key in this step is to really feel the love and care in your body. Practice staying with this for at least three to five minutes.

Step 5: Repeat steps 1–4 one more time. The key is to juxtapose the negative image of God, along with the positive image of a loving, protective, compassionate being, and to repeat that process a few times. Hold them in your consciousness, side-by-side, having almost an experiential awareness of *both* at the same time.

A JOURNEY TOWARD FREEDOM

After completing the process, the original image as a memory will be reconsolidated and stored in your memory banks in a less distressing form. And, after practicing the sequence, there should be less emotional baggage associated with it when you revisit the original image in the future. Tim Desmond encapsulated the memory reconsolidation process very simply:

Distressing Memory + Care-Circuit = Less Distressing Memory.[5]

We can seldom *think* our way out of childhood or religious trauma. Instead, we must engage in practices that rewire our brains for the better. These healing practices must involve our nervous system experiencing new information alongside old beliefs and feelings, integrating them in both the cognitive and emotional aspects of our mind and body. To accomplish this, we can rely on positive memories of nurturing figures like parents or mentors, or experiential practices like forgiveness, self-compassion, and serving others. These pathways and practices can help us reconstruct and rewrite our beliefs, faith, and behaviors in a more positive and adaptive way, creating a more fulfilling future.

Memory reconsolidation can help. *Why?* Because our experiences, especially those that are full of intensity and emotion, after a period become *consolidated* and wired into our brain at the entrenched, synaptic level. And we can work with that through experiences with compassionate others, patient therapists—even emotional support animals! A foundational principle of memory reconsolidation is that new experiences *can* inform and transform past interpretations of events (and our uninformed reactivity to them). "Neurons that fire together with new experiences, wire together"—creating a kinder, gentler reality for us and offering the potential for greater peace and happiness.[6]

Let's turn to other important psychological principles and experiential practices, some of which incorporate the memory reconsolidation mechanism that can help you on your healing journey.

CHAPTER 13

"AVENGERS ASSEMBLE!": INSTALLING POSITIVE INTERNAL RESOURCES

"Imagination gives us the opportunity to envision new possibilities—it is an essential launchpad for making our hopes come true. It fires our creativity, relieves our boredom, alleviates our pain, enhances our pleasure, and enriches our most intimate relationships."

—Bessel van der Kolk, *The Body Keeps the Score*

In a small, quiet village, a disheveled but charismatic shaman with a long coarse beard placed a curse on a mischievous village thief who had beaten a defenseless woman and stolen her food a few nights before. The thief learned that the shaman's hex was a curse of death and that he was doomed to die before midnight. The thief panicked. He became unbearably anxious and began to sweat profusely. He felt a large lump in his throat and couldn't breathe. He said to himself, "Surely the curse is taking a hold of me. I am going to die." He darted from his home and ran furiously as far as he could from the village, hoping to somehow outrun the curse. The next day he was found dead about six miles away from the village being eaten by jackals.

Some might see this tale as an example of supernatural forces at work. Others, though, might understand the story as showing how absolute belief in the supernatural can lead to risky decisions and harmful consequences. The thief may have experienced something akin to the *nocebo effect,* which refers to how a belief that something is harmful leads to actual harm occurring. The effect is the opposite of the better-known *placebo effect,* in which the mere belief that a thing has a positive effect leads to a real positive outcome. Another term we could have used to describe the thief's fate is a "psychophysiological death," or even a "voodoo death".[1] It was the thief's certainty in the shaman's curse, and not the "curse" itself, that did the damage. The belief produced fear, which became overwhelming terror. The physiological response to this stress, which likely involved a bombardment of ghastly glucocorticoids (stress hormones), caused the thief to have a heart attack, keel over, and die.

The brain is fascinating in that if it believes something to be real, it can seemingly produce that reality. Studies of depression have shown that taking sugar pills can have an antidepressant effect if participants believe them to be genuine medication.[2] A piece of rope in a bush may be mistaken for a snake and cause the release of associated stress hormones. Someone who believes in demons may see these behind every bush, filling them with fear. Others who have no belief will have no such experience. Our mentality creates our experiential reality, and vice versa. Our thoughts have power over our moods, our immune system, and our quality of life.

Our imaginations have power too, and brains are not always able to distinguish between fantasy and reality. If we imagine engaging in an activity, neurons in the brain become activated as if we were actually doing that activity. For example, someone imagining playing the piano along with their favorite music, hitting the precise keys with the exact fingers that they would in real life, can show patterns of brain activity that are identical to those of people who were really playing. It is an extraordinary thought that someone could become a better piano player just through imagination.[3] Just as extraordinary is how memories can elicit powerful images and feelings in the present. At this very moment, I am visualizing myself and my family on a trip we took to Hawaii. I feel the white sands between my toes, see the gorgeous blue water, taste the great food, and enjoy the lovely company. As I think about it, I feel a burst of joy, likely stimulated by a release of neurochemicals and hormones. It is as if I were really back there.

Many models of therapy use visualization exercises to facilitate healing. Studies have consistently demonstrated the positive effects of healing imagery. These include a healthier immune response, reductions in stress, anxiety, and depression, a better capacity to stop unhealthy habits, and the ability to better manage one's pain. The imagination is such a powerful tool for altering our states and promoting healing that it can also be used to heal religious trauma.

Before we continue, a quick caveat: I do not believe in quick fixes. The exercises we are about to explore are not meant to heal instantly. They are meant to help. For some, you may find these exercises to be an incredible benefit to you on your healing journey. Others may not find them as helpful or may feel they do not work at all. Some may have a difficult time using their imaginations in new ways and may need the assistance of a trusted guide or therapist. All of this is okay. Be kind to yourself. If you find the exercises challenging, hopefully you can take away some of the healing principles and practices as you move to the other chapters.

EMDR AND BILATERAL STIMULATION

Eye Movement Desensitization and Reprocessing (EMDR) is an empirically validated model of psychotherapy originally designed to help trauma survivors. The aim of EMDR is to help people work through traumatic memories and adverse life experiences. In Bruce Ecker's book *Unlocking the Emotional Brain,* one chapter is dedicated to EMDR and memory reconsolidation. In it, Ecker describes his belief that EMDR involves the memory reconsolidation process, which is why the method is so effective at promoting lasting change.

In my own EMDR training, I discovered a number of visualization techniques that have since proved potent for myself and my clients in working through the effects of religious trauma. Before we explore the benefits of these techniques, I want to introduce the reader to the topic of bilateral stimulation.

Francine Shapiro, the psychologist who developed EMDR, explains how when walking in a park one day, she realized that some distressing feelings she had been experiencing were suddenly gone. When thinking about why this might be, she noted that just before the feeling stopped she had made some spontaneous eye movements. It was in this moment that she had a revelation. She wondered whether moving the eyes in a rhythmic pattern while focusing on a distressing memory might reduce emotional suffering. This hypothesis has now been tested in more than two dozen randomized controlled studies and the evidence suggests that EMDR can indeed be very effective at reducing suffering.

Bilateral stimulation (BLS), usually in the form of visual, tactile, or auditory stimuli, occur in a rhythmic left-right or right-left pattern. For example, think of moving your eyes repeatedly from side to side. Then imagine tapping your thighs like a drummer in a rhythmic left-to-right or right-to-left pattern.

How or why BLS works is still a scientific mystery. One prominent belief is that the left-right pattern creates a calming effect and allows for a greater connection between the left and right hemispheres of the brain.[4] This helps with trauma because there is typically emotional material that remains frozen and unprocessed. As the negative memory is recalled, BLS seems to allow this information that is lodged in memory to become "unstuck," clearing the pathways between the two hemispheres and contributing to healthy memory integration and healing.

Before we begin exploring exercises that can assist in dealing with religious C-PTSD symptoms or other difficult memories, I encourage you to find a BLS technique that works for you. Going back and forth tapping on your thighs like a drummer works for some. Others perform a simple technique of tapping their middle finger and thumb, switching from left to right hands. My personal favorite is The Butterfly Hug. To do this, you cross your arms in front of you with your left hand on your right shoulder and vice versa, then you tap your hands over and over on each shoulder (an example of The Butterfly Hug can be found at https://youtu.be/iGGJrqscvtU). With any of these techniques, if any pain or discomfort is felt, you should use another BLS technique. Wherever you can tap with a rhythmic side-to-side motion, that will work just fine. The speed and rhythm of the BLS is up to you. Take a moment, give it a try, and find what works for you.

Once you have found the BLS method that feels most comfortable for you, we can begin exploring visualization exercises that can help when religious trauma is activated. These exercises can be used for the healing of religious trauma and to help you stabilize your thoughts and feelings when C-PTSD symptoms are getting the best of you. For example, they can be used when feelings of worthlessness, shame and guilt are difficult to shake, or if you are struggling with insomnia and finding it difficult to fall asleep. The interventions might also be used if you are triggered by being exposed to religious dogma and find yourself anxious and disoriented. Basically, you can use these practices whenever you need to feel supported, uplifted, and balanced.[5]

Before starting the exercises, do be aware that they can be challenging for some. If you find yourself feeling emotionally overwhelmed, stop the exercises immediately. You can always try this deeper work with a trusted guide or therapist. Audio files of the activities in this chapter can be found at https://markgregorykarris.com/meditations (password: HEAL) .

PEACEFUL PLACE

This exercise will guide you to find your peaceful place and to integrate it with BLS. When your religious trauma is activated, or you feel triggered for any other reasons, being able to visualize your own peaceful place while using BLS will help you to shift away from overwhelming emotions and negative self-critical thoughts. Some people choose a serene lake or tranquil beach as their peaceful place. One client used their home overlooking a beautiful city. Others choose places they have watched in a movie or read in a book. I invite you to close your eyes and to pick a place that feels right for you. Perhaps you would like to add elements to your peaceful place that were not there originally. For example, my peaceful place is a beach, and around that beach I imagine a force field that offers me added protection. If you need protective barriers, dinosaurs on the perimeter, or radiant light all around, just add it. This is your place, and you can make of it whatever you want. Once you're ready, follow these seven steps:

1. Make sure you're seated and comfortable. Set an intention to be open to engage with this exercise.

2. Once you feel safe, close your eyes, and become aware of your breath. Do this non-judgmentally and with compassion. Feel the air moving into your nostrils and into your body. Notice if the air is warm or cool.

3. Next, using your imagination, identify a place that evokes a sense of safety, calm, relaxation, and peacefulness. This can be a real-world location or a completely imaginary place.

4. Now, with your peaceful place in mind, begin the BLS of your choosing. Try to get a felt sense of this peaceful place. Are you seated in this image, or are you standing? The task is to really imagine yourself being there. Feel what it is like to immerse yourself in this place. As you look

at your surroundings, what do you see? What is close, and what is at a distance? Do you notice any smells? What do you hear?

5. As you continue the BLS, notice what you feel in your body. Notice positive sensations in your chest, hands, head, and other areas. If you notice positive feelings, stay with those for a minute. Then, go back to each of the positive sights, sounds, smells, and tastes. Appreciate each of the elements in your peaceful place.

6. When it feels good, positive, and strong, you can open your eyes and appreciate the moment.

Congratulations! You just installed your peaceful place. Hopefully this exercise helped you feel peaceful, calm, or whatever adjective feels right for you to describe your experience in this moment. You may want to give your peaceful place a short code name. For example, if you name it *forest*, then you can immediately use that word next time you want to enter your peaceful place, which could shorten the time needed to arrive there in your mind. If you are an artist or like to create, you can draw your peaceful place and return to that visual when needed.

If this exercise was not effective for you, or if you found that it destabilized you emotionally, then do make sure to engage in self-care in whatever way is best for you. You can take a walk, listen to music, watch a movie, go to the gym, or call a friend. Do whatever feels nurturing and stabilizing. That is the same encouragement I offer you as you engage the rest of the exercises.

NURTURING FIGURE

This next visualization will invite you to install a nurturing figure. This should be someone who embodies the qualities of care and warm support. Your nurturing figure could be a real or imaginary figure. It could be an animal, a person, or a divine being. It might be a character from a movie or a book, or even a historical figure, as long as it has a nurturing quality. Your nurturing figure should be conflict-free and without complications. A romantic partner or a parent can make a great nurturing figure. However, if these relationships are at all complicated and you have any mixed feelings toward them, or you can easily think of times these people were not there for you, then they will not be the best figures to use for this exercise.

Finding a nurturing figure may be difficult, especially if you grew up in an abusive or neglectful home environment. It may be even harder if you have internalized an image of a God with a perpetual scowl on His face. If this sounds like you, take it slowly and be kind to yourself.

Remember, you can use your imagination. If you cannot find a figure, you can always create one. Many clients find it helpful to create an *ideal parent*. This may sound strange to you, but you could create an ideal mother, for example, who embodies the characteristics you wish a mom would have. As we have seen, the brain doesn't care about what is objectively real, and cannot easily distinguish between reality and an image in your mind. Creating a visual of an ideal mother who is engaged, responsive, warm, nurturing, and caring can be an important resource for you on your healing journey. Another option is to use your most compassionate, adult self, with the understanding that at this point in your life, you know what you need to feel supported, nurtured and cared for. The nurturing figure exercise has six steps:

1. Make sure you're seated and comfortable. Set an intention to be compassionate and open to engaging with this exercise.

2. If you can, take a sitting position and place your feet on the floor. If it feels comfortable, close your eyes, and mindfully become aware of your feet on the floor. Feel the sturdiness of the ground with your feet firmly on it. Let this be symbolic of you being grounded in this moment.

3. Next, using your imagination, call up the nurturing figure you have chosen.

4. Once you have a good sense of your nurturing figure being a positive presence, you can begin the BLS. Remember to tap in a rhythmic left-right or right-left pattern. With your nurturing figure in mind, bring to your awareness their nurturing qualities. Imagine them responding to you in a warm, kind, and compassionate manner. If there is a particular memory of the person that encapsulates them being nurturing and supportive to you, then immerse yourself in that memory while continuing the BLS.

5. As you continue the BLS and you are aware of your figure's nurturing qualities, notice what you feel in your body. Notice sensations in your chest, hands, head, and other areas. If you notice positive feelings, then stay with those for a minute and explore them further. Allow your nervous system to benefit from these feelings.

6. When it feels good, positive, and strong, you can open your eyes and appreciate the moment.

PROTECTIVE FIGURE

The next figure I want you to install is a protective figure. Again, this figure can be real or imagined. It may be a person that you have encountered on your journey, or someone from a fictional story, mythology, or even dreams. Some clients have used Thor, Super-woman, or Gandalf. Others have used a momma bear or dragon. Whatever protective figure you choose, it should embody strength, fierceness, and protection. This figure can be called up at any time you feel powerless, or after you feel you have been taken advantage of or treated unjustly. As above, this is a six-step exercise.

1. Make sure you're seated and comfortable. Set an intention with an attitude of compassion to be open to engaging with this exercise.

2. If you can, take a sitting position and place your feet on the floor. If it feels comfortable, close your eyes, and mindfully become aware of your feet on the floor. Feel the sturdiness of the ground with your feet firmly on it. Let this be symbolic of you being grounded in this moment.

3. Next, using your imagination, call up the protective figure you have chosen.

4. Once you have a good sense of your protective figure being a positive presence, you can begin the BLS. Remember to tap in a rhythmic left-right or right-left pattern. With your protective figure in mind, think about their protective qualities. Imagine them being fierce and willing to step in to protect you when you need support. If there is a memory that you recall of this figure offering you protection in the past, then immerse yourself in that memory while continuing the BLS.

5. As you continue the BLS and you are aware of your protective figure's powerful qualities, notice what you feel in your body. Notice positive sensations in your chest, hands, head, or anywhere else. You may notice that you feel safe. If so, stay with that feeling for a minute and enjoy the positive sensations this brings about. Allow your nervous system to feel protected.

6. When it feels good, positive, and strong, you can open your eyes and appreciate the moment.

WISE FIGURE

The third and final figure I want you to install is a wise figure. As before, this figure can be real or imagined, but it must embody wisdom. Previously, some people have chosen a spiritual figure such as the Buddha, Gandhi, Dalai Lama, an Imam, Jesus, or the Holy Spirit personified. Others choose an animal who is wise, like an owl, and who in their imagination can speak to them. You could also choose an aunt, uncle, teacher, or a parent. You might even choose the adult you. This advisor will be useful to you when you are feeling stuck, helpless, and down, and you are at a loss of what to do in a given situation. Installing this figure is another six-step process. Read the steps first and try them when you're ready.

1. Make sure you're seated and comfortable. Set an intention with an attitude of compassion to be open to engaging with this exercise.

2. Once you feel comfortable, close your eyes. Be mindful of your breath, your life force that provides your body the oxygen it needs to survive. Take some deep breaths and slowly exhale. Relax and release any tension you might be feeling.

3. Using your imagination, call up the wise figure you have chosen.

4. Once you have a sense that your wise figure is a positive presence, you can begin the BLS. Remember to tap in a rhythmic left-right or right-left pattern. With your wise figure in mind, feel grateful for their compassion and wisdom. Hear the soothing tone of their voice.

5. As you continue the BLS, and you are aware of your figure's wise qualities, notice what you feel in your body. Notice positive sensations in your chest, hands, head, or anywhere else. If you notice feeling more at ease thanks to your figure's wisdom, then stay with that for a moment and appreciate the positive sensations you feel. Allow your nervous system to take in their wise qualities.

6. When it feels good, positive, and strong, you can open your eyes and appreciate the moment.

AVENGERS ASSEMBLE

You should now have a team of three helpful figures. You may want to come up with a name for this team. Some clients have chosen to name them "The Avengers," while others have gone with "Team Love" or "The Fellowship of Sanity." These figures will become great allies for you as you continue your healing journey. If it feels natural, you may try to combine them and use them together. Though if you prefer to keep them separate, that's fine too. If you wish to combine their powers, take a moment to close your eyes. Think of them together with all of their nurturing, protective, and wise qualities. For added effect, why not have them hanging out with you at your peaceful place. Perform a set of BLS exercises until the image feels good, positive, and strong.

EXAMPLES OF HOW TO USE THE INNER RESOURCES

Religious trauma inevitably results in a plethora of potential triggers. There are the encounters with religious parents still desperate to save us. There's the conservative friend or family member on social media whose posts occasionally get us into a terrible state. There are the random ads for church events. Then there's the ghosting by people we thought cared about us but decided to reject us because of our emerging beliefs. More triggers might come from reading or watching the news; for instance, hearing about a reputable pastor who had an affair or was guilty of keeping a cache of child porn. Or seeing a narcissistic politician quoting Jesus while speaking about others in a devilish manner. We may be triggered by observing people in church sing about Jesus and literally kiss the American flag. Any such triggers can come out of nowhere and launch us into a negative mood or bring about feelings of anxiety, shame, hurt, anger, and fear.

But distress does not only come about due to outside triggers. Sometimes the triggers are within. When our inner wounds are bothered, we can struggle to get a good night's rest. The rigid, hyper-moralistic religious system we were formerly a part of may have given us an oversensitive conscience to struggle with. A simple lustful thought might trigger senseless shame; a selfish consideration might unleash our harsh inner critic. We might also feel shame about our bodies, our unspiritual foreign lands with their forbidden pleasure centers. The peaceful place and our inner allies can help us to face these triggers and internal struggles, as well as any other life challenges that come our way.

LEAH, AUNT PATRICIA, AND MUFASA FROM THE LION KING

I would like to share the illustrative story of Leah, a young woman from a Pentecostal background who was in counseling with me and working through her disorienting faith shift for about six months. Her mother, who was still in the Pentecostal tradition, called her one day to check in on her. Their conversation was going fine until Leah's mother brought up religion, telling Leah that she was being led astray and expressing concern for her salvation. Leah thanked her mother for caring but told her she had to go. Even though Leah was making excellent progress in therapy, after this conversation she found her self-critic saying things like "God is mad at you," "Don't stray too far or you will wind up in Hell," and "You are going to be alone if you don't go back to church." These thoughts left her feeling anxious and depressed, with frustration and resentment directed toward her mother. This time, however, instead of using one of her usual avoidance strategies to distract herself and suppress these difficult feelings, she chose to call on a couple of her inner allies whom she had installed two weeks prior in counseling.

Leah set an intention to be with her feelings that were welling up inside her. She closed her eyes, took a deep breath, and did a quick scan of her body. She noticed with curiosity the anxiety, hurt, and frustration she felt toward her mother. She noticed that her heart was racing, her palms felt slightly sweaty, and there was some tension in her shoulders. Leah did a grounding exercise with her feet on the floor. She felt the ground underneath her feet. When her mind wandered, she brought her attention back to her feet.

Leah then imagined herself as a young girl in her bedroom, feeling the same feelings she was experiencing in the present. Her younger self was lying on the bed, looking up at the bare ceiling, feeling alone and anxious. At this point, Leah invited her nurturing figure into her imagination. The figure was her dear Aunt Patricia who had passed away four years earlier. Leah also invited her wise figure into her imagination. This was the character Mufasa from *The Lion King*. With her aunt and Mufasa there with her in her childhood bedroom, she allowed her imagination to take the lead, and then began the BLS.

As Leah proceeded with the butterfly hug exercise and gently tapped herself on each shoulder, she noticed that Aunt Patricia sat on the bed with her and held her. Patricia then whispered gently to Leah "It's going to be okay. You are going to be okay. I'm here now." Continuing the BLS, Leah acknowledged Mufasa, standing at the front of the bed, telling her "Listen, your mom is not going to change. However, you are changing, and that is okay. You have done great work. God is not mad at you. There is no place of eternal torment called Hell. Dear one, you are not alone." Leah accepted her aunt's soothing words of comfort and Mufasa's timely wisdom. She did the BLS until she felt good, positive, and strong. She then concluded the exercise and felt an immediate sense of calm.

KEVIN, AND BEING A KIND HOST

My next story involves Kevin, a young guy in his early twenties who considers himself "spiritual but not religious." He came out as gay to his friends, family, and church community about two years ago, and has been in therapy for about a year, where he has been doing incredible work. Kevin has largely dealt with his parents not being receptive to his coming out, though of course he still feels sad on occasion. The loss of his church community was hard too. However, he found a new community in a progressive church not too far from his college.

One area that Kevin still struggles with is his relationship with God. Kevin is trying to believe that God loves him. He knows it in his head, but his emotional self is less convinced. Kevin was raised in a conservative Christian home, and so has received many messages about God's wrath, the coming judgment of "sin-sick America," and the fact that many people will burn in Hell for eternity. He was taught that God hated "fornicators" and "homosexuals," and that He would send them to Hell for their wickedness. Kevin, having known from an early age that he was gay, was forced to hide his sexuality and pretend to be something he was not. But eventually this took a huge emotional toll on him. Once at college, he slowly started to embrace his sexual identity and distance himself from the fear-based religious roots of his past. Kevin still occasionally feels distant from God. One week, this distance felt especially difficult, and Kevin felt tension and heaviness in his body. Before he knew it, the tentacles of toxic shame started to grip his mind and body.

My encouragement to Kevin when he struggled emotionally like this was always to reach out to trusted others. Sometimes we can feel like we are falling apart. At these times we need other people alongside us. Aloneness can be utterly excruciating, and the bouts of heaviness and anxiety can feel unbearable. Fear of the unknown can be suffocating and brutal. The overwhelming stream of contradictory thoughts and mixed emotions during our healing process forces the mind to attempt to manage the mayhem and make sense of it all. Compassionate witnesses can help. Other people do of course inflict wounds and cause our deepest pain, but they can also be the most vital sources of healing and growth.

One night, Kevin needed support, but it was late and his close contacts were sleeping. Kevin decided to engage in a healing practice I call HOST, which involves setting for oneself the intention to be *Honest, Open, Self-Compassionate,* and *Thankful.* The fundamental qualities of a good host are to be friendly, make guests feel welcomed and at home, and genuinely seek to take care of them. With the HOST practice, Kevin attempted to do that for himself.

He set an intention to be *honest* about his experience. He wanted to stop relying on defensive mechanisms that made him avoid the anxieties he was having. It always takes courage to face the difficulties in our lives. He was ready to face his heaviness head on.

He then decided to be *open* to his experience. He put on soothing music and turned it down low in the background. He chose to sit on the floor, meditation style. He gently asked himself, "What am I feeling right now?" He tried to put aside any preconceived ideas and instead allowed a childlike curiosity to guide him through his experience. He wanted to be open to whatever sensations, impulses, emotions, and thoughts he was having. He noticed feeling heavy, with some pressure in his head and chest. He noticed feeling sad. He became aware that he was struggling with self-critical thoughts about his gay identity and whether God truly accepted him. One part of him knew that God loved him, but another part was coming to the foreground. Reflecting on his mental chatter, he noticed a critical part of him saying "See, God is so distant because you are a sinner," and "God doesn't love you." This inner critic became more biting, saying "You are a loser," "No one is going to love you being such a hot mess," and "Just give up."

Kevin made the decision to exercise some self-compassion. He decided to tap into his internal resources and visualize his peaceful place and his team of inner allies, which he had named "The Crew." He started BLS and imagined himself at "The Cliff." This was a gorgeous spot that overlooked the ocean. He noticed birds flying high in the sky and the vast blue ocean stretching as far as the eye could see. He allowed himself to be fully immersed in this experience, even imagining the sea breeze brushing his face. He felt a calmness in his body, taking in all the peaceful qualities of that special location. He then invited his inner allies to join him in his peaceful place.

Kevin's protector was a samurai. Kevin felt safe and secure knowing that the samurai had his back, literally. The samurai was behind him standing guard, so that no one could harm him. Kevin's nurturing figure was there too. This was the Holy Spirit personified as a young woman who radiated light. Kevin allowed the Holy Spirit to sit next to him. She didn't need to do much, just sit with him so that they could enjoy the moment together. Kevin's wise figure was sitting on his other side. This was a pastor and mentor whom Kevin had been meeting with monthly. As his wisdom figure enjoyed the moment, he shared with Kevin some words of comforting wisdom: "Kevin, I am sorry you are suffering. Let me encourage you. The Divine ain't mad at you. She loves you just as you are. You have friends who love you. I love you too. Don't listen to that inner critic. You are not a loser. You will get through this."

Kevin eventually opened his eyes, symbolizing the end of this meditative experience. But before he was completely finished, he went back to the peaceful place one more time so that he could complete the last letter of the HOST acronym—being *thankful*. He took a moment to express gratitude for his peaceful place and his supportive team. He was also thankful for his feelings of calm and that his nervous system was now at ease. He opened his eyes.

CONTINUE TO ENGAGE THE FINE ART OF NEUROHACKING

As we have seen, the mind can make the unreal feel real. A Hell of eternal torment watched over by an angry and vengeful God is not real, but if we believe this place exists, it will surely create some hellish experiences within us. The effects of Hell indoctrination can persist long after one has concluded it is nonsense and made the intentional decision to free oneself from its tenacious grip over the mind and body. But these negative religious projections and images that have been implanted in our minds must not get the last word. We can fight them by using our imaginations to engage in something called neurohacking, which refers to the ability to change our mental states using various forms of technology.[6] The technology in this case is simple enough, and is comprised of our imagination, our allies, and bilateral stimulation.

In life, just when we think we are doing well, the rollercoaster of emotional instability can sometime get the better of us. When crippling thoughts and overwhelming feelings start to cause us suffering, or if we can't sleep, or if we need to tap into our inner pharmacy for a dose of feel-good neurochemicals, then our peaceful place and the nurturing, protective, and wise figures can be our allies. In the next chapter, we'll look at some additional principles and practices that can help you heal from and cope with the religious trauma of Hell indoctrination.

CHAPTER 14
SELF-COMPASSION: SHAME AND SELF-CRITICISM'S KRYPTONITE

"One of the most powerful weapons in our arsenal is caring force. Tender self-compassion harnesses the energy of nurturing to alleviate suffering, while fierce self-compassion harnesses the energy of action to alleviate suffering—when these are fully integrated, they manifest as caring force."

—Kristin Neff, *Fierce Self-Compassion*

Occasionally, our phones ping with the dreaded alarm of an Amber alert. Imagine your child has been abducted and held against their will until one day, they courageously escape. After coming home from work, you find them on your porch, scared and crying. You immediately call the police. While waiting, your teen, with tears in their eyes, tells you how terrible their captor was. They tell you how the captor belittled them and constantly reminded them of how worthless they were. They tell you they were constantly threatened with torture and that same threat extended to those they love.

How would you respond to them amid their suffering? What would your tone be like? What attitude toward them would we see in your body posture? What things would you say? Would you be encouraging or discouraging? Would you be comforting or rude? Would you be tender or detached? Would you be up close or distant?

Now, think about those times when you are suffering; when your mind fearfully warns you about not straying too far from your abusive captor, God. Think about those times when thoughts of Hell or images of a wrathful God creep up and try to scare you into submission. What about when you have felt anxious, depressed, or even suicidal? What about those moments when you didn't have the bandwidth to be the best version of yourself and then hurt someone you love? How did you respond to *yourself* in those times?

Did you respond to yourself as you did to your teenager who was suffering? What was your tone? Were you gentle? Did you normalize and validate your experience? Did you speak tenderly and offer words of kindness and reassurance? If you did, wonderful! However, if you didn't, this chapter is for you, offering guidance on how to cultivate more self-compassion as you heal from the trauma of Hell Indoctrination.

WHY SELF-COMPASSION?

To put it simply, self-compassion is the most powerfully effective antidote to self-hatred, fear, shame, and the other cascading effects of the doctrine of Hell-Bound People. The benefit of self-compassion has often come from woo-woo spiritual gurus who proposed sappy and hollow statements to mask the reality of suffering in our lives. However, in recent years, some of the world's leading scholars have done incredible research on self-compassion, the fruits of which is a set of ideal and practical ways to love yourself in the midst of life's struggles. At this point, there are many hundreds of research studies and the results are clear—self-compassion is linked to just about every beneficial facet of human well-being.

Kristin Neff is one of the world's leading self-compassion researchers. She has shown that self-compassion increases motivation, forgiveness, happiness, hopefulness, positivity, wisdom, curiosity, engagement in new experiences, agreeableness, extroversion, and conscientiousness. At the same time, it decreases shame and depression.

Self-compassion is also beneficial for relationships. In one study, participants ranked their partners' level of self-compassion and then listed the characteristics that influenced their ranking.[1] Participants who scored higher in self-compassion were described as significantly more warm, considerate, and affectionate. In contrast, participants who ranked lower in self-compassion were described as more self-absorbed, detached, and controlling.

As might be expected given the above benefits, practicing self-compassion benefits those with complex PTSD symptoms, especially when those symptoms include shame and harmful self-criticism. Gilbert's compassion-focused therapy (CFT) is a model with an extensive evidence base. CFT places self-compassion at the core of its approach. It was developed specifically for individuals with significant trauma in their history and who are struggling with psychological problems linked to self-criticism and shame.[2] A recent study (2021) explored the benefits of self-compassion through a CFT lens for group treatment of eleven women with complex post-traumatic stress.[3] They found that self-compassion and the group treatment was beneficial for the participants in a number of ways.

Several of the participants experienced a shift in identity. Instead of the shame and self-criticism that came with believing that the trauma was their fault, self-compassion practices helped them release that burden. Self-compassion psychoeducation and exercises also helped many of the women feel empowered, stronger, and more resilient. For example, one participant shared, "It's made me feel like I've put on like a compassionate armor where ya know I'm able to handle each day better and I feel like I've got a security armor on and I'm able to just be compassionate with all aspects of my life. . . it makes me feel stronger and feel more empowered."[4] Self-compassion is revolutionary!

WHAT IS SELF-COMPASSION?

Kristin Neff describes self-compassion in a very practical way: Respond to yourself in the midst of struggle as you would a dear friend. Neff's research has focused on three main elements to self-compassion: self-kindness, common humanity, and mindfulness. First, respond to yourself in the midst of struggle as you would a dear friend. She calls this self-kindness; treating yourself as you would a loved one in pain and suffering—with kindness, warmth, and genuine care. Rather than engaging in self-hatred, harshness, judgment, and criticism, self-kindness is treating oneself gently and compassionately despite personal flaws and foibles.

Second, become aware of your common humanity; the recognition that all human beings are imperfect, wounded, struggle, and are prone to making mistakes. The opposite is the tendency to isolate oneself when in distress and believe that no one else suffers the way you do. One might neglect this important aspect of self-compassion and say, "I'm alone on this journey. I am the only one having these doubts about God and faith." Isolation breeds self-judgment and leads to disconnection from other human beings. On the other hand, if when one experiences a personal failure or a period of mental and emotional turmoil, one recognizes the universal human tendency to make mistakes or go through suffering, then the hardship can be used as an invitation to bring compassion into one's experience.

Third, practice mindfulness; an awareness and acceptance of the present moment with an attitude of gentle curiosity and wonder. Before we extend kindness to ourselves, we need to know what we're feeling. Engaging in mindfulness allows us to be open to everything that we are experiencing in the present moment, such as our physical sensations, thoughts, feelings, urges, and impulses.

Mindfulness is the ability to distinguish thoughts and feelings from the self. In other words, when you practice mindfulness, you observe the thoughts and feelings passing through your mind and understand they are not *you*; instead, it *is you* having thoughts. A lack of mindfulness can lead to *overidentification*, where people identify and fuse themselves together with negative thoughts and feelings. Mindfulness, however, allows people to view negative emotions and experiences from a self at a distance, to recognize that the negative thoughts may not be accurate, while also facilitating an open and flexible perspective.

If you're thinking to yourself again, *That's a great concept. But what does mindfulness look like in real life?* Well, here's a practical application as you continue the path of healing from religious trauma. If you're like most people with Hell trauma, it's easy to have thoughts such as: *I'm spiritually dead. God is angry at me and going to send me to Hell. I'm a sinner deserving of punishment.* Instead of looking from the self and recognizing that your brain is just doing what it does best—spitting out thoughts which you may have no good basis for accepting—you can end up believing that those thoughts and feelings describe who you are as a person.

The alternative is to be mindful, or aware, of those thoughts when they occur. The phrase *I'm a sinner deserving of punishment* morphs into *I'm having the thought* that *I'm a sinner deserving of punishment.* The gist is that mindfulness creates space around thoughts so you can choose to believe them or not, to identify with them or not. It not only increases your free will, but it also increases your "free won't"—the ability to choose *not* to believe or act in a particular manner.

THE YIN AND YANG OF SELF-COMPASSION

In her book *Fierce Self-Compassion*, Neff distinguishes between the Yin and Yang of self-compassion.[5] I think this distinction is helpful. Some people have a negative conception of self-compassion as something just for women. They perceive it as too weak or feminine to be effective. Others may view it as something for over-indulgent narcissists who just want to be spoiled and pampered all the time with no potential for active change. That is just not the case. Self-compassion is strong, fierce, and practical to protect ourselves from potential harm and oppressive dynamics relationally and systemically.

Drawing on ancient Chinese philosophy, Neff distinguishes between the Yin and Yang of self-compassion. The Yin quality is the softer, nurturing energy of self-compassion. It motivates us to be present with our suffering in a tender way. A good example would be a mother gently holding and caressing a crying child. Yin has a very soothing and accepting quality to it. The Yang quality, or fierce compassion, is more action-oriented. Imagine the fierce and compassionate motivation of a firefighter thrusting him or herself into a burning building to save people from suffering. One can also think of a momma bear who is ready to fiercely protect her cubs, no matter the cost. The type of self-compassion we need can be determined by asking ourselves, "In the midst of this suffering, what do I need right now?" And, more importantly, "What specifically can I do for myself to ease my suffering?"

For example, Jared, a 37-year-old-man, told me about a rough day he had last week. He met up with a Christian friend of his whom he had not seen for a while. He was anxious because he didn't know how it would turn out. He knew his friend was kind but feared he would say something critical about him not being at church for a while. Everything was going well until they were saying goodbye. As his friend was shaking his hand, he said to Jared, "I want you to know I am praying for you. Just don't stay out of church too long, cause, you know, Satan can get a hold of you when you're not under a covering." Jared kindly thanked his friend and left.

When Jared got home, he found his Inner Critic was out front and center. He felt anxious and fearful about whether he was doing the right thing by distancing himself from what he perceived as rigid rules and toxic doctrines. He had the thoughts: *Without staying in the church, I will go to Hell. Maybe Satan is poisoning my mind.*

He then practiced the Yin of self-compassion. He was able to be *mindful* of the tension in his shoulders and tightness in his stomach. He recognized his anxiety and noticed that his Inner Critic had put on the familiar religious "Doom and Gloom" radio station. With gentleness, he reminded himself that he was not alone in his struggle (*common humanity*). Then, he put his hand on his heart and said to himself, "May I be kind to myself in this moment. May I be loved. May I be at peace. May I be free from my religious past and move forward toward my authentic self (*kindness*)."

And then there was Chrissy who started counseling with me to work through her religious trauma. We had been building her self-compassion and assertiveness skills, especially in relationship to her conservative Christian family. Her parents would continually react to her views about the Bible and question her emerging atheist beliefs. Chrissy tried to answer their questions as best she could but would always leave her parents place feeling sad, hurt, and angry. She was naturally shy and didn't share with them how she felt about their interactions. She avoided conflict at all costs.

One day Chrissy came into her appointment and excitedly shared, "I did it! I tapped into the Yang of self-compassion and stood up for myself to my family."

Chrissy shared that she went over to her parents' house for dinner on the weekend. When her parents started being critical about her spiritual journey, she was *mindful* of her body and what she was feeling. She felt herself becoming anxious and was surprised at the anger rising up within her. She knew she was not alone in her experiences with religious parents (*common humanity*), as some of her friends had shared their same struggles with their parents.

Then, with the Yang of fierce self-compassion, she mustered up the courage to protect her heart. She told her parents, "Mom. Dad. I know your faith is really important to you. I know you care about my salvation. However, if I am going to visit, I need you to promise you won't talk about religious stuff anymore. I know how you feel already. I am in a different space and place and want you to honor that. If you can't, then I think I need a break in coming over (self-kindness)."

I said, "Wow! You go girl!" "What was their response?"

Chrissy said, "I could tell they were surprised. It was an awkward silence for a few seconds. Then my dad looked at my mom and said, "We could do that."

I then asked her, "How did it feel to be brave and be kind toward yourself?"

She told me, "It felt great! I was concerned how they would respond, but I did it because it was the kindest thing I could do for myself in the moment. I am worth being honest with myself and my parents."

Self-compassion means being willing to act and respond in ways that reduce our pain and suffering. It can be soothing and comforting, and it can also be brave and courageous. It can offer an emotional hug to our nervous system when we are tired, worn-out, shame-ridden, sleepless, and feeling anxious. In this way we can tap into our inner drug store and release oxytocin, the neurochemical that triggers feelings of warmth, calm, trust, and safety. Self-compassion can also be fierce. It can help us feel energized and provide the resources we need to liberate ourselves from the tyranny of religious propositions and judgmental persons.

SELF-COMPASSION AS A SUBVERSIVE ACT

We have plenty of anecdotal evidence and qualitative research that shows perpetuating the message of original sin and eternal torture, especially to children, can bring grievous, monumental, pathological ramifications from which a person might take a lifetime to heal. Marlene Winell writes,

> In conservative Christianity you are told you are unacceptable. You are judged with regard to your relationship to God. Thus you can only

be loved positionally, not essentially. And, contrary to any assumed ideal of Christian love, you cannot love others for their essence either. This is the horrible cost of the doctrine of original sin. Recovering from this unloving assumption is perhaps the core task when you leave the fold.[6]

In Amy Phillips' research study of 35 American Christians who deconverted and became atheists, the doctrine of original sin was noted as being instrumental in their emotional and spiritual suffering. Further, most of the participants did have a history of abuse, some at the hands of their religious parents, making the picture even more complex. It was this combination of abuse and indoctrination with the notion of original sin that caused their future feelings of toxic shame, guilt, depression, and anxiety. Phillips writes,

> It seems that childhood/adolescent rejection and trauma, combined with religious teachings such as Original Sin, led the respondents to see themselves as defective or bad in some way. When respondents experienced abuse or punishments from their parents or religious leaders, they may have believed that authority figures punished them as a means to correct their defective or sinful nature. This shaming led the respondents to feel guilty for the bad or wrong that they had done. Based on the religious teaching of Original Sin, the respondents may have rationalized that this was due to their innately "defective" nature. Feelings of guilt then led the respondents to experience extreme anxiety.[7]

Being brave enough to be accepting and kind toward ourselves when we walk away from toxic religious propositions like original sin, or when we don't have all the answers, or when we are questioning the answers that we were once fed, is subversive. When religious folk tell us we are listening to Satan as we throw antiquated doctrines in the trash and that we should feel guilty and condemned, self-compassion is a subversive middle-finger. When a punitive and critical God whispers in our ears that we are evil worms who are Hell-bound, fierce self-compassion says, "Screw you!" When someone like Chrissy loves herself enough to be assertive to religious family members to diminish anxiety, fear, and suffering in her life, that is subversive self-compassion.

So much of our emotional suffering comes from the way we shame and criticize ourselves. We have internalized negative messages and believe them uncritically as though they were our own original thoughts which we have every reason to trust. Once internalized, these negative messages become authoritarian gods in our psyches who, whip in hand, drive us to always think about our supposed unworthiness. We need to kill these gods. Sometimes the most Christ-like act is to put into action the last part of the greatest commandment ("You shall love your neighbor as YOURSELF"). Self-love in the form of self-compassion is powerful. It is fierce. Anxiety, fears, shame, pain, and loneliness will still arise at times, but self-compassion helps us to float above the quicksand of distressing emotional states. Self-compassion has drastically changed my life, and I absolutely think it can do the same for you.

COMPASSIONATE ANTHROPOLOGY

We were told we were born into sin and that we are sinners saved by grace. We were told our righteousness is like filthy menstrual rags.[8] We were told that no one is good, and there is nothing good within us. We were told that our hearts are deceitfully wicked. We were told that we can do nothing except through Christ. We were told our desires are sinful. We were told that we couldn't trust our minds and intuitions but should trust only the biblical text (or what is found in our pastor's favored interpretation of the biblical text). We were told the Creator of the Universe despises us as we are. We were told our bodies are corrupt, our emotions are deceptive, and that spiritual things are more important than all else. We were told we are evil. We were told we were dead in our trespasses and sins. Oh yeah, and to be fair, we were told we are the apple of God's eye and deeply loved at the same time (crazy-making indeed).

While all these negative statements seem extreme, believe me, these were the messages that many have received in churches. I know I did. If you didn't experience those messages, then that is wonderful. There are some healthy churches out there. However, many of us received this cyanide-laced doctrinal cocktail. Sadly, some received weekly cups starting from a very young age.

If we embody fierce compassion, and we say "hell no" to this toxic anthropology, then how should we understand ourselves? What is our nature? How should we think of human beings? Sinners? Saints? Good? Evil? Neutral? Or maybe it is best not to use categories at all?

What would it mean to see ourselves through a compassionate instead of a shame-filled lens? And how could we achieve that? While I invite you to come to your own conclusions about humanity that feel honest and healthy, allow me to share a few brief thoughts on the topic.

A COMPASSIONATE, EVOLUTIONARY LENS

Was there really an innocent state of "perfection" with God, where sin was non-existent, and when God and people lived happily ever after? Was there really a never-changing state of blissful, original perfection without the hint of evolving processes? Was there really a time when the interdependency of decay, chaos, novelty, growth, life, and death did not exist? Were there really no plants growing and dying before Adam and Eve sinned? Before the Fall, were there really no insects that were drowned by heavy rains or eaten by other hungry critters? Was childbirth originally created to be a painless experience full of pure physical and sensational delight? Could moments of joy, love, and peace exist without moments of loss, fear, and anxiety? The notion that Adam and Eve, before they were influenced by bad company on the playground, were living in some pristine paradise where pain, death, suffering, and sin were non-existent, just doesn't add up, either scientifically or philosophically.

If we believe in evolution, then that changes the theological game when it comes to our origin story and original sin. It helps us construct a compassionate anthropology rather than an overly judgmental one. We don't have to view humans as originally without sin, who, leaving a life of pure perfection in utopia, became prideful, guilty sinners— godlike beings who defied God. A more compassionate approach is one in which we view ourselves as creatures who, through the ripple of time, have courageously fluttered, splashed, crawled, clawed, and slowly evolved into complex sentient beings.

I have some Christian friends who tell me I am a Hell-bound sinner and a heretic. I have spiritual folks who say, "Mark, we are all gods and goddesses." One is too dark. The other is too fantastical. I think both are nonsense. Both are tiring. One is a shame narrative. The other is a narrative that can easily produce shame. I tried the whole "I am a god and one with the universe" thing. I can never measure up to that. It is like climbing a hill that goes up to infinity without a beyond. How many hours of meditation do I need to perform to achieve nirvana and this godlike state? I just want to be the best, imperfectly perfect version of myself without the Hellish tropes and mystical metaphysical mountains to climb.

I don't think humans are all good or all bad. When it comes to our nature, we defy binary and rigid categories. We are wonderfully and scarily *human*. Just as light can paradoxically display properties of both waves and particles, we are paradoxically both sinners and saints. We all have the capacity to be sinners. We can also be saintly. We can be violent, selfish, judgmental, and apathetic, like animals in the wild. We can also be sacrificial, loving, courageous, and creative, which can also be said about animals. (We do, however, seem to have more awareness than other species, a meta-awareness that transcends primitive instincts and can connect with a greater spiritual whole.).

There is nothing new under the sun about our complex nature. It is what we have always had since our coming onto the evolutionary scene. Sometimes we progress; other times we regress. A compassionate anthropology allows us to be who we are—the good, bad, beautiful, and ugly—without the frenetic need to be anything else. At the same time, in a wonderful dialectic, we are invited to become the best possible versions of ourselves.

Enough philosophical ponderings. Let's explore a few practical self-compassion exercises to help you heal from the trauma of Hell indoctrination, and religious trauma in general.

SELF-COMPASSION BREAK

I invite you in this moment to put self-compassion into practice. This self-compassion break is an exercise you can do at any time of the day, whenever you notice you are being overwhelmed by heavy emotions such as sadness, shame, fear, and anger. You can also engage in this exercise when you are noticing discomfort in your body or are being rocked by self-critical thoughts. An audio file of this activity can be found at https://markgregorykarris.com/meditations (password: HEAL).

Take a moment to think of a current area of suffering in your life.

Are you experiencing a little too much anxiety? Are you feeling depressed? Have you had distressing thoughts about God or Hell today? Did you recently feel the sting of rejection from people you thought cared about you? Is life feeling a little overwhelming?

Bring the difficult experience to mind. Then, close your eyes and allow yourself to feel the pain of that experience. Make note of the emotions that arise when you think about your suffering. And then be aware of your body's physical response to that emotion (*mindfulness*). Remind yourself, in this very moment, that you are not alone in this hurt and that many people recovering from religious trauma have felt the very same feelings (*common humanity*). Place your warm hands on your tender heart and gently repeat to yourself at least three times:

"I feel the sharp arrow of this deep hurt. Other people feel this way too. May I be kind to myself in this moment. May I be loved. May I be at peace. May I accept myself as I am (*self-kindness*)."

Allow yourself to really feel the benefits of self-compassion breaks. If they do not bring total relief, that's okay; notice even that with compassion, and remember that healing can take time.

ENGAGE IN COMPASSIONATE SELF-TALK

Julio, a young guy in college, was one of the best trash talkers around —about himself. He would beat himself up for not attending church: "I think God is punishing me for not going to church." He constantly *should* on himself: "I *should* just do what my parents want." "I *should* be a more spiritual person." "I *should* be a better friend." He continually criticized himself: "I am sinful." "I am not worthy of being truly loved." "I am not good at anything, so what is the point of trying new things?" He criticized his future: "You are probably just going to go to Hell." and "You will be alone for the rest of your life."

Julio's chaotic Inner Critic was out of control. Life is hard enough without a live-in enemy who tries to tear you down every minute. Moving from incessant self-criticism toward warm, friendly, and empowering compassionate self-talk was not easy. Using the acronym INK (Intention, Noticing, Kindness), let me share a few strategies that helped Julio over time become less critical and more compassionate.

SETTING A SELF-TALK INTENTION

Julio realized that his harsh self-criticism was holding him back and affecting his life negatively. He made a conscious decision to address this issue and set an intention to counteract the negative self-criticism by incorporating self-compassion principles and practices into his daily routine. This process took some time, but was worth the effort.

For a long time, Julio believed that being self-critical was valuable. There were some cultural factors at play here. He thought he had to be tough and macho, as that was how all the males in his family and peer group were. Julio shared, "I thought my self-criticism helped me. I thought it made me a hard worker." However, after exploring the costs of his self-criticism and considering how he would never want to speak to his children in the same way he spoke to himself, Julio was ready for a change. He began to see the benefits of compassionate self-talk and was ready for the next step.

NOTICING SELF-TALK

After Julio set an intention to work on his self-talk, he committed to becoming mindful of how he talked to himself. I asked him to look out especially for *DARK* thoughts, an acronym I use that stands for Despair, Alarm, Ruin, and Killjoy. We can think of DARK FM as a radio station within us which generates these thoughts. Whenever Julio noticed that DARK FM had switched on, he filled in these blanks in his journal (I encourage you to fill them out as well):

- My mind tells me that I am a ...
- My mind tells me that I am too ...
- My mind tells me that I am not enough of a ...
- My mind tells me that I do too much of the following:
- My mind tells me that I don't do enough of the following:
- My mind tells me that I lack the following:
- My mind tells me that God thinks I am ...
- My mind tells me that my family thinks I am ...[9]

KIND SELF-TALK

Once Julio set an intention and noticed when his self-critical part became activated, he would practice kind, compassionate self-talk. The goal was simple. If he noticed he was the subject of harsh, critical thoughts, he would switch to the voice he used when speaking to his older children when they were struggling.

During a session Julio shared with me an example of how this practice helped him. One day he was beating himself up for not knowing what he believed about God. He said to himself, "I can't be on the fence. I must have an answer to what I believe about God. I must figure this out. If I don't, then I will just be lost, and maybe wind up in Hell."

He then caught his Inner Critic at work. He stopped himself. He asked, "If my kids were struggling with issues of faith, how would I respond to them?" Julio paused, and with an attitude of warmth told himself, "It is okay that you haven't figured it all out. Be kind to yourself. Faith is a journey, and not a destination. Trust yourself to figure it out and be okay."

Julio adopted the INK exercise into his everyday living. Give it a try and see if it works for you.

HEALING THE PAST WITH COMPASSION

Think back to the chapter on memory reconsolidation. I proposed the simple equation that "Distressing Memory + Care-Circuit = Less Distressing Memory."[10] We can use compassion and the care-circuit to target painful memories to change how they impact us. We can't change what happened in the past, but we can certainly change the emotional valence, or power, of the memory. We can unlock the memory, expose it, and update it. This will allow us to process the traumatic energy embedded in the memory and address unresolved emotions so that they no longer cause us distress.

For example, I earlier shared the story of a well-known pastor who looked me in the eye and threatened me with hellfire because I had drunk wine at a wedding. He cited Leviticus 10:9, where Aaron the high priest and his sons were told not to drink wine unless they wanted to face death. The pastor seemed to believe that I, like all true Christians, was a high priest, and that my punishment for drinking wine would be death and eternal torture. That event was traumatizing and triggered a fear response in me for years to come. It made me fear not only the consequences of drinking wine, but also of making countless small and seemingly harmless choices, such as listening to non-Christian music, missing a church service, failing to pray for people, or even drinking soda. Eventually, as my eyes opened to the toxicity of religious beliefs and dynamics of spiritual abuse, I started to feel anger at this pastor for harming me spiritually and emotionally.

Armed with the knowledge of memory reconsolidation, a brilliant brain-hacking technique, and the transformative power of self-compassion, I decided to rewrite the emotional experience of that event, to heal and move forward. Being your own advocate and therapist can be a beneficial and empowering experience, and I highly recommend it. This is how I did it.

I began with a relaxing breath exercise to engage the parasympathetic nervous system and help me feel more relaxed. While there are many such exercises, the one I found most helpful was the 4-7-8 technique, which I learned from a book by Andrew Weil, an integrative medicine practitioner. First, let all of your breath out through your mouth, making a whoosh sound at the end. Then, close your mouth and inhale through your nose for four counts. Then, hold your breath for seven counts. After that, exhale through your mouth, slowly for a count of eight. Repeat this process two to three times. Do not continue if you feel dizzy and lightheaded. The goal is to enter a relaxed state.

After completing this calming breathing exercise, I connected with my compassionate self by imagining sitting with my brother who was in pain. I could feel my compassion welling up within me. I became aware of my gentle tone and my desire to encourage and empower him. Once I had established this connection with my compassionate self, I set it aside and moved on to the next step in the process.

I thought back to that day with the preacher. I remembered where we were sitting, what he looked like and how angry he got when I mentioned drinking wine. But more importantly, I paid attention to my body. I could feel the fear and anger come back just by thinking about it. It was like my nerves were on edge all over again. I asked myself: "What does this moment make you believe about yourself?" I could hear answers in my head, *I'm not good enough. I'm in danger. I'm going to hell.* It was tough to feel all that again but it helped me realize what I had experienced in the original moment.

I then imagined my adult compassionate self at the scene and allowed this self to do and say whatever he wanted. The Yang of my compassionate self was angry at the injustice of this moment. As he entered the scene, he pushed the preacher down, making him seem tiny, and said: "How dare you! Don't you dare fill him with that theological rat poison. Do you have any idea the suffering you are creating in him?"

The younger version of me was nervous but felt protected by my compassionate adult self. The next thing I knew, the preacher just left, like a dog with his tail between his legs. At this point, the Yin-filled compassionate part of me held me, saying, "I am so sorry you had to go through that. That was not fair. You were so open to wanting to please God. You were so sensitive and that man, or little boy inside a man's body, didn't see what a beautiful soul you were. You are going to be okay. I've got your back."

The younger version of me, with tears in his eyes, felt protected and relieved. In the here and now, I was able to give myself what I had needed back then and there. With my eyes still closed, I asked myself "What do you believe now about yourself?" My younger self said, "I am safe now." "I am loved." and "I am not going to Hell." I then performed a butterfly hug with a round of BLS, repeating those life-giving phrases until the message felt internalized and truly installed in my nervous system.

Once I finished this exercise, I found that my *experience* of the memory had changed. It didn't have the same emotional charge. All the anger, fear, sadness, and anxiety I had felt was gone. I performed enough of the memory reconsolidation process to experience transformational change.

PUTTING IT INTO PRACTICE

To try this exercise yourself, first read through these instructions. Ensure they are clear to you and make sense. Then, in your own time, give the exercise a try. An audio file of this activity can be found at https://markgregorykarris.com/meditations (password: HEAL).

1. Make sure you're seated and comfortable. Become aware of the compassionate space you are about to create to nurture and heal yourself. Notice your breath. Feel the air moving into your nostrils and into your body. Breathe in; breathe out.

2. Get in touch with your compassionate adult self. Imagine yourself being kind, nurturing, and protective toward a friend or loved one who is suffering. You may doubt your ability to be similarly compassionate toward yourself, but know that this person, the one who can be compassionate with others, is within you. If you prefer, you can get in touch with one of your nurturing, protective, or wise figures.

3. Find a distressing memory you want to rewrite, update, and work with. I would recommend not starting with anything too traumatic. On a scale where zero is no distress and ten is highly distressing, you may want to start with a memory that is a three or four. Save the fives and beyond to work through with a trusted therapist.

4. Once you have decided on a memory you want to update, allow yourself to work your way through that memory. Start from the beginning of the memory and relive it moment by moment. If this feels too painful, try imagining the memory as if you were watching it on a screen in a movie theatre. You may have different memories come up during this thought process. Just focus on one at a time.

5. Ask what image represents the worst part of the incident. What do

you notice feeling in your body? What feelings are coming up for you? What negative beliefs do you have about yourself?

6. Hopefully, by this point your emotions have not become too overwhelming. Try to put the memory and its attached emotional content to the side for a moment. Ground yourself if you need to, either by feeling your feet on the ground, or by engaging in some mindful breathing. Next, get in touch with your compassionate adult self, or inner ally.

7. Invite your compassionate adult self or inner ally into your memory. Allow them the freedom to show you love and care in the spirit of protection, nurturing, and wisdom. Notice what they say to you, and the loving gestures they offer.

8. Observe how it feels for you to receive their love and support. If it feels positive, allow the version of yourself that first experienced the event to accept the care of your compassionate self.

9. If it feels good, consider what positive beliefs you have about yourself now. Once you think of a positive belief, begin the BLS. Begin tapping until it feels good, positive, and strong.

10. Open your eyes. Take an additional moment to revel in the good feeling. Close your eyes one last time. Place a hand on your heart and extend gratitude to yourself for the good work you did. Then gently finish the practice.

CONTINUE TO LOVE YOURSELF WELL

It's important to note that, while the exercises in this chapter can aid in healing religious trauma, they may not produce immediate results. However, with consistent practice and incorporation of self-compassionate practices that we discussed in this chapter and that we shall explore in later chapters, you can learn to cope more effectively with troubling emotions and feel more whole. Self-compassion practices can even create new neural structures that decrease shame, self-criticism, and fear, while increasing the ability to accept one's feelings, both positive and negative. As you learn to embody compassion, you will feel freer to be your authentic self with others. Living a life where you feel lighter on the inside and can express greater confidence on the outside is what healing is all about.

CHAPTER 15

TAMING THE INNER CRITIC

"Those of us who prospered best in society had a little voice telling us to try harder, be better, and to achieve more. The humans in history who had this critical voice then survived more often, had more babies, and passed their genes down to their offspring."

—Cheryl Bradshaw, *How to Like Yourself*

Aliyah, a kind-hearted woman in her twenties, sat before me, undergoing the harsh experience of being berated. It was heart-wrenching to see her going through this. The words being used against her were vicious, with *shaming statements* and *fear statements* coming at her one after the other, like a barrage of verbal bullets. Each hurtful remark seemed to take a toll on her, and I could see her shoulders droop under the weight of each penetrating blast that pierced her sensitive heart.

You don't belong.
You can't trust yourself.
You don't have any real friends.
You don't deserve to be happy or successful.
God will punish you if you keep abandoning core doctrines.
If you don't obey God, you will go to Hell!
You will be alone, and you won't find another community again.

I'd finally had enough. I had to step in. I stared at the perpetrator of these sharp criticisms. With a gentle voice I said to her, "Can we pause for a moment?" Then, with tears in her eyes, she said, "Okay."

You guessed it. It was Aaliyah who was saying those vicious things, to *herself.* To be more precise, it was a *part* of her saying those cruel things, an internalized part that I have referred to as the "Inner Critic."

During the pause, Aaliyah looked at me with defeated eyes and said, with frustration, "I am so tired of Satan beating me up like this." I responded, "I am so sorry you are suffering in this way. Before we explore some skills to help you *unhook*[1] and create some distance from those thoughts, may I share with you another way of looking at where these thoughts may come from?"

"That sounds great! Thank you," Aaliyah said. And so our work together began....

THE EVOLUTION OF THE MIND

One of the most brutal consequences of religious trauma and Hell indoctrination—and *trauma in general*—is the tendency to use nasty, shame-based, self-critical statements that attack our identity, our present condition, and our future reality. The Inner Critic can ravage our self-esteem and self-worth, leaving us feeling discouraged, deflated, and defeated. It can prevent us from seeking out the happier existence we deserve. But there is hope. In this chapter, I will explore some liberating principles and practices that have helped Aaliyah and countless others on their healing journeys. These principles, when practiced consistently, can effectively tame the Inner Critic, allowing people to live out their values more freely, experience self-compassion, and lead to a truly more meaningful life.

THREE SYSTEMS

Recent neuroscientific research has put forth the idea that the human brain has three major systems that work together to manage and regulate our emotions.[2] The *threat system* helps us detect danger and avoid harm, producing emotions such as anger, anxiety, and disgust in order to move us toward safety. The *drive system* propels us to accomplish important tasks, such as acquiring the resources necessary for survival. Emotions propelled by this system include joy, pleasure, and excitement. The third is the *soothing system,* which encourages us to rest and relax and is involved in forming bonds with others and maintaining attachment relationships.

To put these systems in a religious trauma context, our threat system will likely be activated if someone we care about tells us that we are going to burn in Hell for eternity. The drive system can motivate us to learn about religious trauma and get passionate about healing from it. The soothing system functions when we spend time with people who love and encourage us on the healing journey; it helps us to feel calm and relaxed. Unfortunately, however, the brain's *default* activity is most commonly to alert and activate the threat system. If this system is not well-regulated and aligned with the others, tremendous suffering can result.[3]

THE THREAT SYSTEM

Today, for most of us, it is unlikely that going outside could be a death sentence. For our primeval ancestors, however, leaving the cave or wandering too far away from the tribe could mean having to encounter threats behind every tree. Wherever they traveled, there was likely to be some animal slithering or sneaking in the shadows, looking for a scrumptious human snack or another Neanderthal seeking an enemy to slaughter!

Of course, the brain has evolved over millions of years, but it still prioritizes its primary motivation to keep us safe. It does whatever it can to help us stay alive. If the brain had a motto, it would sound like the *Star Trek* character, Mr. Spock, who famously greeted and took leave of others with the salutation: "Live long and prosper!"

Since the brain's main objective is to protect us, it has a particularly sensitive monitoring system that is constantly on alert and scanning for threats. This monitoring takes place largely subconsciously, outside of our awareness. Stephen Porges, a well-known neuroscientist, calls this latent subconscious monitoring *neuroception*.[4] It involves our nervous system being responsive to what is happening (both in our environment and within ourselves), as it looks for cues of safety or danger and responds accordingly. Neuroception brings about the physiological changes needed for us to connect with others, to engage in fight-or-flight responses to danger, or to shut down for survival.

THE INNER CRITIC—AND OTHER PARTS WITHIN US

The Inner Critic, the voice inside each one of us that is often responsible for triggering our feelings of worthlessness and shame, appears to be linked to the threat system and neuroception. The Inner Critic's influence can be found in most forms of depression, anxiety disorders, eating disorders, and addictions. It is the voice that repeatedly judges, shames, and criticizes us, induces fear, makes us second-guess ourselves, and causes us to have poor self-esteem.

This voice likes to bring up DARK thoughts (recall that this is an acronym for thoughts to do with Despair, Alarm, Ruin, and Killjoy). The songs that DARK FM plays can make us despair of our future, alarm us about what we are doing wrong in life, or tell us what we should be doing more, or less, of. They can ruin our day and kill off any joy we have inside.

Let's return to Aaliyah. She has many brilliant facets to her character—a creative part, a caring part, a logical part. Yet, above all these, her Inner Critic stood, berating her, shaming her, and declaring negativity about her identity.

Cleverly, the Inner Critic was also able to construct a negative feedback loop. Each self-critical statement was felt as an attack which set off Aaliyah's threat response system. The attacks increased her feelings of shame, manifesting physically as a heaviness in her body and slumping of her posture. The more her threat response system was activated and the more shame she felt, the more reasons the Inner Critic would find to attack her. For some, this loop can last just a few moments. For others, it can last for days, weeks, months, even years.

IT AIN'T THE DEVIL. IT'S YOUR "FRENEMY"!

Some say that the self-critical voice in our heads is the Devil's doing. This idea is foreign to some Christians and, fortunately for them, they may not have this aspect of religious trauma to work through. However, for those coming from more Pentecostal and charismatic traditions, and some Evangelical denominations, the belief that the Devil implants negative voices in our minds is likely to be a familiar one. Joyce Meyer, a charismatic speaker and author of *Battlefield of the Mind*, shares a common belief about how Satan influences thoughts. She writes:

> For most of my life, I didn't think about what I was thinking about. I simply thought whatever fell into my head. I had no revelation that Satan could inject thoughts into my mind. Much of what was in my head was either lies that Satan was telling me or just plain nonsense —things that really were not worth spending my time thinking about. The devil was controlling my life because he was controlling my thoughts.[5]

Terry L. Ledford, PhD, a Christian psychologist and author of *Para-*

bles of a Wounded Heart, concurs with her, writing that, "Satan benefits from our self-demeaning and self-critical thoughts. In fact, I believe that Satan feeds us self-critical and self-demeaning thoughts because it serves his purposes."[6] Bill Bright, American evangelist and founder of *Campus Crusade for Christ,* offers an example of what Meyer and Ledford discuss in his book *Witnessing Without Fear.* Discussing the timidity of some Christians in sharing their faith, Bright describes specific "lines" Satan plants in the mind, such as: 1) *Mind your own business—you don't have any right to force your views on someone else,* 2) *You're going to offend this person. Don't say anything,* 3) *That person will think you're a fanatic,* and 4) *This person will say no, and you'll be embarrassed.*[7] After delineating this list, Bright tells us to, "notice that each one of the Devil's lies is targeted at our own insecurities."[8]

Personally, I disagree with Bright's position that Satan is filling Christian minds with self-critical lines. Attributing to Satan what happens naturally in human beings is yet another form of projection. To illustrate, I remember once talking to a passionate environmentalist who was trying to get me to sign a petition relating to forest conservation. He was new to the job. During our discussion, I asked him what it was like being, as I called him, *an evangelist* for the environment. Though he was not a Christian and was not witnessing for Jesus, his internal struggles showed a distinct similarity to the insecurities that Bright discusses, with the same self-criticisms and uncomfortable concerns.

The environmentalist was worried about forcing his view on others and didn't want to make people feel bad or offend them. He was self-conscious about being viewed as a fanatical tree-hugger. He was also worried about potential rejection and embarrassment. His inner self-critical thoughts reflected those worries.

Was Satan feeding the environmentalist self-critical thoughts to attack his insecurities? I don't believe so. Understanding the nature of the mind and the motivation of the Inner Critic can help explain self-criticism; there is simply no need to appeal to an unseen metaphysical entity called Satan to explain what is going on.

Becoming aware of how the activation of the threat system can unleash the Inner Critic to do its destructive work can be life changing. Remember, our threat system has evolved to protect us. The Inner Critic can be viewed as something like the threat system's handyman. Its job is to keep us safe—emotionally, physically, and spiritually. Jay Earley and Bonnie Weiss, authors of *Freedom from Your Inner Critic*, offer this superb definition of the Inner Critic's role:

> Your Inner Critic thinks that pushing and judging you will protect you from hurt and pain. It thinks that if it can get you to be a certain way—perfect, successful, cautious, nice, slim, outgoing, intellectual, macho, and so on—then you won't be shamed or rejected, and you might even get approval from people who are important to you. It tries to get you to fit in by prescribing rules and then attacking you if you violate them. Even though attacking you actually backfires and causes you more suffering, your Inner Critic is doing what it thinks is best for you.[9]

From this description we can see that the Inner Critic is a handyman who is a "frenemy" (both an enemy and a friend). Its actions may be well-intended, but its tactics cause us suffering. Once fully comprehended, this is a profound realization!

Let's test this theory in relation to Aaliyah's self-critical barrage. If the theory holds, we should be able to see a positive motivation behind Aaliyah's self-directed attacks. Looking again at her negative internal accusations, it can be hard to see any well-meaning motivation for comments such as, *No one loves you. God will punish you if you keep abandoning core doctrines. If you don't obey God, you will go to Hell.* However, examining them a little more closely, can you see the Inner Critic's *positive intent?*

What the Inner Critic is trying to do here is to get Aaliyah to change course, to avoid what it sees as potential future pain. It is thinking: *Stick with what you know. Stay with the religion you were raised in. Don't change course.* It hints to Aaliyah: *You'll be fine as long as you follow the community's morals and beliefs. If you do so, nothing in your life will get worse. You'll have the love of God and your community will be intact. If you don't, doom is in your future!*

Perhaps we can better understand the Inner Critic's harsh methodology with an analogy. Imagine you're walking on a hiking trail and you encounter another person rushing frantically toward you. They tell you there is danger ahead, that a bobcat is nearby. You don't take the stranger seriously and keep walking. But then they start yelling and criticizing you: "Hey, stupid!" "Don't do it!" "Stop walking!" "You are going to get killed!" "Don't be an idiot." The stranger says these things to get you to change course, so that you will avoid what the stranger perceives to be your certain demise!

In the same way, Aaliyah's Inner Critic perceives that if she continues to deconstruct her faith, it will ultimately end in rejection and hurt for her. It also senses the possible future punishment of Hell. So, it does what it can to convince Aaliyah to change course. The problem, though, is that Aaliyah's Inner Critic stems from the *threat system*, which means it is immediate, instinctual, and non-rational. It doesn't bother to consider how its strategy might cause Aaliyah more harm than good in the long term, because its only motivation is the immediate cessation of perceived—and sometimes not necessarily actual—danger. It is not aware that as it tries to be a friend, it acts like a vicious enemy.

THE POTENCY OF THE INNER CRITIC

Before we dive into the helpful principles and practices that can allow you to work with your Inner Critic, I want to briefly discuss how potent this inner voice can be. One key thing to note is that the Inner Critic's strength can vary depending on the environment in which we were reared.

Many are fortunate to have grown up in loving homes which, while not perfect, were a place where parents were largely accessible, responsive, and engaged. These people likely have a *secure attachment* style and have healthy ways of relating to others. They view themselves as lovable and worthwhile, exhibit stable self-esteem, and see others as mostly trustworthy. For these people, the Inner Critic can be a healthy and positive influence. For example, if someone with a secure attachment style of relating said something cruel to their partner, they may hear their Inner Critic say, *That wasn't cool. You can do better. Why don't you apologize to the person you love?* The Inner Critic notices the threat of rupture in the romantic bond and tries to provide critical feedback to repair it quickly.

However, if a child grew up in a home where there was abuse or neglect, the potency of the Inner Critic can be greater, its words more severe. In the same scenario, the Inner Critic might say something like: *You are such a jerk. You've got so many issues. What is the point of apologizing? You are just a loser who is going to keep doing the same thing.* There is a spectrum of self-criticism; it ranges from healthy to unhealthy. At the healthy end, positive criticism can help us become the best version of ourselves. At the opposite end of the scale lies self-hatred and self-critical wishes, ones that may even extend to encouraging us to end our own life.

As an aside, what could be the positive motivation be for an Inner Critic to suggest suicide? Many people who are suicidal say, "It's not that I don't want to live; it's just that I don't want to feel this pain anymore." Again, in these cases the Inner Critic is trying to alleviate suffering, even though the method is extreme. Its intention is good, but its strategy is destructive.

The Inner Critic's potency is dependent on the toxicity of a person's early childhood environment and can be worsened by later experiences of trauma. Our idealistic culture, with its promotion of perfectionism, does not help matters either. It seems that every time we turn on the television or scroll social media, we are led to compare ourselves to others, to judge and assess ourselves in all manner of unhealthy ways.

Indeed, companies pay creative, innovative advertisers millions of dollars to tell us, as succinctly and persuasively as possible, who we are *not* and what we are missing. We then learn to judge ourselves for not being attractive enough, successful enough, smart enough, masculine enough, feminine enough, rich enough. In short, we learn that *we are not enough.* And what do you know, it just so happens that marketing companies know exactly what we need to remedy our shame-based identities—their products!

For Aaliyah, her strict religious parents and the experiences she'd had at church provided ample fuel for her Inner Critic. Her experiences of moralistic and constricting propositions, practices, policies, and persons within her church and her family, combined with her own sensitive temperament (and exacerbated by the toxic cultural messages she received), meant that as she got older her Inner Critic had taken on ample atomic fuel. Thankfully, psychological principles were available that helped Aaliyah temper her Inner Critic and increase her self-compassion.

GET TO KNOW YOUR INNER CRITIC

Try to imagine what would happen if a friend were visibly upset at something you were about to do, and you told them, "Just stop it!" "I wish you didn't even exist." "You are such a damn nuisance." and "I hate you." Your friend would probably become quite angry and reactive. Such sentiments are often expressed by people toward their Inner Critic and it reacts in much the same way. The more we push back, the louder it gets and the more it wants to be heard. So, the first principle is to not attack or shun the Inner Critic. Instead, we must get to know it and befriend it.

It may seem strange to try to form a positive relationship with a part of you that speaks so cruelly. But this turns out to be much more effective than hating it. That which you resist, persists. Once the Inner Critic feels understood and taken seriously, it tends to soften its voice. So how do you get to know your Inner Critic? In the same way you would get to know anyone else. You approach it with curiosity and an open mind. An audio file of the activity below can be found at https://markgregorykarris.com/meditations (password: HEAL) .

EXERCISE: ENGAGE YOUR INNER CRITIC WITH CURIOSITY

1. Close your eyes and try to think of a self-critical statement you often hear from your Inner Critic. Perhaps it's something about your relationship with God. Or about your future. It could be about your identity, or even your body.

2. With your eyes still closed, try to hear the tone that your Inner Critic takes. Can you get a sense of what your Inner Critic looks like? Can you form an image of it in your mind? Some describe their Inner Critic as a monster, large or small. Some see an image of a critical person they encountered at some point in their life. Some describe it as an abstract shape made up of varied colors. Once you can see an image, you could even try to draw it, if you are so inclined.

3. It's now time to find out your Inner Critic's positive intent—its reasons for attacking you. Get in touch with the Inner Critic and try to picture yourself talking to it. You can ask, *What are you trying to achieve by criticizing me and judging me the way you do?* Listen to what it says. You could also ask, *What are you afraid might happen to me if you didn't criticize and judge me?*[10]

4. Once the Inner Critic reveals its motivation for criticizing you, try your best to express gratitude for its intention, perhaps responding with something like: *I appreciate you trying to protect me and looking out for my best interests.*

5. What does your Inner Critic share in response to your gratitude?

6. If your Inner Critic is feisty and doesn't want to cooperate, then you can normalize its concerns, telling it: *I totally understand it's hard for you to receive gratitude right now. Thank you for trying to protect me, and let's reconnect soon.*

Now, you may not be the go-inside-type person that likes to engage in imaginative work like this. That's *okay.* If the exercise feels difficult or odd, my recommendation would be to try being mindful of the Inner Critic over the course of the next week. When you notice that it is active, see if you can be aware of its intent. Remember that it is genuinely trying to help you.

TREAT YOUR INNER CRITIC WITH COMPASSION

The Inner Critic can be biting. If it decides to team up with shame, together they can profoundly affect your mood and self-esteem. Its criticisms may contribute to feelings of depression and anxiety, making us feel defeated and overwhelmed. Yet, instead of berating the part of us that feels scared, we must try to show compassion. One way to do this is to encourage this part of us to think about what caused it to become so hypervigilant. Behind every judge and every bully is a painful story.

Our Inner Critic, much like a bully on the playground, needs to be heard and loved in order for it to transform. To find out its story, close your eyes and ask: "*What happened in your life that made you so hurt, scared, and vicious? What made you feel that you must be so critical toward me?*" Listen to what it says.

What you'll likely find out is that the Inner Critic started off wanting to be helpful, not hurtful. Its purpose was to look out for danger. However, it was forced into the cruel and bullying position it now takes because of what it experienced. Behind each harsh Inner Critic is often a story of hurt, abuse, or neglect. When a child experiences their parents or caregivers as neglectful or abusive, they may do what psychoanalysts call *splitting*, seeing their harmful parents as totally good so that they may keep the love and care they need from them intact. How could they stay angry toward their parents, given that their parents are their only source of love and comfort? Rather than being angry at them for not meeting their needs, children may internalize their anger and criticism and turn it toward themselves. So, the most savage Inner Critic is created in a child who was treated most savagely by others.

For those who have experienced religious trauma, either within the family, within the church, or both, it makes complete sense how years of teaching about our inherent sinfulness and a punitive God could put our threat system on edge. If our parents often criticized us harshly, and if every Sunday we heard messages that attacked and denigrated the self, this would of course add fuel to the fire for our Inner Critic. If we constantly received messages that we deserved punishment, it makes sense that we would make a habit of punishing ourselves. Albert Ellis, a psychologist who introduced Rational Emotive Behavior Therapy (REBT), wrote in 1962:

> Religion (Christianity), by positing absolute, God-given standards of conduct, tends to make you feel self-deprecating and dehumanized when you err; and encourages you to despise and dehumanize others when they act unethically. Since self-deprecation is the main cause of anxiety, overweening guilt, and depression, and since damning others is probably the chief source of hostility, rage and violence, religious moralism patently produces or abets enormous amounts of severe emotional disturbance.[11]

The moral police, believing they are on the Highway to Heaven, cannot wait to catch us going over the behavioral speed limit so that they can remind us we are traveling on the Highway to Hell toward eternal punishment by a wrathful God. As Ellis astutely noted, this constant moral judgment leads to emotional pain. Excessive emotional suffering causes an overactive nervous system, which then creates a powerful Inner Critic.

So, the Inner Critic is not the Devil. Given the things you have gone through, of course your Inner Critic would be the way it is: harsh and accusatory. It has suffered devilish experiences that have caused it to become overactive and always on high alert. I hope this new understanding of the reality of what it has been through allows you to feel compassion toward it. Every time your Inner Critic is telling you how you don't measure up, or what your gloomy future looks like because you left the faith (or a certain version of it), think of its struggle, and thank it for trying to keep you safe.

While maintaining this compassion, you must also acknowledge that, sometimes, you *do* need to get things done. You can't always coddle your Inner Critic. In times like these, your compassion needs to be firm. Think of the *Yang* form of compassion, discussed in a previous chapter. For example, let's say you are about to give a workshop on healing religious trauma and your Inner Critic says to you: *You are going to suck. You are not smart enough. No one is going to listen to you,* or *Who are you to talk about this material?* The Inner Critic thinks that if it can persuade you to *not* give the workshop, it will have saved you from embarrassment and social rejection. It imagines a future where someone criticizes you for not sounding smart enough, where people judge you because you don't understand the material. So, it tries to save you from the pain, thinking that *no presentation equals no pain.*

To respond appropriately, you need to be loving but firm with this part of yourself. You will have to say something like: "I know you're anxious. I get that you care for me. But I must focus. Chill out right now, while I take care of business. I got this." Just as it can be comforting for an anxious child when a busy parent takes a moment to firmly reassure them that they will make sure they're okay, this is the same attitude we need to extend to our Inner Critic. Once you have shown your loving assertiveness, you can get on with the task of presenting well.

GET ANGRY AT THE FUEL TRUCKS!

Another useful strategy to tame the Inner Critic is to have a head-on collision with the trucks that provide its fuel. If the Inner Critic's potency is determined by the level of trauma it has experienced, it is important to heal the scars of those original traumas. The Inner Critic will then be able to do its job effectively, with a focus on the positive end of the self-criticism spectrum. In a coming chapter, we'll focus specifically on the intersection of wounds caused by parents and wounds originating from religious trauma. For now, I want to point out that it is important and helpful to express your anger in a healthy manner toward the original perpetrators of your trauma.

When getting in touch with your core feelings in this way, you can also, at some point in the healing process, express yourself from a place of vulnerability and share what you needed from them and did not get. This multilayered process is done in imaginative work, and not face-to-face. For example, some may choose to do an "empty chair" exercise, where they imagine the one who has inflicted pain on them sitting in the empty chair and speak to them as if they were really there. I highly recommend that you only attempt this piece of deep trauma work, which usually involves the expression of repressed anger, with a professional therapist to guide you.

Anger is a natural emotion, rooted in our tribal evolution and signaling that we, or those we care about, have experienced wrongdoing or injustice. Anger has a strong physiological component. When we are angry, we can feel our muscles tense, a response that prepares us to fight an enemy or flee from the danger. Anger raises our heart rate and increases adrenaline, mobilizing us to take necessary action for our very survival.

Negative or harsh self-criticism and self-attacks result from the justified anger one holds toward those who hurt them. Sometimes, as with parents, it does not feel emotionally safe to direct anger toward them. In these cases, when anger is repressed, pushed down inside, it can later emerge with a vengeance and become directed toward the self. For Aaliyah, it was easier to repress her anger than to allow herself to be angry at her parents or the church. Expressing anger toward others was just not in her emotional repertoire. Her parents and her church had made it seem that anger was an *ungodly* emotion. So, instead of directing her anger toward those who deserved it, she felt shame for feeling it and unknowingly engaged in an attack on her own self.

Part of Aaliyah's healing journey was to learn to express her anger at her parents and the teachings of the church in a healthy manner. Doing this helped her to develop needed assertiveness. Once she was in touch with her core self, her self beyond thought/feeling/criticism, thus directing her anger toward the true source of her pain, the Inner Critic had less fuel to keep it active. It also felt reassured, knowing that Aaliyah was now more confident, in the driver's seat of her life, and going in a congruent direction. With the Inner Critic part running on empty, Aaliyah now possessed the ability to advocate for herself when necessary.

Jamie Marich, a licensed therapist, trauma-focused author, and director of The Institute for Creative Mindfulness, recalls her experience of being young and growing up with her evangelical Christian father and attending a conservative Christian church.[12] While Jamie has many memories of adverse religious experiences growing up, she recalls her yearly attendance a theatrical production called *Heaven's Gates, Hell's Flames*. The Christian play explores the lives of different people who make various life choices that ultimately decide their eternal fate. After they die, whether by natural causes, accidental life events, or suicide, they eventually face their eternal destiny—Heaven or Hell. It is a play filled with dramatized scenes with high stakes, along with angels, Satan, demons, and of course, Jesus. The epic drama was meant to scare the hell out of her, so she would accept Jesus as her savior and avoid eternal conscious torment.

The play reinforced a message Jamie constantly received from her father since the age of five: "If you don't accept Jesus Christ as your Lord and Savior, no matter how good of a person you are or regardless of how hard life was for you, then you will be sent to eternity in the lake of fire where Satan will torture you forever." One of Jamie's protective defensive strategies to deal with witnessing such fear-based events was going numb. She writes, "I was a queer young person attracted to all genders, and I viewed these vignettes with an extra special sense of: If I don't shove this shit down, look at the end I'm going to meet." It was not until she was an adult that she experienced the full weight of betrayal trauma and allowed herself to feel the authentic and adaptive power of anger.

A deep wounding for Jamie was her sense of "feeling trapped" in her religious environment growing up. Her healing journey involved getting in touch with her anger, a powerful emotion that communicated what felt unjust and unfair to her. Before that, however, her anger and perpetual constricting emotions also added fuel to her Inner Critic and "crime-punishment orientation."

Jamie took a big step in her healing process by giving herself permission to express her anger. She writes, "I first had to unpack some baggage that it was horrible or shameful or forbidden to even be angry at God/Jesus." Through the expressive arts and her own EMDR therapy, she was able create a safe and empathetic internal environment which allowed her to courageously express her anger, along with her sadness, grief, and experiences of loss. Due to her authentic expression of her emotional truths in a safe and empathic environment, her Inner Critic, while still present and active on occasion, is "less destructive" and more manageable. Instead of Jamie's anger turning inward, causing her somatic symptoms and fueling her Inner Critic, she now uses that anger to fuel her social justice work and educate others on spiritual abuse, trauma, and pathways toward healing.

At this point you might be saying to yourself: "But I've been angry for some time and it has not been healing for me." The key in this healing task is not to hold the anger inside or wield it like an out-of-control firehose, but to get in touch with, and so understand, the specific experiences that made you angry. The next step is to express your vulnerability, state what you needed and how this differed from what you received, allowing yourself to feel sadness and hurt because of what you missed out on at the time. Lastly, if possible, invite yourself to see those who hurt you through a lens of compassion. You can journal through these steps alone, yet this is all done most effectively in the company of a compassionate wit(h)ness, whether a licensed therapist or a trauma-informed spiritual director. I encourage you to seek one out and work with them toward healing!

RAPID-FIRE STRATEGIES TO DEAL WITH YOUR INNER CRITIC

I now want to explore some additional quick tips that can help you tame your Inner Critic and more generally calm your mind.[13] Find what techniques work for you by trying out different methods. Stick with the ones that you find helpful and don't waste time on the ones that don't suit you.

1. Speak to yourself kindly. Compassionate self-talk arises from your soothing system, rather than your threat system. Think whom you would prefer to have as a spiritual teacher: someone who is cruel and punitive, or someone who embodies compassion and grace. I am sure it is the latter. Be a wise and compassionate companion to yourself. Some of us have had harsh taskmasters in our families or in our churches, with the harshest figure embodied in an imaginary, punitive God. We don't need to be a stern taskmaster to ourselves. Compassionate self-talk is the much healthier option.

2. Remember, thoughts are just thoughts. Our thoughts are not always the problem. Rather, the problem is that we are prone to fuse with our thoughts and believe them as if they were the truth. We need to create distance from them, and we can do that by reminding ourselves of the nature of the mind. To do this, let's try a quick experiment.

Recall one of the self-critical religious statements you have often thought; for example, *I am going to Hell*, or *God hates me*. As you say these to yourself, notice what it feels like to really believe them. Next, take one self-critical statement and insert this phrase in front of it: *I'm having the thought that....* For example, *I'm having the thought that God hates me*. Do you see the difference? Many find this thought-distancing technique very helpful. It's a good one to have in your tool belt!

3. Name that tune. Another simple technique is to give a name to the tunes on your DARK FM radio station. For example, if the *I'm a Loser* tune starts playing, you know, the one with the lyrics that go: "I suck. Nobody likes me. There is something deeply wrong with me." Then you can name it to tame it. For example, if you are going about your day and notice a shame spiral start to consume you, and you hear all the familiar lyrics from that song playing in your head, you can say: "Oh, I recognize this song. This is the *I'm a Loser* song." Instead of the lyrics of the song mesmerizing you and making you feel distressed, you can simply acknowledge it as an annoying oldie your mind likes to play sometimes, and then move on with something that feels more purposeful.

4. Focus on what is helpful and not on what is true or not true. When deconstructing and reconstructing what we believe, we can easily get stuck focusing on what is true or not true. While figuring out what's true is important, we can spend too much time and energy worrying about things such as whether we are saved or unsaved, going to Hell or not, or whether God is angry with us. Such endless ruminations can keep us frozen in time. One strategy to deal with this negative mind-chatter is not to ask whether these thoughts are true, but whether they are *helpful*. For example, if your Inner Critic keeps reminding you that God is angry at you, ask yourself: *"Is the thought that God is mad at me helping me live the best version of my life today?"* Or, when your Inner Critic informs you that *You're a loser,* rather than trying to determine whether you are, objectively, a loser or not, just ask: *"Is the thought that*

I'm a loser adding value to my day?" If not, then toss it. This subtle shift in focus can be a game changer.

5. Engage in compassionate mindful breathing. Setting aside time each day to gently focus your attention on your breath can be helpful to reinforce compassionate self-talk. This doesn't require you to be a monk or to spend time in a monastery. You can do it in bed, at work, or anywhere you like. Either close your eyes or defocus with your eyes open, so that you're not paying close visual attention to anything in particular. Then attend to your breath to find a natural rhythm. Notice your breath as it moves through your nose or mouth. Notice the coolness or warmth of the air. If your mind wanders, gently bring your attention back to your breath. You can occasionally wish yourself positive things such as kindness and healing. Or, as you breathe, you can silently repeat, *Inhale, my love; exhale, my love.*[14] This can activate your soothing system, making you feel more relaxed, and reinforce your motivation to continue to engage in compassionate self-talk.

MOVING FORWARD WITH YOUR INNER CRITIC IN CHECK

In this chapter, we've seen how the Inner Critic is a frenemy. While it is concerned with our safety and protection, it does not particularly care about whether we are filled with inner peace and joy. To its credit, the Inner Critic was instrumental in helping us find the faults within toxic religious practices, propositions, policies, and persons—and giving us the freedom to move in a more positive and healing direction. Yet its strategies can often cause more harm than good, making us feel terrible—as if it is our true enemy.

The goal is to *temper* the critical voice and gain access to our compassionate voice, to replace the hyperactivation of our threat system with the switching on of our soothing system. As we practice compassionate self-talk and engage in effective strategies to tame the Inner Critic, we will be able to live with less shame, less self-criticism, and more vitality.

As you are healing from religious trauma, particularly from the trauma of Hell indoctrination, may you befriend your Inner Critic and talk to this aspect of your self in the way you would talk to a dear friend who is on the same journey. The Inner Critic has been with us throughout our life and will be with us until our final day. May we train it to become our ally rather than our enemy as we appreciate its ability to warn us, protect us, and keep us from harm. May we allow it to balance our reckless tendencies with caution, yet not allow it to keep us from living a meaningful life.

CHAPTER 16
WORKING THROUGH PARENT WOUNDS

"Trauma is personal. It does not disappear if it is not validated. When it is ignored or invalidated the silent screams continue internally heard only by the one held captive. When someone enters the pain and hears the screams healing can begin."

—Danielle Bernock, *Emerging with Wings*

I went through a time when I could no longer ignore the splinters in my mind—those sharp, pesky shards of neural dissonance pushing deep down into the recesses of my puzzled and disoriented psyche. I was aware of the appalling God who, in one breath, told me I was loved and, in the next, told me my heart was deceitfully wicked; a God who let me know that if I didn't do what He told me to do, I would soon be sizzling in a barren land ruled by conniving demons waiting to have their way with me.

I started to become aware of all the fear and shame messages pumped into me by my church. I was shocked that God could be mad at me for listening to progressive metal music. I was saddened that I was afraid to have long hair as a Christian. As a man, I thought there was an acceptable and unacceptable hair length to God. I recall many angry preachers ranting about biblical gender requirements and quoting a verse in the Bible where it says, "Does not the very nature of things teach you that if a man has long hair, it is a disgrace to him?"[1] I believed demons were lurking everywhere, and I had to be on guard against their influence at all times. I was living in a sick, twisted, religious fantasy world.

Here is what was on the menu: Fear for the appetizer. Judgment for the main course. And more fear for dessert! I was angry, disappointed, hurt, afraid . . . and I blamed the church, along with its venomous teachings, for all my trauma and misery.

However, I came to realize that I couldn't blame the church people for *all* my trauma. Guess who else was cold, harsh, "loving," caring, punitive, violent, and moody? You guessed it. My mom and dad.

I had a mother who did the best she could, but she was addicted to drugs as far back as I could remember. She would eventually die from a drug overdose. I had a father who was mentally, emotionally, and physically abusive. As a kid, he never told me he loved me, never told me he was proud of me, and never showed me affection. I can't tell you how many times I was told, "You're an f'ing loser, just like your mother," "You're a lazy piece of shit," "You're weak," "You're clueless," and other wonderful, life-affirming phrases (note the sarcasm). I also had a stepfather, a man with a big heart but who was also very violent. He was high ranking in one of the most notorious motorcycle gangs in New York, which was known for dealing drugs, extorting others, perpetrating violence, and committing murder (*Hmm, I wonder where my shame infestation and suicidal tendencies came from?*).

The same level of fear that I had of my dad and my stepfather was transferred to God. The same fear of violent physical punishment by my dad because of my "misbehaviors" was the fear I had of God. The same primal panic that I had of my mom abandoning me and shutting off her love and presence was the panic I had at times of God. The same doubt I had about my parents' love for me was the doubt I had about God's love. The same poisonous arrows of verbal put-downs, criticisms, and gaslighting I received from my dad was what I perceived coming from God. I had a diverse trauma tapestry and the web of connection between my parents' message and God's voice was difficult to tease out.

Clearly my life was full of traumatic imprints long before my pastoral and church experiences came along. Looking back now, I can see that, while I was angry that the church profoundly hurt me, let me down, and abused me in many ways, I was hurt and wounded long before this. The church was merely a place onto which I displaced the enormous amounts of pain and anger that I carried. This is not to say the church or, more specifically, people in the church, didn't threaten me, reject me, let me down, or seek to control me. Yes, they were responsible for their actions and the pain those actions caused me, but the pain and *lostness* I felt in the deep recesses of my heart predated my even knowing them.

As I was healing from religious trauma, I began reflecting on the deprivation of my early childhood. I realized that I unconsciously wanted the church people to become the parents I had never had. I saw that I had unfairly projected my need for the love, acceptance, attunement, encouragement, and nurturing that I never received from my parents onto a bunch of imperfect, wounded people in my church.

Not only did I learn I was displacing unresolved negative emotions due to my abusive parents onto the church members, but I found that other existential realities were also causing me pain. I was hurt by the unfairness of life. I was hurt because my brother was rotting in prison. I was hurt by the crappy decisions *I* had made that caused heartache for me and other people. I was hurt seeing that I had to work so hard just to inch my way through life. I was hurt by the fact that people in power marginalized and oppressed others. I was hurt when my heart got broken in several failed romantic relationships. I was hurt when I saw that nothing lasts—that everything is fluid and changes repeatedly over time. I was just plain hurt, and somebody had to pay. Someone, or some entity—specifically, the church—had to be the scapegoat!

One of the most important moments in my life was when I realized I was dumping my own hurt onto the church members. Some of that hurt was warranted, for sure. Some of it was not. I unconsciously expected the church to fix me or provide me with the idealized family I'd never had. The problem with that was that I set the standards much too high. The payment for my hurt was more than the church could afford. The truth was that *no one* could fill the emotional void left in the wake of neglectful and abusive parents and an unfair, ever-changing, and sometimes harsh existence—not even the church. Once I started realizing this truth, my heart shifted, and I began to feel compassion for the church and its people.

Was repeatedly being taught Hell-Bound-People theology damaging to my soul? *Hell yeah!* Were anxiety, shame, and self-criticism present in my life because of those teachings? Absolutely! But there were additional threads to my *trauma tapestry* that could also help explain my complex post-traumatic stress disorder (C-PTSD) symptoms.

Truth be told, as I took a hard look at parent trauma and its effects on my life, there had long existed a low-level hum of generalized anxiety and toxic shame within me, even before my harmful religious experiences. These crept their way into me as the many negative thoughts I had about myself and the way other people saw me. I also had major trust issues, which is a no-brainer in that the most powerful people in my life had wounded me to my core. False doctrines and painful church experiences just magnified my deep-seated belief that I was unlovable and worthless, reinforcing messages I'd received growing up with my parents.

This is not to say I didn't have short moments of love and connection with my parents. However, it is the cumulative traumatic ones that had more staying power in my brain. Rick Hanson, renowned psychologist and author of *Hardwiring Happiness,* writes, "The brain evolved a negativity bias that makes it like Velcro for bad experiences and Teflon for good ones."[2] Adverse childhood experiences (ACEs) have a long-lasting impact. They certainly did for me.

What I realized in my own healing journey was that I had an inner child who was a *wounded exile*, who had existed deep within me long before those traumatic church experiences. The more I sat with clients working through religious trauma, the more I saw that they, too, had young, wounded exiles, deeply affected by parent abuse, living within them.

RELIGIOUS TRAUMA AND CHILDHOOD WOUNDS

For many of the clients I work with, the themes that show up in the therapy room are not only issues surrounding religious trauma, but also trauma experienced at the hands of parents or primary caretakers. Untangling the roots of these can be further complicated when people are reared by religious parents. That is where I see the deepest levels of religious trauma. Kids who are raised with *Hell indoctrination*, which includes negative images of God, self, and others, suffer the worst forms of C-PTSD.

What makes healing so complex for "adult children" who grew up with religious toxicity is that God, family, friends, and church become so intertwined that it is challenging to tease out which negative beliefs and feelings are tied to which specific person or incident of trauma. The web of many false religious doctrines is tangled up with them all.

ASSESSING OUR RELATIONSHIP WITH PARENTS

When we are young, our parents, our primary attachment figures, are the most important people in our universe. Apart from our inherent genetic code, they determine the trajectory of our lives more than any other variable. Research done on *attachment style* in human relationships is clear: how our parents relate to us when we are young creates *internal working models* that profoundly affect our very capacity to form healthy relationships later on, both with ourselves and others.

Internal working models are mental and emotional representations that originally formed through our relationship with our primary caregivers, then become a template for all future relationships. These mental and emotional maps tell us how much we can trust that people will show up for us if we are hurting and need care. They tell us which relationships feel safe and which don't. They inform us of our lovableness and desirability when in contact with important people in our lives. They influence our ability to communicate our needs, longings, and desires. They influence our thoughts, emotions, and behaviors in significant, long-term relationships.

For example, if an infant has repeated interactions with primary attachment figures who are accessible, responsive, and engaged, it gives rise to implicit expectations and beliefs about the self and their key attachment figures. Although babies do not have complex language skills, if their nervous systems could talk, they might say: *Ah, I feel taken care of. I can trust that if need something, my parents will be there for me. My parents are trustworthy. People are okay. I am okay.* This creates an internal working model in which there is an implicit, positive view of self. The child grows up carrying that same positive, trusting mind map, superimposing it upon other people in relationships. As an adult, they tend to be secure within themselves and with others.

Unfortunately, not everyone grows up with a consistent set of the ABCs of attachment: *Acceptance, Belonging, Comfort,* and *Safety.*[3] I know I didn't. The lack of relational nutrients when I was younger created an internal relief map with a rocky and frightening terrain built up on it. I looked out at the world through lenses with a darker tint. I had acute abandonment issues, along with powerful, ingrained, shame-based beliefs about myself and my worth etched upon my soul. I believed, mostly on an unconscious level, that I couldn't count on anyone—that no one would ever really love me for who I was, and that men in authority disliked me and were always angry with me.

Many others grow up with parents who were aloof, busy, distracted, shut down, abusive, controlling, addicted, in a season of personal grief in our early years, or with a host of other dynamics going on in the home. This unsafe environment created internal insecurities and negatively impacted my internal working model of self.

While some have a *secure attachment style*, many people have what is called an "insecure" attachment style. Without getting bogged down in the research, the insecure styles of relating, which are typically consistent across relationships, are due to core *attachment wounds*. They develop due to primary caregivers not providing enough accessibility, responsiveness, and engagement to the child. They are also due to abuse or neglect. Those core wounds can affect how children see themselves and others, largely in negative ways.

For example, a child with an inconsistent parenting experience can create an *anxious attachment style* of relating. They yearn for love that never seems to arrive. They need constant reassurance they will not be abandoned. As a result, they may over-accommodate to people's needs to keep relationships intact. They end up with a low view of self. They are desperate to be loved and feel insecure about most of their relationships. (If attachment theory interests you, there is a wealth of pertinent research that can help you identify and work with your own attachment style.)[4]

The topic of parent wounds is a potentially triggering and emotionally vulnerable one. Think about and reflect on your own childhood and relationships with your parents, and then describe those relationships in your own words. Be kind to yourself as you explore your early childhood relationships with your parents. If it feels like too much to reflect upon at any time, set the work aside and revisit it later when you are feeling more centered.

Here are some questions that can help you reflect on your parent wounds (or primary caregiver wounds). Notice the feelings that arise within you as you answer them (e.g., anger, sadness, shame, fear, surprise, or joy):[5]

1. Can you describe your relationship with your parents as a young child, as far back as you remember?

2. Choose five adjectives or words that reflect your relationship with your mother, starting as far back as you can remember.

3. Choose five adjectives or words that reflect your relationship with your father, starting as far back as you can remember.

4. Which parent did you feel the closest to, and why? Why isn't there this feeling with the other parent?

5. When you got hurt, who did you go to for comfort and care? Can you think of specific memories?

6. Were your parents threatening in any way? What memories come to mind?

7. Do you remember feeling rejected by your parents? Is there a specific incident that comes to mind?

8. Did your parents model the ability to share their feelings? Were you able to share your feelings with your parents?

9. Did your parents force religion on you? Did they use God as a weapon to threaten you? What was the negative impact of their religious belief system upon you? What was the positive impact, if any?

10. Would you consider any behaviors of your parents as abusive? What were they? What specific incidents come to mind?

11. Were your parents receptive to new ideas, or did they engage in all-or-nothing thinking?

12. What did you need from your mom that you didn't receive?

13. What did you need from your dad that you didn't receive?

14. In what ways do your parent wounds reflect your church wounds?

15. How do the ways you relate to your parents mirror your relationship with God?

16. If your parents were religious, what specific doctrines did they teach you that affected you the most?

17. What beliefs were formed about yourself due to how your parents related to you (i.e., "I am _____")?

GORDON

The point of these questions is to help you reflect on possible parent wounds. Did you notice how your parent wounds intersect with your religious trauma wounds? It is often helpful to tease out the specific *soul wounds* you carry. This is precisely the task of processing our life story, or *integration*. When a person allows their left brain (thinking brain) to know what their right brain (feeling brain) feels, why it feels that way, who the feelings were originally directed toward, and what negative beliefs were formed out of that experience, that person begins to feel less crazy, more in control, and more whole.

For example, Gordon, a self-described "exvangelical," was able to delineate the emotions he felt toward each aspect of his core wounds. He was able to express anger toward his parents for their rigid rules and constant shaming, especially around his being gay. He felt sad because of the good relationship he longed to have with them, which never came to be. He also felt sad that he couldn't bring his feelings to his parents. He felt alone, never feeling like he could truly connect with other kids in his youth group.

He felt guilty for having hate-filled feelings toward his parents and for wanting to distance himself from them. He felt generalized anxiety, believing that God was constantly mad at him. He felt shame for never measuring up to his parents, God, or himself. He felt fear, thinking that he could go to Hell in the afterlife. He felt rage when he thought of how he was "brainwashed" by his parents and how they contributed to his self-hatred. Gordon also felt angry at the church for the way they treated LGBTQIA+ people. He felt sad because he lost close connections at his church when he came out. *Whew!* That is a whole lot of feelings and diverse painful experiences. They definitely took a toll on Gordon's wellbeing.

Prior to entering therapy, Gordon carried around those jumbled feelings inside himself for a long time. It took a lot of energy to push them down and keep them at bay. Because they were unprocessed, Gordon felt heavy, stuck—and he experienced a chronic, global sense of distress. But once he allowed himself to feel the depth of all those emotional experiences, to grieve them and to heal from them, he was able to move forward toward a life that felt lighter, without the weight of heavy unprocessed and unintegrated trauma in his life. *How did he do it?* Allow me to share a few helpful suggestions as you are reflecting on your own parent wounds.

SELF-COMPASSION

Compassion, compassion, compassion. We may have it for others yet find it very difficult to extend it to ourselves. If the parenting questions brought up some painful material for you, take a moment to engage in a self-compassion break. Perhaps you can close your eyes, bring your hand to your heart, and with a warm and gentle quality say to yourself: *In this moment, I feel the pain around my parent wounds. It hurts. It sucks that I still must deal with this. I know a lot of other people deal with it too. May I be kind to myself in this moment. May I be loved. May I be confident that I will work through this trauma. May I accept myself as I am.*

FIND A GOOD THERAPIST

Books are great. However, the best place to adequately work through your parent wounds and religious trauma is with a licensed therapist. Make sure it isn't just "talk therapy," as well. Notice if the therapist is active, engaging your body language and emotions, not just your mind and "talking" about things. In other words, make sure they have training in how to work with trauma. Inquire how much of their work is with religious trauma. You can also ask about their religious orientation if it makes you feel more secure.

There are a lot of great therapists out there. Remember, you are in control! If you meet with a therapist, and they seem bright, but you don't feel a connection with them, feel free to find someone else. We all need competent wit(h)nesses in our lives, people who know how to navigate the draconian seas of trauma. If you can't afford a therapist right now, take a risk and ask someone you trust to be a compassionate story-dweller—someone who will sit with you, listen well, and engage your story with curiosity, compassion, and hope.

JOURNALING

Where I come from we need to be wary of stagnant pools of water. Because of the location and high humidity, standing water becomes discolored and smelly. It also becomes a breeding ground for weird and unsightly insects—including nasty, blood-sucking mosquitoes that especially enjoy snacking on humans.

The same thing happens when all your anger, sadness, shame, and pain remain stagnant and unprocessed. If those emotions sit in your self unprocessed for a long time, your self can become a breeding ground for nasty critters like self-doubt, bitterness, unforgiveness, and hate, eventually becoming a pond of depression. Journaling can be helpful, even essential, in clearing the emotional swamp. Journaling is a practice that helps you take what is on the inside and bring it to the sunlight outside. It keeps your inner world moving outward, flowing like a vibrant and lively river, rather than an icky, murky pond.

Journaling is a powerful practice you can use to help work through religious trauma and parental wounds, heal your delicate heart, and gain transformative insights into your past, present, and future. Many studies have shown that expressing yourself through writing can reduce the symptoms of depression and anxiety, improve your mood, and increase the efficiency of your immune system, promoting your overall physical health.[6]

Imagine a movie scene where a character is packing for a trip. In a rush to leave, he throws everything into his suitcase, wrestles it closed, and runs toward the door. But the bulging suitcase hits the door frame on the way out and busts open, sending its contents flying. The same thing can happen with our "emotional suitcases."

Perhaps looking through and reflecting on those questions about your parents feels disorienting. So, you may have tried to cope by shoving many of your thoughts and emotions down into your over-flowing suitcase (the unconscious) to deal with later. Unfortunately, since it is overfull with stuff (negative thoughts and emotions), your emotional suitcase will fly open if you bump it against something (triggers, e.g., reading someone's religious comments on social media, hearing an old church hymn, etc.), and your *stuff* will fly out (self-criti-cism, withdrawal, impatience toward others, etc.). Many people quickly pick up their T-shirts (negative thoughts), jeans (anger), and underwear (grief) and try to cram them back inside the suitcase. This way of dealing with an upset can occur over and over—until you either get rid of some of the items you're carrying or pack them in a different way.

Journaling enables you to unpack your emotional luggage in a rational way. It can help you pay attention to what is going on in your innermost being and help you separate and label feelings of guilt, loss, anger, and sadness. Once you label your emotions, your nervous system gradually calms down and you start to feel a little saner and more relaxed. That is just how we are wired. We like to make sense of things. We like things neatly ordered. It makes us feel safer and more secure.

You can also incorporate self-compassion in your journaling. As you work through those parenting questions, be mindful of what thoughts and feelings arise within you and write them down (mindful-ness). You can connect your experiences to the larger human experi-ence (common humanity). In other words, you can write down how others' experiences intersect with your own. Lastly, you can include some kind and encouraging words for yourself with each entry (kindness).

Late at night when everyone is sleeping, except you because you're struggling with insomnia, or at times when you still feel like you cannot confide in someone else, even in the daytime when everyone's awake, your journal can become a sounding board and a powerful instrument of healing. I invite you to journal about your parent wounds and religious trauma, especially if you are looking for an effective, research-based practice that promotes the healing of soul wounds.

BEFRIENDING YOUR INNER CHILD

Internal Family Systems (IFS) therapy is an approach to psychotherapy that posits that we have within us many sub-personalities, or an *internal family system*, within us. IFS maintains that the various sub-personalities or *parts* of us within have their own thoughts, emotional experiences, impulses, motivations, and personalities. You may remember a time when you struggled with your belief in Hell and heard one part of yourself thinking: *I believe that Hell is a bunch of bullshit!* Another part saying: *I think Hell is real and I am scared that God will send me there.* A further example could be one partner getting upset at their spouse, saying something very hurtful, and then stating, "I am so sorry. I don't know where that came from. I wasn't myself." There was a fiery, reactive part at work within, and there was another part that was sorry for the outburst.

We have secure parts of ourselves and insecure parts. We have adventurous parts and parts that enjoy familiar comforts. We have very young parts and older parts. We have apathetic parts and parts that are deeply sympathetic. Some parts believe in an angry, wrathful God. Other parts feel that this is superstitious nonsense. Some parts are healed, and others are wounded. We have parts that want to be close to and connected with people, and we have parts that just want to be left alone.

When reflecting on your parent wounds, perhaps you can befriend your inner child, or what IFS calls your *exile*. The inner child or exile is the vulnerable, younger part of you that feels all the complex emotions of your early childhood experiences. This part was once full of life, curious, friendly, wanting to play and pursue adventure. However, it may now bear the scars of painful, traumatic experiences. The inner child part may be frozen in time at the age of their initial wounding. Those tender parts within us feel all the loneliness, isolation, anxiety, shame, and pain of the original injury. They also hold painful schemas, or negative internal beliefs (e.g., *I'm not lovable, I'm broken, I'm worthless*).

The inner child parts are exiled by our *protector* parts. Our protector parts do whatever they can to keep the wounded exiles locked in a cell in our psyches. Our protector parts try to manage our lives by keeping us in check emotionally and motivating us to maintain the status quo, to "not rock the boat."

There can also be left-brained-leaning parts that "logic" our way through life and keep us from the vulnerability of feeling the pain and burdens that our exiles carry. There might be highly reactive parts who, when they perceive emotional danger, try to numb us out quickly. And there can be *firefighter* parts that may want to run to drugs, alcohol, sex, shopping, and overworking or just explode with anger and rage to keep themselves and other people away from the vulnerable inner child.

PUTTING IT INTO PRACTICE

Go inside yourself and connect with your inner child. Yes, for some of you, that may seem weird. However, if you feel up to it, give it a try. Close your eyes and allow your mind to take you to an image of what best represents you as a wounded child. Notice what image comes to mind. Then, ask the inner child how old they are. What age do they say? Next, ask that vulnerable part of you to share how they felt going through the questions earlier. Allow them space to share. What do they say?

Ask that part what they need from you in this moment in the form of care and comfort. If it is something you can offer, then close your eyes and, in your imagination, offer them the love, care, and comfort they desire. Ask that part of you how it feels to receive that from you. Hopefully, they feel loved. If they do, wish that part well and let them know you will see them again soon. If they still feel raw, then acknowledge the difficulty of the moment, and reassure them that you are doing what it takes to help them continue to learn, heal, and grow.

If this was a difficult exercise, or felt too strange, don't be concerned. As I shared in the beginning of this section, if it didn't feel effective or comfortable, no worries. Move on. Keep going. Don't quit! If this felt like a beneficial exercise, then I encourage you to continue to befriend and reparent your inner child.

Here is a hard truth: your parents can never give you the loving presence you need in the present due to the hellish events you experienced in the past. Some parents can hold a compassionate space for their adult children to share their early childhood wounds. Others can be defensive, make it all about *them*, and leave us feeling like we are the crazy ones who are making a big deal about nothing. Sometimes the healthiest thing to do is to grieve what we went through and come to accept that we can never get in the *here and now* what we needed in the painful past. Sometimes we need to relinquish the desire for a parent to provide now what they didn't provide for us as young children. Sometimes we must just let go. . . and find ways to reparent ourselves.

GLORIA'S STORY

Gloria is a 35-year-old woman seeking healing from religious trauma. We did a lot of work exploring the ways the church had traumatized her. We worked through her trauma of being coerced to stay in an abusive marriage. She talked to her pastor about how her husband constantly ridiculed her and how he was violent toward her when he was drinking. Sadly, the pastor's advice was: "Continue to submit to him and trust in the Lord. Your love for him will bring him back. Be patient."

Gloria worked through her fear of Hell. She worked through her hypervigilance being around other people, thinking she had to save them. We also worked on identity concerns which enabled her to find her authentic voice. Then, as we did work around her religious trauma, her parent wounds surfaced.

Gloria had a dad who was a workaholic—strict, very religious, and who did not have a lot of time to spend with her. Gloria's mom was very anxious, also very religious, and was overbearing. Gloria always yearned for her dad's attention and affection. She tried to be a "good girl" but felt like she could never please her dad. Gloria also felt like she had to always listen to what Mom had to say, or her mom would become angry and critical toward her. Her mother would also use God as a scary figure when Gloria didn't do what was demanded. Her mom would say, "God loves good girls," and "Is that something God would want you to do?" Gloria's parents would also talk about how other people were "following Satan" and were "on the broad road that leads to destruction."

Gloria carried inside an inner child who craved affection, was desperate to be seen, and was highly anxious. When Gloria pictured her inner child, she was in her room all by herself, playing with her dolls. Since she was an only child, she remembers feeling lonely a lot. Thankfully, Gloria had a loving grandmother. Gloria shared, "When grandma visited, I felt like I could be myself. I felt like she loved me without conditions."

Her protector, people-pleasing part developed early since it would keep her inner child at a distance, away from the possibility of experiencing anger from others. The strategy embraced by her main protector part was that of trying to be the perfect daughter; this then developed into a drive to be the perfect Christian, the perfect wife, and the perfect friend. If people were happy with her, and there were no conflicts, the veneer of protection gave her a pseudo feeling of being loved and safe. However, the inner child was always there, tucked away, longing to be seen, heard, and comforted.

After some inspiring work in our sessions, Gloria was able to begin befriending and reparenting her inner child. What does 'reparenting' mean, in practical terms? Gloria would check in with her inner child.

She would pause throughout the day and ask her tender part: *How are you doing?* If her inner child was hurting, she would offer her reassurance.

For example, one day one of her Facebook friends posted about the "Hell-bound dechurched who worshipped the god of social justice," and alluded to those folks as not being saved. Gloria had done great work reconstructing her faith journey, but in that moment, she felt her inner child become anxious. She took a moment to pause with the precious little one: *What are you feeling?* The vulnerable, younger self shared, *I am feeling anxious again. I am scared that maybe I am believing the wrong things. Maybe they are right. And maybe Hell is real, and I could go there....*

Gloria, in a spirit of compassion and in touch with her core self, reassured her younger self: *I know you are feeling anxious right now. Remember all the hard work we've done, and that we are doing. Remember our truth, that we can trust our wise hearts. We don't have to buy into others' fear-based ideas of who God is and what happens in the afterlife.* Gloria imagined herself giving her inner child a hug, and in that moment her younger part felt heard, loved, and cared for. Slowly, and patiently, she was reparenting herself and becoming symptom free.

As you continue your journey, I invite you to get to know your little one within, the dearest part of you that wants to be free again, that wants to love, laugh, and enjoy adventures, that longs to be seen, heard, cherished, and supported. When we are accessible, responsive, and engaged with them, they feel loved, respected, and valued. Their trauma begins to heal.

It is beautiful to see the *marginalized* parts and the exiles within us feel safe enough to leave their damp and dark corners, courageously venturing out and daring to risk sharing what is on their tender and bruised hearts. They can feel so alone, wounded, insecure, and scared at times. As we undo their aloneness, and help them share the unshareable, it can be so liberating for them...and for us! And as we heal them, they heal us as well.

CHAPTER 17
LIVE YOUR VALUES, DESPITE YOUR HELLISH SYMPTOMS

"I wish I'd had the courage to live a life true to myself, not the life others expected of me."

—Bronnie Ware, *The Top Five Regrets of the Dying*

L et's conduct a thought experiment. Imagine for a moment that in front of you are all the things you really care about, everything you love, value, and appreciate. Examples of these might include your family, friends, pets, the delicious food you savor, the sports, books, and fashion you love, television shows, hiking trails, concerts, and any other activities you enjoy—all the things and people that add value to your life.

Also before you are the goals and hobbies that interest you and the tasks you need to get done. These may include chores, such as cleaning the garage and doing yardwork—or more deeply meaningful tasks, such as taking good care of the kids and being a loving partner.[1]

Now, place your hands together, palms up, as if they were pages of a book. Imagine that your hands are symbolic of your passionate determination to heal your overactive Inner Critic, and to avoid shame, fear, anxiety, questions of identity, feelings of emptiness, and so on. Imagine that placed on your hands are all the religious questions you are trying to solve about God, faith, humanity, and the afterlife. If relevant, you might include your anger toward the church as well.

Now, let's see what happens when you put your hands up until they are covering your eyes. Notice a few things. First, observe how disconnected you are from all that you love, value, and appreciate. If a loved one were in front of you, how connected could you be with your hands held up like this? If your favorite television show were playing, how much of it could you see? If the goals that bring meaning to your life are there, how much could you realistically accomplish with your hands covering your eyes? What aspects of life would you miss out on completely?

Now, let's see what happens when you drop your hands down and put them on your lap. If your loved one were in front of you, wouldn't it be easier to connect with them now? If you were watching a show, wouldn't it be easier to watch and enjoy it? If a relationship were strained, could you be more intentional about repairing it? If there were a task or goal you needed to accomplish that would enhance your life in some way, is it easier to focus on now that you have let go of the negative blockages?

One of the challenges for those working through the trauma of Hell indoctrination, and trauma in general, is that they can become hyperfocused on alleviating their symptoms. They might, for example, truly hate their Inner Critic and want nothing to do with this part of themselves, which is more of a *fight* response towards it. The problem with this strategy is that the more the Inner Critic feels despised and ignored, the louder and more active it becomes!

Other people might engage in a *flight* response when facing difficult emotions. In many ways, this is understandable. If we are experiencing hurt, pain, or discomfort, it makes sense that we would want to avoid these feelings. The idea seems to be that moving away from disturbing thoughts and feelings can allow us to move toward "health-ier" and "more positive" ones and live a life we truly want. However, these strategies are often unsuccessful, because the more we try to flee from our painful urges, thoughts, feelings, memories, and impulses, the more they persist. It's like the old adage: *"Don't think* of a pink elephant," in that the more you tell yourself *not* to think or feel a certain way, the stronger your desire to think and feel that way becomes.

Try this experiment: Close your eyes and say to yourself three times, *Don't think about Hell with a Devil in a polka-dot dress holding a pitchfork.* Really, really try to *not* think about it.

How did that work out for you?

There are other flight strategies. Many, for example, escape into using drugs or alcohol to numb their painful feelings. Others turn to pornography, using it to get a temporary rush and distract themselves from their loneliness. Some run into the arms of a new lover in order to feel powerful or to be reassured that someone finds them desirable or lovable. Some become workaholics, laboring ever harder for ever-longer hours. Others constantly pray and read their devotionals, subconsciously trying to ward off anxiety about whether they are loved by God. While all these avoidance strategies can have short-term payoffs, in the long run the consequences can be very harmful.

DENNIS

Let me introduce Dennis, who has been experiencing a spiritual meta-morphosis across the past year. Because his cognitive dissonance had started to boil over, he felt as if he finally had to distance himself from the doctrines of Hell, a wrathful God, Christian nationalism, and an us/them and in/out group mentality. He stated that he was "spiritual" and "loved Jesus," yet he couldn't stomach institutional religion.

At the time I was helping Dennis, he had not attended church for five months. He lived in a small town and didn't want to run into any members of his congregation. He was afraid they would ask him where he'd been and he didn't want to feel uncomfortable. Some had already made judgmental comments about him not being in church. Because Dennis was avoiding possible future discomfort, he gave himself minimal opportunities for social interaction. Because he was isolated, he felt more alone and more depressed, creating a negative feedback loop. The more he didn't go out, the more alone, rejected, and depressed he felt. The more he felt depressed, the more he wanted to stay inside. Dennis had been experiencing an unfortunate cycle of suffering and his avoidance strategies seemed to be keeping this painful loop going. To interrupt it and gain freedom, he had to do one thing differently: change the *avoidant* strategy.

Another way many people become stuck on their healing journey is through thinking they need to have all the right answers. They convince themselves that the life they are piecing together since moving away from toxic religion can't blossom until they have figured everything out. They press "pause" on their lives, presumably until they have found definitive answers as to who God is, what God requires, or how to be completely healed. They also become stuck in doubt as to whether they can trust their intuition without fear of consequences in the afterlife, i.e., burning in Hell.

Others are not fixated on the question of God's existence, but rather on their own past, spending their days ruminating and daydreaming about a life they wish they had lived instead of the one they did. Unfortunately, this rumination can lead to the *paralysis of analysis*, causing the ruminator a constant sense of frustration. *Why?* It's simple: focusing on one's regrets leads to a stagnant life devoid of vitality.

Religious trauma is real—and focusing on healing from it is healthy and positive. What doesn't help, though, is the adoption of a mindset that is too focused on trying to eradicate symptoms or to avoid them entirely. Such a mindset ignores the possibility that our religious trauma had devastating and lasting effects on us that may take years to overcome. What if we can't eradicate the unwanted symptoms quickly? What if trying to rid ourselves of suffering is like flailing in quicksand, in that it only makes our lives worse? Sometimes, being overly focused on healing and having all the right answers keeps us from focusing on what matters most: compassionate acceptance and living out our values. Fortunately, there *is* an alternative to a *symptom eradication* focus.

COMPASSIONATE ACCEPTANCE

Suppressing or trying to get rid of your painful memories of church experiences is like pushing an annoying inflated beach ball under the pool water, hoping it will disappear, while trying to enjoy a swim party. Instead of enjoying being with your friends and relishing the coolness of the water on a hot, sunny day, you find yourself frustrated, struggling with a ball that keeps popping back up. With all the energy you can muster, you push it down, hoping it will go away, once and for all. Eventually, though, it bursts back up with even greater force than it took to push it down!

But what if you just allowed the ball to be there, without struggling with it? The ball would be near you, and at times might even float by and brush up against you. However, after you have accepted its presence and stopped struggling with it, you would be able to do what matters most: have fun, connect with friends, and enjoy life!

Compassionate acceptance means facing and allowing our experiences to unfold with a welcoming tenderness, as opposed to anxiously grasping for defensive or avoidant strategies. For example, Jory believed that *his* actions had caused his wife to start questioning her faith. To avoid the guilt and anxiety surrounding this feeling, he turned to using substances. His wife was a strong Christian and remained that way for several years after his deconstruction. That was, until recently, when she fell into a depression and started questioning everything she had previously believed.

Jory and I worked on his ability to accept his guilt and anxiety with self-compassion. The more he was able to courageously face his feelings, the less he felt the urge to use substances to numb his emotional pain. In turn, the less he used substances, the more present he was for his wife and children, and the less depressed he became.

Instead of using endless energy-draining control strategies to suppress your religious trauma symptoms, you can try to welcome and accept them kindly, even as they arise. Then, you can use that freed-up energy to live a life that feels more meaningful.

Some hear the word *acceptance* and have a visceral reaction, thinking this means one should have a relaxed attitude toward injustice. They may think acceptance condones toxic doctrines and excuses what happened to them, with no attempt at healing or righting wrongs. But this is not the case. Acceptance simply means *accepting what is* at the present time. It is the ability to see things as they are, not as we wish they might have been, had we done something different in the past. It is not fighting or avoiding reality; nor is it fantasizing about another you who exists in a different part of the multiverse. It is the intention to be honest about what is occurring in the present and facing suffering head on. Compassionate acceptance is the intention to be with our rage, sadness, anger, pain, shame, ruminations, boredom, fear, and joy when they arise, and to approach all of these with an attitude of curiosity and warmth.

In Part II, we explored several strategies that can be used to practice compassionate acceptance. For example, when difficult thoughts, feelings, and other internal experiences arise, you can engage in a self-compassion break. You can also face your experiences with courage and, in your imagination, invite an inner ally to support you while performing bilateral stimulation. Try practicing the *Honest, Open, Self-Compassionate,* and *Thankful* (HOST) exercise. If a distressing memory comes up, you can choose to heal the past with your compassionate adult self instead of avoiding that part of yourself. If you find your Inner Critic getting the best of you, try engaging in the INK (Intention, Noticing, Kindness) exercise. These can all help you move away from a dependence on unhelpful avoidance strategies and face your internal experiences head on, with self-compassion.

Acceptance is hard. At first, it might even seem rather *masochistic.*

Who would ever want to sit with uncomfortable and distressing thoughts and feelings? However, as we face reality with courage, a reality not weighed down by heavy, unprocessed emotions, we can start to live a more authentic and meaningful life. When we compassionately make room for our present reality, we can move toward taking committed actions that are guided by our true values.

VALUED LIVING

Imagine that sometime in the future you are able to attend your own funeral.[2] You've lived a long and rewarding life. As you listen to the eulogies spoken by those closest to you, what would you want or expect them to say? As you peer into the future, also look at your tombstone epitaph. What strengths, qualities, and characteristics would you want to see carved there?

Our core values signify the way we want to engage with ourselves and those around us. Values are what we want to stand for in the world. They are our inner compass. What we would want to hear our friends and loved ones say about us at our funeral and what we would like to be written on our tombstone can give a good indication of our deepest values.

Values differ from goals. While goals can be attained, values cannot be. For example, if you want to start a new business, that's a goal. If you want to be inclusive, that's a value. Inclusivity is a quality that can never be fully achieved; rather, it is something you must continually aim for in decision-making. To earn six figures is a goal; to be authentic is a value. To write a book is a goal; to be creative in expressing yourself is a value. Values guide us as we work to achieve our goals and endeavor to experience a meaningful life.[3]

Can we live out our values while struggling with anxiety, depression, and negative thoughts? Absolutely. Can we stay true to our values and at times still feel terror as we reflect on what happens in the afterlife? Definitely. Can we live a values-driven life but still have doubts about the existence of God, or a nagging guilt for having doubt about the existence of God? We can indeed. The beauty of knowing our values is that, regardless of how we think or feel, a *commitment* to live out our values anchors us to a life with meaning and purpose. Admittedly, being guided by our values is no easy task, especially for those who have experienced religious trauma.

RELIGIOUS TRAUMA, IDENTITY, AND VALUES

After running away from the Christian cult I was part of over a decade ago, I embarked on a fearful zigzag toward an unexplored destination. At the time, a friend was attending a less conservative Christian college. I packed my bags and headed there. Going to school was a monumental experience for me. I had always wanted to be the first person in my family to go to college. My dream was that I would learn, grow, and avoid the ignorance and dysfunction that had infested my family for generations.

Before my exodus, the pastor of the cult discouraged me from going to school, saying it would "contaminate God's Word in my heart." More importantly, he didn't want to lose his *armorbearer*, a concept in the Hebrew Bible that referred to the right-hand man of powerful leaders headed into battle. In a modern religious context, the concept is used to justify having a servant to take care of a pastor's practical needs while he prepares for the epic battle of prayer and sermon preparation. So, I obliged.

Who was I to go against the man whom I naively perceived at the time to be "the Lord's anointed"? Yet after some time, I knew I *had* to go to college. While I was not consciously aware of all my reasons for this, I just knew I had to get the heck out of there! Actually, I needed to get myself out of religious hell. So, in a strange way, going to college was my first act of rebellion. And while it felt scary at the time, it also felt really, really good.

While leaving the familiar would end up being the best decision I had ever made, it also left me disoriented. During one brisk night in the first week of school, I found myself in the fetal position on the unusually cold, hard floor of my dorm room—feeling like I was going out of my mind. I was distraught, scared, sobbing uncontrollably, and frantically questioning everything I had done. I was afraid of going to Hell. I didn't know whom to trust. I didn't know what was real. I didn't know what "truth" even meant. *God? Who the heck was that? My values? What in the world were those?*

Loss of identity during a spiritual metamorphosis can be traumatic. While we are fused together with God, or with other people's views of God, and with our tribe's beliefs, norms, and practices, we can lose our sense of uniqueness. Unfortunately, many churches become religious cookie-cutter machines that seek to produce Christians who walk, talk, and think like everyone else. As we unplug from this religious matrix and become born again—*again*—our first steps into the vast new world can shake us to our core. As we start to think for ourselves and question a reality that had previously been presented to us as absolute, we can feel like we have been catapulted onto a new planet. Navigating this new terrain can be disorienting, to say the least.

It also doesn't help that we are taught the conflicting messages that we are loved *and* that we are terrible sinners with wicked hearts who deserve to burn in Hell. The message seems to be that the self is bad, and that God is the only One who is good. Our uniqueness must therefore be suppressed. Marlene Winell says it well:

> Selfishness and pride are considered terrible things in a traditional Christian context. Thus, when you leave the fold, it can be very difficult to know how to think for yourself. At one time, your individual identity was subsumed in a local expression of the body of Christ. Now, you may need to get to know yourself and learn how to appreciate your uniqueness.[4]

Katie, a participant in the *Breaking Up with Jesus* study, shared her struggle in losing her worldview and, ultimately, her identity, after deconstructing her faith. She writes that religion "is your worldview, it's how you understand your place in the world, how you understand the things that happen to you, how you understand what you are supposed to do with your life. And then that all falls apart and you have got to try and find a way of making sense of everything again from a completely different place."[5]

Author of *Post-Traumatic Church Syndrome*, Reba Riley has written about leaving her faith and struggling to find her identity:

> Placing your "identity in Christ" is lingo for church-approved code-pendence: you allow your church's brand of Jesus to dictate what you do or don't do or don't wear, eat, read, discuss, watch, and listen to. You let your church's Jesus pick out your lipstick and your friends, run your bank accounts, and prescribe your wardrobe. Having my identity in Christ was the problem, the entire reason I fell apart when I could no longer believe. When I left my faith, I didn't have anything of my own.[6]

Some on the journey away from toxic religion find that when the foundation of their beliefs starts to crack, there is an undeniable shaking of their sense of self. They can find themselves in an existential dilemma. For years, they plugged their brains into the mothership of religion, constraining any need to think critically about their beliefs and values, or to ponder the nuances of life. They certainly did not feel it appropriate to ask difficult or divergent questions about God. Their brains were wired with the teachings of a book, a priest or pastor, and other people in the faith community. A stream of homogeneous beliefs was slowly pumped in, a pipeline from their tribe to their brain.

Coming untethered from the *religious matrix* can be unsettling and even traumatic. The loss of a community, the loss of a secure connection to the Bible, the loss of God, and the loss of identity cause confusion. Yet, the process of figuring out who you are and healing from the traumatic effects of unhealthy religion can be liberating. Learning about what *you* think, what *you* love and desire, what *your* purpose is, what brings *you* joy, and what *your* values are—alongside wise and compassionate travel companions—can be a pure delight.

WHAT ARE YOUR VALUES?

Have you ever taken the time to think about what your own values are and list them? If not, I invite you to do so. Below are some examples of values to jumpstart your reflection on yours:

1. Acceptance/self-acceptance: to be accepting of yourself and others.
2. Authenticity: to be genuine with yourself and others.
3. Spirituality: to connect with that which is transcendent.
4. Love: to put another's interests above your own.
5. Gratitude: to express appreciation for the people and experiences in your life.
6. Justice: to advocate for and support those who are oppressed and marginalized.
7. Curiosity: to ask questions with the intention of gaining understanding.
8. Adventurousness: willingness to take risks and explore new experiences.
9. Cooperation: to partner with others and work toward common goals.
10. Forgiveness: to acknowledge a wrong done to you by yourself or another, but to let go of any wish for vengeance.
11. Courage: to act to achieve a goal in the face of threat or difficulty.
12. Honesty: to speak truthfully and completely.
13. Integrity: to act in accordance with your values in private, as well as in public.
14. Self-control: to exercise restraint over desires that go against your values.

15. Patience: to wait for a desired goal with no sense of entitlement.
16. Persistence: to continue to act toward a goal in the face of obstacles or fatigue.
17. Kindness: to treat others with friendliness, consideration, and care.
18. Humility: to act without any desire for praise or recognition from others.
19. Transparency: to open your actions to the visibility and scrutiny of others.
20. Safety: to provide an environment for yourself or others that is sheltered from harm.
21. Community: to belong to a group with similar beliefs, values, behaviors, and interests.

Do you see some of your own core values on that list? Which ones take precedence in your life? Can you select a top five? What values do you have that weren't on the list? During your spiritual metamorphosis, it is crucial to know what your values are because they guide you.

Your feelings and moods can change. Your mind may get stuck in the past, regretting all those wasted years spent in toxic religion. Your thoughts might run wild, worrying about a tormenting afterlife at some point in the future. Once you identify and prioritize your values, they become like a compass, helping you to navigate the stormy mental sea of thoughts and ideas vying for your attention in life. Despite the ill effects of religious trauma, and the difficulty of not knowing exactly what you believe, letting your values be your inner guide can help ensure that you live a life worth living in the present. After all, the present is all that we have. Let's live in it!

CHOICE POINT AND VALUES

At any given moment we are doing something. Whether we are engaged in contemplative meditation, eating, taking a shower, working, sitting still and being mindful of our breath, sleeping, or reading, we're always engaged in some form of activity. When our actions move us *toward* a life that feels authentic and meaningful, we might call those "toward moves."[7] When our actions pull us *away* from an authentic and meaningful life, those are "away moves."[8]

Visualize an image of a fork in the road. If you go left, that is an away move, moving you away from your values and the life you want to build. If you go right, that is a toward move, moving you toward your values and the life you want to live.

When veering right, engaging in toward moves, you are choosing activities that feel good to your core self. Toward moves are unique to each individual, but might include actions such as eating healthily, being kind to others, advocating for the marginalized, being creative, getting adequate rest, exploring nature, writing music, taking a warm bath, and connecting with friends and family.

Away moves, by contrast, do not enhance your life in the long run. They might include consuming unhealthy foods or substances, avoiding healthy exercise, stonewalling, or criticizing loved ones, scrolling on social media for hours at a time when there are important deadlines to meet, going on shopping sprees when you don't have the cash, or self-harming.

We are each faced with many dozens of choices daily. When life goes according to plan, it is easier to make *toward moves* that are in line with our values. When we encounter life stressors, however, some of us are more prone to veer left, moving away from our values down a well-worn pathway to unhelpful responses. For example, if we have thoughts such as, *Those church people don't want to be around you*, and, *You will be alone for the rest of your life*, it may be easy to believe what your mind is saying as if it were true.

Here, though, we have a choice. We can choose *away moves*, such as eating junk food, taking our negative feelings out on our dog or someone close to us, gambling with money we don't have, or attacking ourselves. Alternatively, we could choose a toward move on a trajectory in the direction of our values. If we value self-compassion, for instance, we might give ourselves a self-compassion break. If we value community, we could acknowledge our feelings and call a caring friend. If we value spirituality, we may be mindful of our thoughts and feelings and share them with the Divine.

EXERCISE: THINKING THROUGH A CHOICE POINT

An audio file of this activity can be found at https://markgregorykarris.com/meditations (password: HEAL).

1. Try to name a common struggle you experience as you heal from religious trauma. Is it emotional? Relational? Spiritual? Theological? Do you have trouble sleeping? Are there challenging relationships with family members or friends? Does your Inner Critic tell you that you should fear punishment by God? Are there unresolved theological questions you feel you need to have answered?

2. As you pick a struggle, try to name the emotions and bodily sensations you experience as they occur. Do you feel sadness, anger, guilt, fear, or loneliness? Do you feel your heart racing, a heaviness in your chest, a tightness in your jaw, or nausea? Do you feel overwhelmed, unable to describe your feelings?

3. Imagine yourself in the middle of that struggle and try to press "pause" on your experience. What thoughts are you having (e.g., *This will never change, I deserve this, I'm a loser, God hates me, I'm tainted goods, I'm going to Hell, I might as well die.*, etc.)?

4. When you think about being in the midst of the struggle, along with the concurrent distressing thoughts and emotions you feel, describe your typical *away moves*. These are the behaviors that take you away from the life you want to build and the person you want to become. They might include drinking too much, isolating yourself, or eating unhealthily.[9] What does engaging in these moves cost you?

5. Now, as you think about your struggle and the distressing thoughts and emotions that accompany them, name the top go-to *toward moves* you use that are in line with your values. These could include connecting with friends, engaging in self-compassion, exercising, meditation, or being in nature. If you find it difficult to think of toward moves, try to list some that could be *go-to's* when this struggle comes up in the future. What benefits would you and others around you experience if you chose toward moves every time this struggle arose?

MY CHOICE POINT

Just like you, every day I have my own choice points. Let me go through the above exercise using one of my own struggles as an example for you. On this occasion I was struggling with one of the residual effects of Hell trauma.

1. I was writing the chapter of this book on projections and suddenly, my Inner Critic told me, *God is mad at you.*

2. I did not want to push that thought away. I chose to sit with it and be present and curious with the thoughts, feelings, and physiological sensations arising. I noticed myself feeling anxious. My heart was beating a little faster. I also felt some heaviness in my chest.

3. I noticed some familiar lyrics of a song being played on the "DARK FM" radio station inside my head. I heard: *You are a heretic, You will be responsible for people going to Hell,* and *God Is going to punish you.* I was surprised, as I thought I'd stopped having these thoughts a long time ago.

4. My *away moves* in the past would have included seeking to avoid these thoughts and physical sensations as quickly as possible. I would have achieved this by suppressing my thoughts and feelings. I would also mindlessly scroll Facebook or browse the news, or watch dumb

videos on YouTube for hours, all distractions to avoid my internal experiences.

5. In this instance, I chose a *toward move* that was in the direction of my values, particularly those of mindfulness, common humanity, and kindness. With an attitude of curiosity, I made an intention not to suppress my thoughts and feelings. After becoming aware of my internal experience in this moment, I engaged in a self-compassion break. With my eyes closed, I placed my hand on my heart and said to my frantic Inner Critic, *I know you are anxious. I know you are just trying to protect me. We have good reasons to no longer believe in this kind of punishing, wrathful God. We also have no need for other people's twisted projections of Hell and the afterlife. You are not alone. Other people struggle with these thoughts, as well. May you be kind to yourself. Know that you are doing the right thing by writing this book. May you also take comfort that you will help other people on their journey.* Then I moved in the direction of my values of authenticity, creativity, justice, and healing—and continued writing.

LANCE'S STORY

Lance left the conservative Baptist church he grew up in after many internal struggles, mostly to do with the moral strictness, politics, and the mundaneness of church life. He was still working out what his spirituality looked like in the aftermath of his departure. Since he'd left, he had been plagued with obsessive thoughts about his relationship with God and Hell. He couldn't shake the belief that he might be going to Hell for leaving his church and many of his former religious beliefs behind. He feared that God would be perpetually angry at him and would punish him with condemnation.

Fear of where his doubts and questions might lead him made him feel depressed and anxious much of the time. Lance would try to busy himself by working extra hours. If the weather permitted, he would have liked to go hiking on weekends, but usually lacked motivation to do so. Over time, his alcohol consumption increased, and he found himself watching porn more than what he thought was healthy. Since leaving the church he had very few friends. He felt alone and hopeless.

In our work together, Lance shared one of the main mental blocks that stopped him from exploring his values. He stated, in therapy: "How can I live out my values, whatever they are, if I am going to Hell? I need to figure out if I am going to Hell first. If Hell is real, who cares about my meaningful life?" This tenacious belief is a difficult blockage to overcome, and I have worked with many others who struggled with versions of it. It can take years to chisel away at this fortified mental construct. The reason for its persistence is that people often feel that "it is better to be safe than sorry." *If Hell is indeed real*, they think, *it is too great a risk not to believe in it.*

Through self-compassion work, healing of parental wounds, and learning to relate to his Inner Critic differently (as well as Lance's own exploration of other ways to view God, Hell, and himself), Lance was able to chip away at the block. Eventually, he concluded that *no one can know definitively what happens after we die.* While he was told by preachers that "eternity is too long to be wrong," he owned his own truth and came up with his own mantra: "Life is too short and precious to be squandered." Although his mantra didn't rhyme, I'm glad he found a cognitive anchor that helped him feel grounded when his Inner Critic would try to stir up some internal storms.

Another of Lance's cognitive anchors was "I don't need to know all the answers. For now, I will simply focus on loving myself and others." Included in that new mantra was Lance's ability to love himself enough to honor who he really was and own his core values.

After I helped him explore some of his values, Lance realized that he valued physical fitness, creativity, sensuality, adventure, and connectedness. Lance came to realize that despite his confusion about many issues surrounding faith, including his understanding of the afterlife, identifying his own values was immediately within his control. Identifying his core values empowered him since they were *intrinsic*, coming from inside of him, rather than *extrinsic*, or originating from outside.

Lance's intentional decision to identify his core values was instrumental in his being able to reconstruct his life after a toxic religious experience. He still felt anxious and depressed at times, and his fears about Hell popped up now and again. He also struggled with insomnia on some days. However, when faced with these struggles and their associated *choice points*, he consistently engaged in toward moves. He didn't wait until he was healed, whatever that meant, before beginning to live a life worth living. Instead of focusing on what he didn't know, he focused on what he was sure of—his values.

Since creativity was one of his core values, Lance started painting again, a pursuit he had ceased many years ago. To honor his value of sensuality, he started appreciating his body more. He now made it a habit to receive a massage once a month, as feeling the touch of another person helped him become reacquainted with his body; this was also a way to care for his body. Recognizing he had not accorded fitness—another of his values—its proper place in his value hierarchy, he decided to hike more frequently. Hiking also helped him to live out his value of adventure, as he now started hiking at new and unfamiliar locations. Instead of isolating himself, he joined a birdwatching group in order to feel connected with like-minded others. His focus was on living a purposeful life, not a symptom-free life. Paradoxically, the more he lived with purpose and in alignment with his values, the fewer symptoms he experienced.

SLAY THE GODS, LIVE OUT OF AUTHENTICITY!

Slaying the false gods in your life, meaning any powerful figures whose beliefs and values you previously internalized, is integral to feeling alive. Sometimes the false gods within you must die and be given a funeral so that your new life, with its authentic self, can spring forth. Identifying your values, being mindful of your choice points, and living out your values despite your hellish symptoms, are all part of the healing journey.

This process can restore your vitality, propelling you to live the life you are meant to live. The healing journey is not an easy one, but it is absolutely worth it! May you no longer conform to people's projections of how you *should* live and what you *should* believe. May you live a life that is true to yourself, not a life others expect of you.

EPILOGUE

Wrathful God

Tormenting Hell

Sinful Self

The religious narrative of a wrathful and punitive God who created Hell so that evil and sinful human beings could be tortured for all eternity is the most depraved and poisonous tale ever created. Its destructive ripple effect through the ages has been incalculable. As theologian and philosopher David Bentley Hart aptly states:

> The belief that a God of infinite intellect, justice, love, and power would condemn rational beings to a state of endless suffering or would allow them to condemn themselves on account of their own delusion, pain, and anger, is probably worse than merely scandalous.

It may be the single most horrid notion the religious imagination has ever entertained.[1]

I *get* how and why this heinous version of a torturous Hell came into existence and has remained with us until this day. We are a curious, creative, and meaning-making species who are wired to belong. Versions of an afterlife with a reward and punishment motif are apparent across eras, cultures, and various religions. We want to know that our suffering is not in vain and that our toil and good deeds will lead to a heavenly existence after we die. We also hope for a Hell, because we want reassurance that those perpetrators of evil who get away with their awful behaviors on earth will receive justice in the afterlife. Another reason the idea of a tormenting Hell has survived is because it has been used as a weapon to instill fear and enforce standards of morality by those seeking to create homogenous communities. The idea of a tormenting Hell was born out of trauma and wielded by traumatized people. Overall, it has done humanity more harm than good.

My hope is that this doom-ridden, poisonous narrative of a furious, fickle, and retributive God, a God who creates a demon-filled Hell so that the human beings God supposedly loves can be tortured forever, eventually withers out and dies. It seems that this may be happening in our times, though slowly.

There have been theologians, pastors, therapists, and spiritual leaders who have come together to rally against such virulent doctrines. While there will always be a handful of Christians who constantly engage in Hell talk, I think many Christians today are realizing how toxic Hell indoctrination really is.

Imagine it is late at night and you're driving down a winding road, coming back from a long trip. It's very late and there are not many people on the road. Your parents are about five minutes behind you. Suddenly, you slam on the brakes because you see a huge sinkhole in the road. You fail to stop in time and your car now teeters on the precipice of a bottomless chasm. Miraculously, you somehow escape from the car. Seconds later, the car inches its way over the edge and drops into the sinkhole!

If you knew there was a hole in the road and your parents were about to drive into it, wouldn't you flail, scream, and do whatever you needed to warn them of their impending doom? If you believed the hole was real and you cared about your parents' fate, of course you would!

Now, we've seen that often when someone leaves a fundamentalist church the person's friends and family do seek to "warn" them, do try to tell them that they are headed for eternal torture in Hell. And we've seen various ways those who've progressed beyond the immoral idea of Hell as a place of eternal conscious torment can seek and achieve psychological healing from the trauma that Hell indoctrination causes. But, we might ask, if those in conservative churches who believe Hell is a place of eternal conscious torment really did believe it with all their heart, wouldn't they be out there every single day trying to warn, not just the odd "backsliding" relative they may or may not have, but every single person they ever met? Wouldn't the right thing to do, given this belief, be to check that every person one encountered had the right beliefs and was thus "going to Heaven"? After all, the random person any of us passes on the street today may drop dead tomorrow. Why is it that many Christians believe in Hell, but do not raise their hands, waving and screaming, to tell every single non-Christian person they meet—co-worker, friend, classmate, or family member—that they are on a road leading to eternal conscious torment? If Hell is an abysmal place where people, including children and the elderly, will be eternally tortured, why would those who wholeheartedly believe in Hell not say anything to the non-Christians they meet daily? I propose that there are many Christians today who profess to believe in Hell but who live in a way which betrays a lack of belief in that Hell they so insistently profess belief in. This is the only way to explain the lack of action by many supposed Hell-believing Christians.

Sure, some who believe in a place of eternal conscious torment may be shy. They may avoid speaking up because they fear other people's responses and they do not want to risk being rejected. That being said, however, when we step back for a minute, it seems absurd to think that a fear of how other people might perceive them, or a fear of being rejected, could trump their chance to save someone from the black hole that is eternal damnation and excruciating eternal suffering. Only the severest phobia of social interaction could justify or come close to excusing inaction in the face of a person's potential eternal conscious torment, and even then it would be a stretch. And of course, most believers in Hell have no such phobia.

In a similar vein, it is possible that belief in Hell is so irrational that people know if they talk about it, they will sound crazy—both to themselves and to the person they are talking to. But, again, who cares about sounding crazy if people could die tomorrow and spend eternity in Hell?

Is it possible that some, if they are honest, do not wholeheartedly buy into the idea of Hell? They might deceive themselves by thinking they hold certain beliefs, but their everyday actions reveal what they *actually* believe. The man who says he values protecting the environment but cannot be bothered to separate his items for recycling is either fooling himself or lying to those around him, saying only what he thinks others want to hear. Similarly, some who profess belief in Hell may be saying only what they think others want to hear.

I think there are people who remain silent about eternal torment because of their unconscious rejection of the archaic idea of Hell. By their silence, they demonstrate the true nature of their intuitions— that the existence of an Infernalist's Hell is a myth. Some may even deceive themselves into thinking they really *do* believe in it. But just as "faith without works is dead," so is belief in Hell without telling every single person one encounters about it. Pointing out these truths is not meant to be judgmental. It is simply meant to demonstrate that some may believe subconsciously what many of us believe consciously (including many other Christians)—that hellfire is irrational and traumatizing.

One could say that the people with their bullhorns in the streets, shouting about Hell and damnation, are the ones who really believe it. But could it also be that the reality of Hell is so traumatizing that some Christians suppress the thought of it because of how horrific and nonsensical it is? Perhaps some Christians know, deep within, that there is no possibility of integrating the idea that God is the utmost of love as well as being the Grand Torturer Supreme. They know that when they look at a naive fourteen-year-old who died a Hindu, had no faith in Jesus, yet was as loving and sincere as he could be, it is preposterous to believe that a loving God would have him tortured forever.

Yet, they push down their doubts. The cognitive dissonance becomes so great, that while they believe in Hell intellectually, emotionally they find the concept to be appalling and indigestible. To hide their own trauma of Hell, they push their beliefs down into those hard-to-access corridors of their psyches, where they can live their whole lives never telling even a single soul about the reality of Hell. *Really?*

Thankfully there are more beautiful versions of the Divine and the afterlife that are being shared, even by faithful Christians and religious leaders. As someone who values authenticity and freedom, I am aware that some of you may have found narratives that center on an atheistic or agnostic view of God, without the belief in an afterlife. I think we should all give ourselves permission to be true to ourselves. I trust that each of us, as sincere, seeking people, can trust our intuition and follow paths that are congruent with who we are, on the journey of spiritual metamorphosis.

As someone whose life has been fundamentally altered by Jesus and his teachings, I am genuinely sorry that you have been traumatized by Hell and its interrelated doctrines. What happened to you is not right. Some of you were young children when you first heard these doctrines. You deserved to be immersed in narratives of love, inclusivity, diversity, and unity, not those filled with terror, shame, and fear. It is not fair. It is unjust. Thankfully, the trauma of Hell indoctrination does not get to define us or dictate how the rest of our life's adventure unfolds.

The subtitle of this book is *Healing from the Trauma of Hell Indoctrination*. I chose *Healing* instead of *Heal* because I believe that healing is a journey and rarely a final destination. To suggest that we can *heal* sounds like an end goal, yet; as I have expressed throughout the book, I do not believe in quick fixes or magic potions that can instantly cure us. While I do believe that healing is very much possible, I am fully aware of trauma's effects on our nervous system. I am aware that, in many cases, healing from the trauma of Hell indoctrination can take some time.

My hope is that the principles, practices, and ideas presented here have helped free you from your ideas of Hell, a vengeful and punishing God, and a view of yourself as a sinful, evil creature. There are countless people who have felt much freer in their lives without these beliefs. I hope this can be the case for you, too. Continuous healing is a possibility for us all.

May you find the courage and strength to navigate the challenges ahead, despite religious trauma's effects, and may each step bring you closer to a life filled with joy, purpose, and meaning.

Peace, Mark

APPENDIX
BOOKS THAT EXPLORE HELL FROM A NON-ETERNAL CONSCIOUS TORMENT PERSPECTIVE

Allin, Thomas, Robin Parry, and Thomas B. Talbott. *Christ Triumphant: Universalism Asserted as the Hope of the Gospel on the Authority of Reason, the Fathers, and Holy Scripture.* Wipf & Stock Publishers, 2015.

Baker, Sharon L. *Razing Hell: Rethinking Everything You've Been Taught about God's Wrath and Judgment.* New York: Wipf & Stock Publishers, 2013

Beauchemin, Gerry, and D. S. Reichard. *Hope Beyond Hell: The Righteous Purpose of God's Judgment,* 3rd ed. Scotts Valley: Malista Press, 2015.

Bernstein, Alan E. *The Formation of Hell: Death and Retribution in the Ancient and Early Christian Worlds.* Ithaca: Cornell University Press, 1993.

Burnfield, David. *Patristic Universalism: An Alternative to the Traditional View of Divine Judgment.* London: T&T Clark, 2011

David Bentley Hart. *That All Shall Be Saved.* New Haven: Yale University Press, 2019

Date, Christopher, Gregory Stump, and Joshua Anderson. *Rethinking Hell: Readings in Evangelical Conditionalism.* Eugene: Wipf and Stock Publishers, 2014.

Ehrman, Bart D. *Heaven and Hell: A History of the Afterlife.* New York: Simon & Schuster, 2020.

Ferwerda, Julie. *Raising Hell: Christianity's Most Controversial Doctrine Put Under Fire.* Edited by Stephen Ferwerda. Vagabond Group, 2011.

Fudge, Edward W. *The Fire That Consumes: A Biblical and Historical Study of the Doctrine of Final Punishment,* 3rd ed. Eugene: Wipf and Stock Publishers, 2011.

Giles, Keith. *Jesus Undefeated: Condemning the False Doctrine of Eternal Torment.* Quoir, 2019.

Gregg, Steve. *All You Want to Know About Hell: Three Christian Views of God's Final Solution to the Problem of Sin.* Nashville: Thomas Nelson, 2013.

Henning, Meghan. *Educating Early Christians through the Rhetoric of Hell: "Weeping and Gnashing of Teeth" as Paideia in Matthew and the Early Church.* Heidelberg: Mohr Siebeck, 2014.

Henning, Meghan R. *Hell Hath No Fury: Gender, Disability, and the Invention of Damned Bodies in Early Christian Literature.* New Haven: Yale University Press, 2021.

J.W. Hanson. Universalism: *The Prevailing Doctrine of the Church During Its First Five Hundred Years.* Boston: Universalist Publishing House, 1887

Jersak, Brad. *Her Gates Will Never Be Shut: Hell, Hope, and the New Jerusalem.* Eugene, Or.: Wipf & Stock Publishers, 2010.

Kronen, John, and Eric Reitan. *God's Final Victory: A Comparative Philosophical Case for Universalism.* Bloomsbury Academic, 2013.

Kvanvig, Jonathan L. *The Problem of Hell.* Oxford: Oxford University Press on Demand, 1993.

MacDonald, Gregory, and Robin A. Parry. *"All Shall Be Well": Explorations in Universal Salvation and Christian Theology, from Origen to Moltmann.* Eugene: Wipf and Stock Publishers, 2011.

MacDonald, Gregory, and Robin A. Parry. *The Evangelical Universalist,* 2nd ed. Eugene: Wipf and Stock Publishers, 2012.

Myers, Kenneth N. *Let's Talk About Hell.* Mayeux Press, 2021.

Ramelli, Ilaria L. A Larger Hope?, *Volume 1: Universal Salvation from Christian Beginnings to Julian of Norwich.* Eugene: Wipf and Stock Publishers, 2019.

Randy Klassen. *What Does the Bible Really Say About Hell?* Kitchener, ON: Pandora Press, 2001

Sprinkle, Preston M. *Four Views on Hell.* Grand Rapids, MI: Zondervan, 2016.

Thomas Talbott. *The Inescapable Love of God.* New York: Oxford University Press, 1999

Toscano, Margaret. *Hell and its Afterlife: Historical and Contemporary Perspectives.* London: Routledge, 2016.

Zahnd, Brian. *Sinners in the Hands of a Loving God: The Scandalous Truth of the Very Good News.* WaterBrook, 2017.

NOTES

INTRODUCTION

1. Burk, D. 'Eternal Conscious Torment', in Burk, D., Stackhouse Jr., J, Parry, R, and Walls, J. (eds) *Four Views on Hell* (Grand Rapids, MI: Zondervan, 2016), 20.
2. Ballenger, Mark. "How Does Hell Glorify God?" ApplyGodsWord.com. Accessed December 27, 2016. https://ApplyGodsword.com/how-does-hell-glorify-god/.

CHAPTER 1

1. See Harris, Russ. *Trauma-Focused Act: A Practitioner's Guide to Working with Mind, Body, and Emotion Using Acceptance and Commitment Therapy,* (Oakland: New Harbinger Publications, 2022), 2.

CHAPTER 2

1. In its critical reaction to Winell's ground-breaking work, the British Association for Behavioral and Cognitive Psychologists specifically cited this type of work (on fringe cults) as accepted forms of religious abuse that they considered uncontroversial. https://www.mindandsoulfoundation.org/Articles/289535/Mind_and_Soul/Articles/Religious_Trauma_Syndrome.aspx
2. Peck, Brian. "Room to Thrive - FAQs." Accessed November 14, 2022. https://www.roomtothrive.com/faqs. The definition of ARE was defined by Laura Anderson and Brian Peck (the co-founders of the Religious Trauma Institute) and Kendra Snyder and Kayla Felten (co-founders of the Reclamation Collective).
3. Koch, Daniel, and Leihua Edstrom. "Development of the Spiritual Harm and Abuse Scale." *Journal for the Scientific Study of Religion* 61, 2 (2022): 476–506. doi:10.1111/jssr.12792. You can find the scale here: https://www.dankochwords.com/uploads/1/1/7/6/117689856/spiritual_harm__abuse_scale_-_screener_v1.3.pdf
4. https://www.rawstory.com/2019/09/religious-trauma-syndrome-psychologist-reveals-how-organized-religion-can-lead-to-mental-health-problems/
5. Peck, Brian. "Room to Thrive - FAQs." Accessed November 14, 2022. https://www.roomtothrive.com/faqs. The definition of religious trauma was defined by Laura Anderson and Brian Peck (the co-founders of the Religious Trauma Institute) and Kendra Snyder and Kayla Felten (co-founders of the Reclamation Collective).
6. Tarico, Valerie. "Religious Trauma Syndrome: Psychologist reveals how organized religion can lead to mental health problems," September 5, 2019, https://www.rawstory.com/2019/09/religious-trauma-syndrome-psychologist-reveals-how-organized-religion-can-lead-to-mental-health-problems/.

7. See Riley, Reba. Post-Traumatic Church Syndrome: One Woman's Desperate, Funny, and Healing Journey to Explore 30 Religions by Her 30th Birthday (New York: Howard Books, 2016).
8. Ibid., 10
9. Elizabeth Baker. Accessed November 21, 2022. https://elizabethkbaker.com/.
10. Baker, Elizabeth. "My Evangelical Church Is Gaslighting Me, But I Refuse to Fall For It Anymore," Huffington Post, November 28, 2018, https://www.huffpost.com/entry/evangelical-christians-trump_n_5bfc326de4b03b230fa57ae9.
11. Karris, Mark. Religious Refugees: (De)Constructing Toward Spiritual and Emotional Healing (Quoir, 2020).
12. See Escobar, Kathy. Faith Shift: Finding Your Way Forward When Everything You Believe Is Coming Apart (New York: Convergent Books, 2014),

CHAPTER 3

1. Graham, Franklin. "Franklin Graham: The Eternal Peril of Progressive Christianity." Decision Magazine, May 2, 2022. https://decisionmagazine.com/franklin-graham-the-eternal-peril-of-progressive-christianity/.
2. Ibid.
3. Cranney, Stephen, Leman, Joseph, Fergus, Thomas A., and Rowatt, Wade C. "Hell Anxiety Scale." PsycTESTS, January 2018. doi:10.1037/t72689-000.
4. Baylor Religion Survey Wave 5. "American Values, Mental Health, and Using Technology in the Age of Trump." September 2017.
5. Shariff, Azim F., and Aknin, Lara B. "The Emotional Toll of Hell: Cross-National and Experimental Evidence for the Negative Well-Being Effects of Hell Beliefs." PLoS ONE 9, 1 (2014). doi:10.1371/journal.pone.0085251.
6. Quoted in Winell, Marlene. Leaving the Fold. (Berkeley, CA: Apocryphile, 2007), 63.
7. Gunnarson, Dennis. "Fostering a Healthy Soul: Escaping Spiritual Disillusionment" (Independently Published, 2022), 95.
8. https://research.lifeway.com/2020/09/08/americans-hold-complex-conflicting-religious-beliefs-according-to-latest-state-of-theology-study/
9. Margaret Steel Farrell, My Mother, My Church in Dann, G. Elijah. Leaving Fundamentalism: Personal Stories. (Waterloo, Ont.: Wilfrid Laurier University Press, 2008.), 74.
10. Streib, Heinz, Hood, Ralph W., Keller, Barbara, Csoff, Rosina-Martha, and Silver, Christopher F. Deconversion: Qualitative and Quantitative Results from Cross Cultural Research in Germany and the United States of America, (Germany: Vandenhoeck & Ruprecht, 2009), 101.
11. Mayfield, Krispin. Attached to God: A Practical Guide to Deeper Spiritual Experience. (Grand Rapids: Zondervan, 2022), 198.
12. Phillips, Amy. 2016. "The Resurrection of Self: How Deconversion from Religious Belief to Atheism Healed a History of Rejection, Trauma, and Shame." Dissertation Abstracts International Section A: Humanities and Social Sciences, 2016. ProQuest Information & Learning. https://search.ebscohost.com/login.aspx?direct=true&db=psyh&AN=2016-37850-257&site=ehost-live&scope=site., 160.
13. Abramowitz, Jonathan S., and Hellberf, Samantha N.. "Scrupulosity." In Advanced Casebook of Obsessive-Compulsive and Related Disorders, (Academic Press, 2020), 71-87.
14. Ibid, 71

15. Ibid.
16. Ibid., 73
17. Peck, Debra. *The Hijacked Conscience: An Informed and Compassionate Response to Scrupulosity*, (SacraSage Press, 2023).
18. Natterson-Horowitz, Barbara, and Bowers, Kathryn. *Zoobiquity: What Animals Can Teach Us about Being Human*, (London: Virgin Books, 2012).
19. van Megen, Harold J, den Boer-Wolters, Dianne, Verhagen, Peter J. "Obsessive compulsive disorder and religion: A reconnaissance." In Verhagen P, Van Praag HM, López-Ibor JJ Jr, Cox J, Moussaoui D (eds.). *Religion and Psychiatry: Beyond Boundaries* (Wiley, 2010), 271–82.

CHAPTER 4

1. Edwards, Jonathan. "Sinners in the Hands of an Angry God (Enfield, CT, 1741)," in Sinners in the Hands of an Angry God and Other Puritan Sermons (Mineola, NY: Dover, 2005), 178.
2. Smedes, Lewis B. *Shame and Grace: Healing the Shame We Don't Deserve* (San Francisco: Harper, 1993), 1.
3. Gilbert, Paul. "The Evolution of Shame as a Marker for Relationship Security: A Biopsychosocial Approach." In Tracy, Jessica L., Robins, Richard W., Tangney, June Price (eds), *The Self-Conscious Emotions: Theory and Research,*(New York, NY: Guilford Press, 2007), 283–309. https://search.ebscohost.com/login.aspx?direct=true&db=psyh&AN=2007-14002-016&site=ehost-live&scope=site.
4. Ibid., 55
5. Gilbert, Paul. *Compassion focused therapy: Distinctive features.* (London, UK: Routledge, 2010).
6. Crocker, Seth C. "Persevering Faith: A Qualitative Exploration of Religious Trauma and Spiritual Resilience in Sexual Minority Christians." Dissertation Abstracts International: Section B: The Sciences and Engineering (2022). ProQuest Information & Learning. https://search.ebscohost.com/login.aspx?direct=true&db=psyh&AN=2022-13252-042&site=ehost-live&scope=site.
7. Downie, Alison. "Christian Shame and Religious Trauma" Religions 13, 10 (2022): 925. https://doi.org/10.3390/rel13100925, 5.
8. Hollier, Joel, Clifton, Shane, and Smith-Merry, Jennifer. "Mechanisms of Religious Trauma amongst Queer People in Australia's Evangelical Churches." Clinical Social Work Journal 50 , 3 (2022), 275–85. doi:10.1007/s10615-022-00839-x.
9. Distefano, Matthew and Collins, Michelle. *Learning to Float*, (Quoir, 2022), Preface.
10. Garcia, Kevin Miguel. *Bad Theology Kills: Undoing Toxic Beliefs; Reclaiming Your Spiritual Authority* (United States, 2020), 40.
11. Ibid.

CHAPTER 5

1. As a side note, someone with schizophrenia does not have "multiple personalities"; that would be *Dissociative Identity Disorder* (which used to be called *Multiple Person-*

ality Disorder).

2. Freyd, Jennifer J., DePrince, Anne P., and Gleaves, David H.. "The State of Betrayal Trauma Theory: Reply to McNally—Conceptual Issues and Future Directions." Memory 15, 3 (2007): 295–311. doi:10.1080/09658210701256514., 297.

3. Ibid.

4. Gagnon, Kerry L., Lee, Michelle Seulki, and DePrince, Anne P. "Victim–perpetrator Dynamics through the Lens of Betrayal Trauma Theory." Journal of Trauma & Dissociation 18, 3 (2017), 373–82. doi:10.1080/15299732.2017.1295421.

5. Phillips, Amy. "The Resurrection of Self: How Deconversion from Religious Belief to Atheism Healed a History of Rejection, Trauma, and Shame." Dissertation Abstracts
International Section A: Humanities and Social Sciences, vol. 77, no. 3–A(E), ProQuest
Information & Learning, 2016. EBSCOhost,
search.ebscohost.com/login.aspx?direct=true&db=psyh&AN=2016-37850-257&site=ehostlive& scope=site, 138.

CHAPTER 6

1. Gungor, Lisa. *The Most Beautiful Thing I've Seen: Opening Your Eyes to Wonder* (Grand Rapids, Michigan: Zondervan, 2018), 104.

2. Klein, Linda Kay, *Pure: Inside the Evangelical Movement That Shamed a Generation of Young Women and How I Broke Free* (New York, NY, Touchstone, An Imprint of Simon & Schuster, Inc, 2018), 250.

3. Ibid.

4. DeWall, C. Nathan, et al., "Acetaminophen Reduces Social Pain: Behavioral and Neural Evidence," Psychological Science 21, no. 7 (2010): 931–37, Business Source Complete, EBSCOhost. 10.1177/0956797610374741.

5. See Cozolino, Louis J. *The Neuroscience of Human Relationships: Attachment and the Developing Social Brain*, (New York: Norton, 2006).

CHAPTER 7

1. van der Kolk, Bessel. *The Body Keeps the Score: Brain, Mind, and Body in the Healing of Trauma* (New York: Penguin Books, 2015), 96.

2. Klein, Linda Kay. *Pure: Inside the Evangelical Movement That Shamed a Generation of Young Women and How I Broke Free* (New York, NY, Touchstone, An Imprint of Simon & Schuster, Inc, 2018), 134

3. Ibid., 8.

4. Amy Phillips, "The Resurrection of Self: How Deconversion from Religious Belief to Atheism Healed a History of Rejection, Trauma, and Shame." *Dissertation Abstracts International Section A: Humanities and Social Sciences*, vol. 77, no. 3–A(E), ProQuest Information & Learning, 2016, 49.

CHAPTER 8

1. See Ehrman, Bart D. *Heaven and Hell: A History of the Afterlife* (New York: Simon & Schuster Paperbacks, 2021).
2. Obayashi, Hiroshi. *Death and Afterlife: Perspectives of World Religions* (New York: Greenwood, 1992).
3. Rosen, Steven J. *Ultimate Journey: Death and Dying in the World's Major Religions*, (Westport: Praeger, 2008).
4. Ibid.
5. Ibid.
6. Ferwerda, Julie. *Raising Hell: Christianity's Most Controversial Doctrine Put Under Fire.* (Vagabond Group, 2011), 48
7. Ibid.
8. See Bell, Rob. *Love Wins: A Book about Heaven, Hell, and the Fate of Every Person Who Ever Lived* (New York, NY: HarperLuxe, 2013).
9. Oord, Thomas. *God Can't: How to Believe in God and Love After Tragedy, Abuse, or Other Evils* (SacraSage, 2019), 180.
10. Ramonas, Arvydas. "Revisiting the Concept of Hell: Contributions of S. Bulgakov and P. Florensky." Lateranum 88, 1 (2022): 43–63.
11. Ibid.

CHAPTER 9

1. Jonte-Pace, Diane. "Religion: A Rorschachian Projection Theory," *American Imago*, 42, 2 (1985): 199-234.
2. Ibid, 205.
3. Matthew 15:19
4. Ibid, 115.
5. Frederickson, Jon. *Co-Creating Safety: Healing the Fragile Patient* (Seven Leaves Press, 2021).
6. Ross, Lee D, Lelkes, Yphtach, and Russell, Alexandra G. "How Christians Reconcile Their Personal Political Views and the Teachings of Their Faith: Projection as a Means of Dissonance Reduction." *Proceedings of the National Academy of Sciences of the United States of America* 109, 10 (2012): 3616–22. doi:10.1073/pnas.1117557109.
7. Aslan, Reza. *God: A Human History* (Random House, 2018), xiii.
8. Bernstein, Alan E. *The Formation of Hell: Death and Retribution in the Ancient and Early Christian Worlds* (Ithaca, NY: Cornell University Press, 1993), 202.
9. Freud, Sigmund. *The Future of an Illusion*, The Standard Edition of the Complete Psychological Works of Sigmund Freud, vol. 21, gen. ed. James Strachey (London, UK: The Hogarth Press and The Institute of Psycho-Analysis, 1927–1931), 28-29.
10. Ostermann, Denise. "Is Christian Belief Just Psychological Wish Fulfillment?" Essay. In *The Harvest Handbook™ of Apologetics* (Harvest House Publishers, 2019), 328.
11. Olson, Roger E. Against Liberal Theology: Putting the Brakes on Progressive Christianity (Grand Rapids, MI: Zondervan Reflective, 2022), 97.
12. Vitz, Paul C.. *Faith of the Fatherless: The Psychology of Atheism*, (Seoul: Holy Wave Plus, 2012)

CHAPTER 10

1. Ehrman, *Heaven and Hell*, 253.
2. Zhang, Hejing, Gross, Jörg, De Dreu, Carsten, and Ma, Yina. "Oxytocin Promotes Coordinated Out-Group Attack during Intergroup Conflict in Humans." *ELife 8* (January 2019). doi:10.7554/eLife.40698.
3. French, David. "Another Pop-Culture Christian Loses His Faith." National Review. National Review, August 14, 2019. https://www.nationalreview.com/2019/08/another-pop-culture-christian-loses-his-faith/.
4. As quoted in Thomsett, Michael C., and West, Ken. *Slavery and Racism in American Politics, 1776-1876* (Jefferson, NC: McFarland & Company, Inc., Publishers, 2020), 137.
5. Douglass, Frederick. "Slavery in the Pulpit of the Evangelical Alliance: An Address Delivered in London, England, on September 14, 1846." London Inquirer, September 19, 1846 and London Patriot, September 17, 1846. Blassingame, John (et al, eds.). The Frederick Douglass Papers: Series One–Speeches, Debates, and Interviews. New Haven: Yale University Press, 1979. Vol. I, p. 407.

CHAPTER 11

1. Steve Wells, *Drunk with Blood: God's Killings in the Bible* (USA: Giordano Press, 2010), 3.
2. Forehand, Karl. *Apparent Faith: What Fatherhood Taught Me About the Father's Heart* (Orange: California, Quoir, 2019), 55.
3. Kang, Jeehye. "Spanking and Children's Social Competence: Evidence from a US Kindergarten Cohort Study." *Child Abuse & Neglect* 132 (October 2022): N.PAG. doi:10.1016/j.chiabu.2022.105817.
4. Kang, Jeehye. "Spanking and Children's Early Academic Skills: Strengthening Causal Estimates." Early Childhood Research Quarterly 61 (2022): 47–57. doi:10.1016/j.ecresq.2022.05.005.
5. Benko, Jessica. "The Radical Humaneness of Norway's Halden Prison." The New York Times, March 26, 2015. https://www.nytimes.com/2015/03/29/magazine/the-radical-humaneness-of-norways-halden-prison.html.

CHAPTER 12

1. See Ecker, Bruce, Ticic, Robin, and Hulley, Laurel. *Unlocking the Emotional Brain: Facilitating Long-Lasting Change in Psychotherapy* (Routledge, 2012).
2. Leahy, Robert L. *Emotional Schema Therapy* (New York, NY: Guilford, 2019).
3. Ibid.
4. Desmond, Tim. *How to Stay Human in a F*cked-Up World: Mindfulness Practices for Real Life* (San Francisco: HarperOne, 2019), 127.
5. Ibid.
6. Hebb D. 1949. *The Organization of Behavior*. New York, NY: John Wiley and Sons.

CHAPTER 13

1. McCarty, R. "The Fight-or-Flight Response: A Cornerstone of Stress Research." In Fink, George, *Stress: Concepts, Cognition, Emotion, and Behavior*, 1:33–37. Handbook of Stress; Vol 1 (San Diego, CA: Elsevier Academic Press, 2016). https://search.ebscohost.-com/login.aspx?direct=true&db=psyh&AN=2016-26280-004&site=ehost-live&scope=site.

2. Peciña, Marta, Bohnert, Amy S. B., Sikora, Magdalena, Avery, Erich T., Langenecker, Scott A., Mickey, Brian J., and Zubieta, Jon-Kar. "Association between Placebo-Activated Neural Systems and Antidepressant Responses: Neurochemistry of Placebo Effects in Major Depression." *JAMA Psychiatry* 72, 11 (2015): 1087–94. doi:10.1001/jamapsychiatry.2015.1335.

3. See Doidge, Norman. *The Brain That Changes Itself: Stories of Personal Triumph from the Frontiers of Brain Science* (London: Penguin Books, 2007).

4. See Hensley, Barbara J. *An EMDR Primer: From Practicum to Practice* (New York, NY: Springer, 2009).

5. Since I was trained under Laurel Parnell, the creator of *Attachment-Focused* EMDR, I will be adapting material from her work. See Parnell, Laurel. *Attachment Focused EMDR Healing Relational Trauma* (New York: Norton, 2013).

6. See Ricker, Elizabeth. *Smarter Tomorrow: How 15 Minutes of Neurohacking a Day Can Help You Work Better, Think Faster, and Get More Done*, (Little, Brown Spark, 2021).

CHAPTER 14

1. Neff, Kristin D., and S. Natasha Beretvas. "The Role of Self-Compassion in Romantic Relationships." *Self and Identity* 12, 1 (2013): 78–98. doi:10.1080/15298868.2011.639548.

2. Gilbert, P. *Compassion focused therapy: Distinctive features* (London, UK: Routledge, 2010).

3. Ashfield, Emily, Chan, Carmen, and Lee, Deborah. "Building 'a Compassionate Armour': The Journey to Develop Strength and Self-compassion in a Group Treatment for Complex Post-traumatic Stress Disorder." Psychology & Psychotherapy: Theory, Research & Practice 94 (April 2021): 286–303. doi:10.1111/papt.12275.

4. Ibid, 296.

5. Neff, Kristin. *Fierce Self-Compassion: How Women Can Harness Kindness to Speak up, Claim Their Power, and... Thrive* (Penguin Life, 2022).

6. Winell, 1.

7. Phillips, 48.

8. See Isaiah 64:6

9. Adapted from Harris, Russ. *Act with Love: Stop Struggling, Reconcile Differences, and Strengthen Your Relationship with Acceptance and Commitment Therapy* (New Harbinger Publications, 2009), 94.

10. Desmond, 127.

CHAPTER 15

1. See Harris, Russ. *Act made simple: An easy-to-read primer on acceptance and commitment therapy, 2nd Edition* (New Harbinger, 2022)
2. See Gilbert, Paul. *Compassion Focused Therapy: Distinctive features* (London, UK: Routledge, 2010).
3. Ibid.
4. Porges, Stephen. W. *Polyvagal Safety: Attachment, Communication, Self-Regulation* (New York: W.W. Norton and Company, 2021).
5. Ibid, 55
6. Ledford, Terry. "The True Source of Your Self-Criticism." Improving Self-Esteem and Self-Worth, November 27, 2014. http://www.terryledford.com/the-true-source-of-your-self-criticism/.
7. Bright, Bill. *Witnessing Without Fear* (San Bernardino, CA: Here's Life Publishers, Inc., 1987), p.13
8. Ibid.
9. Earley, Jay and Weiss, Bonnie. *Freedom from Your Inner Critic: A Self-Therapy Approach,* (Sounds True, Inc., 2013). 8.
10. Ibid.
11. Ellis, Albert. "The Case Against Religion" (New York: Institute for Rational Living, n.d.), quoted in Bruce S. Narramore, *No Condemnation* (Grand Rapids, Michigan: Zondervan, 1984), 156.
12. Jamie's story is coming from an email exchange we had in Nov. 2022
13. Most of these are adapted from Harris, Russ. *The Happiness Trap: How to Stop Struggling and Start Living, 2nd* edition (Shambhala, 2022).
14. See Turow, Rachel Goldsmith, *The Self-Talk Workout: Six Science-Backed Strategies to Dissolve Self-Criticism and Transform the Voice in Your Head,* (Boulder, CO: Shambhala, 2022).

CHAPTER 16

1. I Corinthians 11:14
2. Hanson, Rick. *Hardwiring Happiness: The New Brain Science of Contentment, Calm, and Confidence,* (New York: Harmony Books, 2016), xxvi.
3. This acronym is taken from a training I did with couples expert Rebecca Jorgensen.
4. See Diane Poole Heller's The Power of Attachment: How to Create Deep and Lasting Intimate Relationships (Sounds True, 2019).
5. The first half of questions are adapted from George, C., Kaplan, N., & Main, M. *The Adult Attachment Interview,* 1985, Unpublished manuscript, University of California at Berkeley.
6. Stockton, Hannah, Joseph, Stephen, and Hunt, Nigel. "Expressive Writing and Post-traumatic Growth: An Internet-Based Study." Traumatology: An International Journal 20, 2 (2014): 75–83. doi:10.1037/h0099377.

CHAPTER 17

1. Adapted from Harris's *Pushing Away Paper* exercise. See also Harris, Russ. *Act Made Simple: An Easy-to-Read Primer on Acceptance and Commitment Therapy.* 2nd ed (New Harbinger Publications, 2019).
2. Adapted from Hayes, Steven. *Get out of Your Mind and into Your Life: The New Acceptance and Commitment Therapy* (Oakland, CA: New Harbinger Publications Inc, 2005).
3. Adapted from Harris, *The Happiness Trap*
4. Winell, Marlene. *Leaving the Fold: A Guide for Former Fundamentalists and Others Leaving Their Religion* (Berkeley, CA: Apocryphile Press, 2007), 20.
5. Lee, Karen Adriana and Gubi, Peter Madsen. "Breaking Up with Jesus: A Phenomenological Exploration of the Experience of Deconversion from an Evangelical Christian Faith to Atheism." *Mental Health, Religion & Culture,* vol. 22, no. 2, Feb. 2019, 178.
6. Riley, Reba. *Post-Traumatic Church Syndrome: One Woman's Desperate, Funny, and Healing Journey to Explore 30 Religions by Her 30th Birthday* (New York: Howard Books, 2016), 114.
7. Russ Harris, an Acceptance and Commitment Therapy (ACT) author, educator, and practitioner, has been helpful in values work. He explores *Toward and Away Moves* and what he calls *The Choice Point* in detail in: Harris, Russ. *The Happiness Trap: How to Stop Struggling and Start Living,* 2nd edition (Shambhala, 2022).
8. Ibid.
9. Ibid., Harris.

EPILOGUE

1. ABC Religion & Ethics. "The Obscenity of Belief in an Eternal Hell." ABC Religion & Ethics. ABC Religion & Ethics, June 13, 2022. https://www.abc.net.au/religion/david-bentley-hart-obscenity-of-belief-in-eternal-hell/13356388.

ADDITIONAL PRAISE

Wrathful God

Tormenting Hell   Sinful Self

"We know hell is bad for those who suffer there eternally. But who knew how bad it is in the present!?! Mark Karris explores in detail the trauma and psychological abuse that belief in hell causes. This book is the go-to psychological resource for rejecting the idea anyone will be forced to endure eternal conscious torment. And the go-to resource for helping us heal from that idea!"

— THOMAS JAY OORD, AUTHOR OF *GOD CAN'T* AND *THE UNCONTROLLING LOVE OF GOD*

"The Diabolical Trinity is deeply insightful and immensely helpful. It shows that religious trauma is real and results in both physical and mental symptoms. If you are one of the unfortunate people raised in such an environment, this book provides up-to-date therapies that will help you on the journey towards healing."

— JOHN SANDERS, *EMBRACING PRODIGALS: OVERCOMING AUTHORITATIVE RELIGION BY EMBODYING JESUS' NURTURING GRACE*

"In his book, *The Diabolical Trinity*, Dr. Mark Karris takes up the mantle of this important legacy by exposing the long-lasting traumatic effects of belief in eternal damnation. His masterful marshaling of evidence ensures that his work will be the new manifesto for helping people heal from their religious trauma by deconstructing the psychological horrors of belief in Hell. *The Diabolical Trinity* is an arresting, empathetic, and conscious-raising book."

— **DARREN M. SLADE**, PHD, RELIGIOUS TRAUMA
STUDIES PROGRAM, GLOBAL CENTER FOR RELIGIOUS
RESEARCH

"As a child barely six years old, I was indoctrinated to believe that my beloved cousins who were "unsaved" would burn alive forever and ever... and that their blood would be on my hands. That poison-tipped spear lodged deep within my heart, tormented my sensitive spirit, and altered my vision of God and humanity for decades. I need no better reason to read Mark Karris' *The Diabolical Trinity*. Thank you for this wise and transformational book!"

— **DR. BRADLEY JERSAK**, DEAN OF THEOLOGY &
CULTURE, ST. STEPHEN'S UNIVERSITY (NEW
BRUNSWICK), AUTHOR, *OUT OF THE EMBERS: FAITH
AFTER THE GREAT DECONSTRUCTION*

"An important and much needed resource! Karris doesn't leave the reader alone on the path of healing, but instead provides a collection of research-based healing practices for religious trauma that will assist both readers and those who walk alongside them in therapeutic settings."

— **JANYNE MCCONNAUGHEY**, PHD. *TRAUMA IN THE
PEWS: THE IMPACT ON FAITH AND SPIRITUAL
PRACTICES*

"*The Diabolical Trinity* offers careful documentation, with numerous case studies, of a specific part of fundamentalist Christianity— doctrine of Hell as eternal conscious torment, and threats of Hell as a routine part of church and family rhetoric. Karris brings his therapeutic skills to bear in providing numerous practical tools to enable those who have been religiously traumatized by Hell theology/parenting/abuse to find healing. As a clinical tool, this book will be enormously helpful both to those recovering from such religious trauma and those who are caring for them."

— REV. DR. DAVID P. GUSHEE, DISTINGUISHED
UNIVERSITY PROFESSOR OF CHRISTIAN ETHICS,
MERCER UNIVERSITY, CHAIR IN CHRISTIAN SOCIAL
ETHICS

"In *The Diabolical Trinity*, Dr. Karris astutely shows how religion can be perverted into a neurosis through the ideology of hell. Further, he shows how the preaching of eternal damnation causes massive psychological suffering rather than salvation. And then this ideology leads to kinds of rationalized sadism to torture others, even if intended as kindness. The book concludes with wise and compassionate strategies to help seekers after God return to their authentic selves after having lived in hell, a living hell caused by this ideology."

— JON FREDERICKSON, MSW, *CO-CREATING
SAFETY: HEALING THE FRAGILE PATIENT*

"As a therapist and Anglican bishop, I believe this book is critical and timely. He explains the foundational aspects of religious trauma, particularly due to Hell indoctrination, and then gives us practical tools to build resilience and help ourselves and others heal from this insidious trauma. *The Diabolical Trinity* is a must-read. I highly recommend!"

— THE RT. REV. DR. JUSTIN MEIER TRAUMA INFORMED AND RESILIENCE BUILD THERAPIST, PROFESSOR, AND BISHOP OF THE ANGLICAN DIOCESE OF THE EMMAUS WAY

"Dr. Mark Karris, with his combined experience as an ex-pastor, reconstructionist, and mental health clinician, is the perfect person to lead us through better understanding and unraveling the impact of Hell Indoctrination. Mark takes on this very heavy and much needed task with great care in his latest book, *The Diabolical Trinity*. I will certainly be adding this magnificently written and very current book to the top of my reading list for religious and spiritual abuse survivors."

— DR. JAMIE MARICH, FOUNDER, *THE INSTITUTE FOR CREATIVE MINDFULNESS* AND AUTHOR OF *DISSOCIATION MADE SIMPLE: A STIGMA-FREE GUIDE TO EMBRACING YOUR DISSOCIATIVE MIND* AND MANY OTHER BOOKS IN THE FIELD OF TRAUMA RECOVERY

"Out of the Abyss bravely addresses arguably the most devastating form of religious trauma impacting 'Exvangelicals' today: the doctrine of Hell. Karris offers readers a wholistic depiction of the impact of religious trauma, connecting its' symptoms to the all-too-common experience of afterlife anxiety. His thoughtful deconstruction of the concept of hell from a non-religious standpoint offers a fresh take on this problematic topic. Survivors of Hell doctrine who read *The Diabolical Trinity* will find validation, education, and practical self-help strategies as they begin their journey of healing from religious trauma."

— **ANNA CLARK-MILLER**, LPC (SPECIALIST IN
RELIGIOUS TRAUMA THERAPY)

"Mark Karris is a wounded healer. He knows the damage of toxic religious doctrines of sin, judgment, and hell from the inside. In *The Diabolical Trinity*, he brings both personal experience and professional expertise to bear in a profound, compassionate, and eminently practical guide to finding hope and healing."

— **RANDAL RAUSER**, AUTHOR OF *PROGRESSIVES
CHRISTIANS LOVE JESUS TOO*, AND PROFESSOR OF
HISTORICAL THEOLOGY AT TAYLOR SEMINARY OF
KAIROS UNIVERSITY

"*The Diabolical Trinity*" is the book I have been seeking for 15 years. If you've recognized religious harm in your life but don't know where to go next, this book is a treasure trove of practical tools for rewiring a nervous system that has trauma written into it. Personally, I found this book validating and empowering; as a clinician, I feel better equipped to meet the needs of my religious trauma clients."

— **CHRISTEN HANSEL**, LPC (SPECIALIST IN
RELIGIOUS TRAUMA THERAPY)

"The Diabolical Trinity encourages readers to augment their beliefs about the doctrine of Hell while also broadening comprehension of the deleterious ramifications teachings of spiritually abusive or controlling religious systems convey. Additionally, Karris provides practical strategies for all who are recovering from religious trauma. *The Diabolical Trinity* is a well-researched tool to aid an individual's psychological and emotional wellbeing while they reclaim their spiritual autonomy."

— **REBEKAH DRUMSTA**, MA, CPLC, SPIRITUAL ABUSE ADVOCATE & CONSULTANT, AUTHOR OF *WHEN FAMILY HURTS: 30 DAYS TO FINDING HEALING AND CLARITY*

"Hell trauma is so common, yet so rarely discussed, and Karris does so with such compassion and clarity. This is essential reading for anyone who was part of a faith tradition that used hell to keep followers in the fold, as well as for therapists seeking to gain a deeper understanding of their clients who have gone through this experience."

— **KRISPIN MAYFIELD**, LICENSED THERAPIST, AUTHOR OF *ATTACHED TO GOD: A PRACTICAL GUIDE TO DEEPER SPIRITUAL EXPERIENCE*

"With the wisdom and compassion of a skilled therapist, Karris guides us through a dismantling of this harmful idea and provides a path to inner peace and healing. I now have a book recommendation for my friends who are still struggling with their fear of Hell!'"

— **DAVID HAYWARD**, AKA THE NAKEDPASTOR

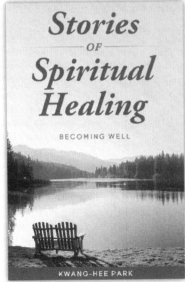

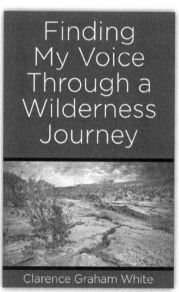

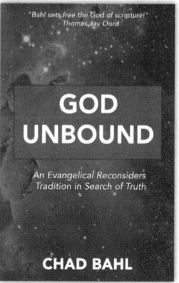

Made in the USA
Columbia, SC
04 October 2023

23927094R00150